THE MID-TUDOR CRISIS
1539–1563

By the same author

THE TUDOR COMMONWEALTH, 1529–1559
NAZI GERMANY

THE MID-TUDOR CRISIS
1539–1563

Whitney R. D. Jones, M.A., B.SC.ECON.

*Senior Lecturer in History, Caerleon College of Education
Research Officer, Schools Council*

BOOKS
10 East 53d St., New York 10022
(a division of Harper & Row Publishers, Inc.)

© Whitney R. D. Jones 1973

All rights reserved. No part of this publication may be reproduced or transmitted, in any form or by any means, without permission

First published in the United Kingdom 1973 by
The Macmillan Press Ltd

Published in the U.S.A. 1973 by
HARPER & ROW PUBLISHERS, INC.
BARNES & NOBLE IMPORT DIVISION

ISBN–06–493390–3

Printed in Great Britain

DA
315
J66
1973

For M.A.W.J.
in memory of
M.A.M.J.

Contents

	Preface	ix
1	Introduction	1
2	The Survival of the Dynasty	7
3	A Crisis of Governance	35
4	The Crisis in Religion	71
5	Economic and Social Problems: the 'Dangerous Corner'	113
6	Foreign Affairs: the 'British Problem'	149
7	Conclusion	190
	Short Titles and Abbreviations	196
	Notes	197
	Select Bibliography	208
	Index	217

Preface

It should perhaps be made clear that this is not a textbook of English history for the period 1539 to 1563, but an introduction to recent studies of important aspects of the mid-Tudor crisis. As such, it will be suitable for upper sixth and undergraduate students rather than for readers who have no prior knowledge of the subject.

The spelling of quotations has been modernised (except in the occasional book title), but idiosyncrasies of punctuation have been corrected only where the sense is rendered doubtful. Exigencies of space have made it necessary to 'group' notes, wherever possible; it is hoped that the provision of a fairly extensive bibliography will compensate for their terseness.

While certain sections of this book reflect my own researches, the extent of my debt to the many historians upon whose scholarship a work of synthesis such as this is so heavily reliant will be obvious, and is gratefully acknowledged. It is also my pleasant duty to record my sincere thanks, for their generous and constructive criticism, to Professor S. T. Bindoff (for Chapter 3), Professor A. G. Dickens (for Chapter 4), Dr C. E. Challis (for Chapter 5), Professor R. B. Wernham (for Chapter 6), Mrs Jennifer Fisher, of Manchester High School for Girls, and Mr John Williams, of Bargod Grammar-Technical School. For errors and shortcomings which, despite their guidance, remain, I must accept responsibility. I am also indebted to the staff of Macmillan for their assistance in preparing the book for the printer. As ever, the writing of this book would have been impossible without the encouragement and patience of my wife and of my mother.

W.R.D.J.

1 Introduction

The first task of this book must be to discuss the concept of the 'mid-Tudor crisis' and to explain the choice of 1539 and 1563 as its terminal dates. That there was a crisis in mid-seventeenth-century England has long been accepted, as has been the notion of a 'general crisis' affecting much of seventeenth-century Europe. While the suggestion of its equivalent for the mid-sixteenth century is more recent, there is no novelty in recognition of the fact that, in retrospect, the trouble-shadowed reigns of Edward VI and Mary stand in apparently sharp contrast with the Tudor 'high noons' of Henry VIII and Elizabeth I. Our purpose will be the study of the problems which seem to have been ever-present in mid-Tudor England – a study which should reveal the close relationship between those problems and also suggest reasons why the dates 1539 and 1563 may perhaps most appropriately mark the duration of the crisis.

We may at once define the fundamental issue of these mid-century decades: that of the continuity, security and power of the Tudor monarchy. Whether it takes the form of Henry VIII's frantic quest to stabilise the succession to the throne; of the reign of Edward VI, a sickly boy destined never to achieve his majority; of the most tragic figure of the 'Spanish Tudor', Mary; or of the precarious circumstances of the early years of the reign of her half-sister Elizabeth, this theme is constant. Throughout, these changes in the fortunes of the monarchy are directly reflected in those of the 'official' religious creed and in the nation's policy and strength in the field of international diplomacy. Meanwhile the security and power of the Crown are affected by these factors as well as by financial and economic problems, and are beset by the perpetual fear that any one, or any combination, of these issues might give rise to civil strife. It is this integral and often causal relationship between its constituent elements – perhaps exemplified in the events of 1549 – which gives the mid-Tudor crisis a certain unity. It was a crisis both of the dynasty and of society, but its focal point was always to be found in the personality of the monarchy. The fact that society recognised this was itself of the greatest significance.

The picture of the brief reigns of Edward VI and of Mary as forming an uneasy and uncharacteristic interlude in the mid-decade of the Tudor dynasty is readily accepted; each was marked by a falling short in the personality of the monarch – at least by Tudor standards. The reign of the boy Edward saw rapid and often unpopular religious changes, a disastrous deterioration in the nation's international standing, a very grave crisis of economic and social stability, and two rebellions. All this under the aegis of two 'over-mighty subjects', one of whom sought unsuccessfully to alter the succession and establish his daughter-in-law as puppet queen. The reign of Mary witnessed a dramatic and even more unpopular reversal of religious policy, a Council torn by conflicting factions, a rebellion which came disconcertingly near to success, and a royal marriage which led both to personal tragedy and to diplomatic disaster and military humiliation. The Queen's intermittent Tudor ability to appeal to the loyalty of her subjects was finally quite submerged by her doctrinal fanaticism, and her death was greeted with the nation's undisguised relief.

Yet alongside this quite traditional diagnosis we may set cogent arguments for extending the time-span of the crisis in both directions. A leading historian has dated the decline in quality if not the outright failure of Tudor government not from the death of Henry VIII but from the execution of Thomas Cromwell in 1540. The disgrace of the minister may be traced from the events of the previous year, which had seen the enactment of the Six Articles, a victory for conservative orthodoxy in the definition of the doctrine of the Church of England. To some this marks the start of a period of 'Catholic reaction', to others it is but one (admittedly important) event in the continuous struggle between the Catholic and Protestant factions at court. Quite certainly it symbolised the surviving vitality of the 'Catholic-conservative' group which was to engineer the downfall of Cromwell. The charge of heresy which was to be used against him may well have been coupled with that of responsibility for the fiasco of the Cleves marriage project which he pushed through in 1539 as a diplomatic counter to the dangerous possibility of a Franco-Spanish entente. In January 1540 Henry found himself yoked to an unpleasing bride who symbolised a dubious alliance which the changing diplomatic situation no longer necessitated. Cromwell's enemies held too many trumps even for his skilful play. On 23 July 1540 he was beheaded.

With this step, writes Professor Elton, the King 'destroyed the efficiency and the purpose of his government.... Of all Henry VIII's follies none cost his country dearer than his illusion that he was an old and experienced King who knew his business and needed no one to do it for him.'[1] Few would dispute that the last eight years or so of his reign saw some weakening in the judgement as well as a further coarsening in calibre of the monarch. Beyond question these years witnessed ambitious military adventures against Scotland and France which were to store up trouble for Henry's successors, while dissipating much of the wealth which the Crown had taken from the Church, and leading directly to the disastrous expedient of debasement of the coinage. The impact of that debasement, especially upon the lower orders of society, was a major constituent of the clearly developing crisis in economic affairs. Social and economic grievances, which had already contributed largely to the outbreak of the Pilgrimage of Grace, found expression in a spate of 'protest literature' during the 1540s. Finally, Henry's concern with his will and with Succession Acts in the last years of his reign testifies to his worries about the future of his dynasty.

At the other end of the period the nation's undoubted relief at the accession of Elizabeth I in 1558 was shot through with apprehension as to the security both of her tenure of the throne and of England's position in face of foreign danger. While her admirers might think the description of a 'shifty princess' ascending an 'uneasy throne' a somewhat ungallant assessment of the personality of Elizabeth, there is no doubting its apt appraisal of her position. Elizabeth might well declare herself 'the only right heir by blood and lawful succession', and style herself 'defender of the true, ancient, and Catholic faith', but in some (Roman) Catholic eyes Mary Stuart, Queen of Scots, was the legitimate successor to the English throne. Mary Stuart personified not only all the doubts as to the validity of Elizabeth's claim to the Crown, but also, by reason of her marriage to the French Dauphin, the menace of the 'auld alliance' between Scotland and France, which much of English foreign policy in the previous decade and a half had served only to cement. Meanwhile, after the fevered excitement of religious passions since 1547, the nature of the ecclesiastical settlement was a major problem in its own right, apart from its obvious relevance in a dynastic and diplomatic context. A recent study concludes that 'the régime seemed to contemporaries to be a very fragile creation with a very precarious future' which included fearful possibilities of 'the sudden death of the queen, a ruinous marriage with Robert Dudley, privy conspiracy in favour of Mary Stuart, or even foreign invasion'.[2]

These issues were not quickly or easily resolved, and the selection of 1563 as a terminal date for our study may seem somewhat arbitrary. Yet it may be suggested that by that time the position of Elizabeth – in regard to her recognition (both at home and abroad), to the apparently imminent danger from Mary Stuart, to the menace from France and Scotland and to the avoidance of damaging extremes in religion – was much improved. Professor Wallace MacCaffrey observes that 'the years between the summers of 1559 and 1563 were formative ones [which] went far in defining the character and goals of the new regime'. We shall see that in fact they were marked by the successful tackling of basic problems and the (sometimes fortunate) surmounting of immediate crises relating to the personal security and health of the Queen and to religious, economic and international affairs. Professor Bindoff cites Cecil's tabulation in 1563 of the achievements of the first five years of Elizabeth's reign: '1559 The religion of Christ restored. Foreign authority rejected.... 1560 The French at the request of the Scots ... sent back to France and Scotland set free from the servitude of the Pope. 1561 The debased copper and brass coinage replaced by brass and silver', and remarks that he might fairly have added: '1563 Many good laws made for the commonweal. Labourers. etc.'[3] In foreign affairs, after burning her fingers in an abortive expedition to aid the French Huguenots (1562–3), Elizabeth settled for a cautious and at times near-isolationist policy for the rest of the decade. It is true that the end of that decade was to bring another major crisis, but it would perhaps be fair to describe its events as the testing-time of an established regime, since Elizabeth had now been enthroned for over ten years.

Thus far we have discussed the period and the aspects of mid-Tudor history with which we shall be concerned. It remains to outline the order of treatment which will be adopted. While important narrative and biographical aspects will not be neglected they will be considered within a framework which is directed to discussion of certain themes. We shall examine in turn each of the constituent elements of the crisis as it evolves throughout the mid-century period. Chapter 2 will be concerned with the fundamental issue to which all else must be related, that of the succession and security of the Tudor dynasty, and will also go some way towards provision of a narrative outline. Next, the closely related problems of constitutional and political development – the alleged deterioration of government, the threat of the 'over-mighty subject', the outbreaks of rebellion, the whole question of order and security in society – will receive attention. The fourth chapter will be devoted to the crisis in religion, and the next to what has been aptly termed a 'dangerous corner' in economic and social affairs.[4] In Chapter 6 we shall trace the evolution of English foreign policy during these crucial decades. The concluding chapter will consider the successful establishment of her position by Elizabeth I and suggest some reasons why, despite the tensions of these years and the many-sided crisis in its fortunes, the Tudor dynasty ultimately triumphed. For it is well to remind ourselves that the conjunction of circumstances which we have observed in mid-Tudor England was almost precisely that which existed in France at the death of Henry II in 1558. For France there followed the struggles for control of the throne between ambitious noble factions, doctrinal fanaticism and foreign intervention, which made up the bloody if intermittent 'Wars of Religion', extending for over thirty years. The fact that England escaped catastrophe – at least, on any comparable scale – cannot simply be taken for granted.

2 The Survival of the Dynasty

It would be no gross overstatement to describe the Tudor dynasty as obsessed, throughout its course, with the problem of its own continuity and security. Nor is this surprising. The first of the royal line, born to a widowed mother, was the only Tudor of his generation. Recollection of his tenuous claim and precarious circumstances of accession to the throne must have been heightened by the memory of the dynastic casualties of the fifteenth century. Perhaps most depressing of all was the recurrent and fatal sickliness of the Tudor line, whose males so often died while still minors. After twenty years of marriage Henry VIII, monarch only by virtue of the death at fifteen of his elder brother Arthur, had no legitimate son. His queen, Catherine, had borne several male children, but none survived for as much as a month; his only legitimate offspring was his daughter Mary. This it was which had led the King to endow his bastard son, Henry Fitzroy, with the evocative title Duke of Richmond, and with a household larger than that of the Princess Mary. This it was, together with his infatuation for Anne Boleyn, which led him to embark upon his matrimonial odyssey, unkindly described as the triumph of hope over experience.

The Act of 1534 'for the establishment of the King's succession' (25 Hen. VIII, c. 22) embodies a full and explicit expression of Tudor preoccupation with dynastic security. His 'Lords spiritual and temporal and the Commons' assure King Henry of 'their remembrance that the good unity, peace and wealth of this realm and the succession of the subjects of the same most specially and principally above all worldly things consisteth and resteth in the certainty and surety of the procreation and posterity of your Highness'. Their 'remembrance' is deepened by that of 'the great divisions which in times past hath been in this realm by reason of

several titles pretended to the imperial crown of the same...
whereof hath ensued great effusion and destruction of man's
blood'. In order to ensure 'lawful succession and heirs, upon
which dependeth all our joy and wealth' the statute goes on
to annul the King's marriage with Catherine and confirm that
with Anne Boleyn, who had borne Henry a daughter in
September 1533. Unfortunately, its prayer that God would
not permit 'your said dear and entirely beloved wife Queen
Anne to decease without issue male of the body of your
Highness to be gotten' was answered only by miscarriage
and the headsman's axe; 'the Lady Elizabeth now princess'
was to be the only child of this marriage.

In January 1536, rejected and disgraced, Catherine of
Aragon died; but royal rejoicings were cut short when, on the
day of her dead rival's funeral, Queen Anne was delivered of
a stillborn child. A few months later, adjudged guilty of
adultery, her own life ended on the scaffold. Two days after
her death Cranmer solemnly declared that she had never been
lawfully married to Henry. Long ago, alluding to the execution of the Earl of Warwick which preceded it, Catherine
had described her marriage with Arthur (from whom Henry
had inherited his bride as well as his expectation of the
Crown) as 'made in blood'; the phrase might well have been
applied to that which Henry now contracted with Jane Seymour only ten days after Anne's execution. In July Richmond
died of consumption. Still, by October 1537 the King could
gaze at last on the face of a legitimate son – although the price
of this moment of triumph was the death, within less than a
fortnight, of his wife. With Henry's genuine grief went a now
almost panic-stricken anxiety as to the safety of his line. He
issued the most stringent and detailed instructions for the
hygiene of the clothing and surroundings of his infant son.
Despite these precautions, young Edward nearly died of
fever in 1541.

Meanwhile, the combination of diplomatic necessity
(Cromwell's determination upon an alliance with the German
Lutheran princes) and of the impact of Holbein's allegedly
flattering portrait of the intended bride brought about the
monarch's fourth marriage in January 1540. But the plain-
visaged Anne of Cleves was soon subjected to an annulment

of her marriage in favour of the pretty face of Catherine Howard – whose charms brought her to the block, attainted of adultery and treason, by February 1542. Catherine Parr, whom Henry married in the summer of the following year, had already survived two husbands and was now to repeat the achievement, in rather more difficult circumstances, by outliving Henry VIII. Complex, sordid, pathetic – whatever adjective is chosen to describe these later royal unions – they had one thing in common: fruitlessness. When the King himself died in January 1547 he left behind only the two daughters and the infant son of his earlier marriages.

Henry had done what he could to stabilise the position. A statute of 1544 had declared the order of succession to the throne: first Edward, then Mary and finally Elizabeth; but against each of these names there rested a question-mark, in terms either of fitness to exercise power or of validity of claim to the Crown. As a final safeguard the King reserved the power of changing the succession by his will, but when he died the order remained unaltered. Edward, not yet ten years old, was clearly not ready to rule for himself, while his half-sisters Mary (aged thirty-one) and Elizabeth (thirteen) had each at some time been solemnly bastardised as their father repudiated their mothers. What were their feelings towards each other? Mary, whose respect and affection for her father had apparently survived the harsh treatment she had received, was on very friendly terms with Edward, to whom she brought fine presents upon her visits. His customary gift from Elizabeth, with whom he had sometimes shared his lessons, was a cambric shirt which she herself had made. A close friend of Edward's childhood, Jane Dormer, was later to recall that the boy preferred the company of Mary to that of Elizabeth despite (or because of?) the gap in age. It is tempting to conjecture that, for Edward, Mary did something to replace the mother whom he had never known, and that, for Mary, the boy went nearest to filling the place of the child she would never have. They had perhaps been closest to forming a united family with their father's sixth wife, Catherine Parr, of whom they became quite fond. Yet already the difference in religion between Edward and Mary had found expression in a letter in which the eight-year-old boy admonished his half-sister to 'attend no longer to foreign dances and merriments, which do not become a Christian Princess'.[1]

It is often alleged that the King became increasingly vengeful and suspicious as his own death approached. Yet in fairness the fate which now befell the great Howard family must be related to Henry's consciousness of the dynastic uncertainty which he must now inevitably bequeath. Norfolk's daughter had been the bride of Henry Fitzroy (Duke of Richmond). His elder son, the Earl of Surrey, now proceeded, amongst his other indiscretions, to speak of his Plantagenet blood and to canvass his father's claim to exercise the Regency when the King should die. Allegedly a plan to murder the Council in order to achieve this object had been concocted. Symbolically, Surrey's ultimate condemnation for treason was to rest on the fact that he had quartered his own coat of arms with those of Edward the Confessor. Surrey was imprisoned and his father soon joined him in the Tower and was subjected to interrogation. The former was beheaded on 19 January 1547, but the warrant for Norfolk's execution remained unsigned when eight days later, Henry VIII squeezed Cranmer's hand as a token of his hope for redemption and lapsed into final unconsciousness. Whether the downfall of the Howards is to be attributed to Surrey's gratuitous folly, to the fears and suspicions of the King himself or to the schemings of the Hertford faction within the Council, it throws into sharp relief the background of dynastic uncertainty against which the rival cliques manœuvred, eager to fill the expected vacuum of power. For all Henry's careful plans for the future now lay at risk. The dead hand could do nothing to prevent the successful attempt to modify, or even to distort, his project for the Regency, in the interest of the new King's uncle, Jane Seymour's brother. Edward Seymour, member of the Privy Council since 1537, created Earl of Hertford three days after Edward's christening, kept Henry's death a secret for two days while he secured his dominant position.[2]

The idea that Henry VIII had selected a Regency Council that was 'balanced' beween Catholic and Protestant advisers in order to preserve his religious settlement after his death has been modified by recognition of a number of indications of his state of mind; yet the issue remains debatable. To some historians the exclusion of Stephen Gardiner, the leading Catholic, from its membership, and the inclusion of Hertford, the significance of whose relationship to Edward he could hardly have missed, suggest that Henry perceived the drift of the tide and, supreme politician that he was, went with it. Such an assumption would resolve the apparent paradox that the King, who died a Catholic, had entrusted the education of his son to distinguished Protestant tutors. But Professor L. B. Smith rejects this interpretation of events, attributing the downfall of the Howards and the exclusion of Gardiner to personal rather than religious factors. He believes that the Prince's tutors, Cox and Cheke (whose Protestantism, incidentally, was not to withstand the threat of martydom in the reign of Mary), were appointed solely on grounds of scholarship, and accepts the statement of Jane Dormer that it was only after Henry died that 'mischievous and heretical governors, contrary to his father's will' transformed the boy into a thorough-going Protestant. He urges that 'it is deceptively easy to forget that Henry VIII might regard resurgent papal Catholicism as a far greater threat to his religious *via media* than a weak and faltering Protestantism'. Whatever the truth as to the direction, or indeed the clarity, of Henry's intentions, for the moment the crucial fact was Hertford's success in establishing himself as Lord Protector of the boy King.[3]

With the accession of Edward VI the first of the suspect links in the Tudor dynastic chain was to be put to the test. Not yet ten years old he was never to reach an age at which he could grasp the reality of power. That power was in fact to be exercised in his name first by the Duke of Somerset (as Hertford now became) and then by the Duke of Northumberland. Their policies and the threat of the re-emergence of the 'over-mighty subject' are considered in Chapter 3; our immediate concern is with Edward himself, his ideas and beliefs (which were not without significance in regard to certain aspects of policy), and with the attempt to change the order of succession to the throne at his tragically early death.

Edward's early childhood was apparently healthy enough – although we need not take at face value the contemporary picture of the exceptionally sturdy infant who would have walked before his time if his nurses had not prevented it. But by the age of four he had almost died of fever. Recovering, the boy displayed a normal taste for games and, upon occasion, an equally normal aversion to prolonged study. Indeed at least once his tutor, Dr Cox, felt obliged to rout out from his royal pupil those enemies to learning 'Captain Will' and 'Captain Oblivion' (as he termed them), by physical chastisement. Thus encouraged, the prince developed into an apt student for languages and scriptures. Nor were his studies mechanical, for he was to show a genuine interest in religious doctrine. As to the qualities of mind and personality which he brought to these studies, interpretation has varied. The contemporary Protestant rejoicings at the coming to the throne of the 'young Josiah' who, like his Biblical namesake, should lead his people to spiritual truth, have been countered by modern allusions to unnaturally precocious bigotry and priggishness. Many have discerned a coldly callous (although perhaps dynastically typical?) streak in Edward's reference in his diary to the executions of his uncles, Thomas Seymour, the Lord Admiral, and Edward Seymour, Duke of Somerset; others would explain this as a natural reaction to the personal discomforts and anxieties to which their actions had exposed a child. Assessments of his personality have ranged from colourlessness to the assertion that Edward inherited all his father's imperious will and that only his premature death prevented him from calling Northumberland to account. Perhaps the truth is that he simply did not live long enough for us to find out.[4]

Yet his education by some of the most brilliant minds of the time suggests that Edward's ideas, even if they be regarded (quite naturally) as a reflection of those of his tutors, merit some attention. He was a convinced Protestant; the religious changes of his reign (see Chapter 4) were undertaken with his full personal approval. Indeed, while Somerset was geninue in his professed beliefs, Northumberland employed a feigned ardour for religious reformation as a means of holding the King's favour and, allegedly, of inducing him to alter the succession to the throne. Edward's religious views embraced the social idealism of several leading Protestant divines who were associated with what has been called a 'Commonwealth party'. While not in any sense an organised party they were moved by the hope that religious, social and economic reform would go forward together. Their influence, especially that of Bishop Latimer, is clear in the boy King's writings, but any significance in terms of policy was cut short by the fall of their sympathiser Somerset (see Chapter 3).

Meanwhile we must remind ourselves that it was a child who reigned in 1547 – a child whose one act of self-assertion during his triumphal entry into London was to halt the procession whilst he watched a tightrope acrobat (a 'stranger' from Aragon, who slid down a cable from St Pauls steeple to the ground); a child in whose interests the coronation ceremony was reduced from the usual eleven or twelve hours to seven. His early impression of his Seymour uncles was coloured by the thought that, on the crucial schoolboy issue of spending-money, 'my uncle of Somerset dealeth very hardly with me, and keepeth me so straight [i.e. short] that I cannot have money at my will. But my Lord Admiral both sends me money, and gives me money.' The Admiral, Thomas Seymour of Sudeley, was moved by ambition rather than by generosity in thus seeking to curry favour, as part of his mad-brained scheme to replace his brother as Protector. Finally, in January 1549, attempting a secret night visit to the royal bedchamber in order to press his claims, Sudeley, with incredible folly, shot Edward's pet dog when it barred his way. This was the last straw. A Bill of Attainder condemned him to death for treason. Probably his schemes were too ill-conceived to pose a serious threat to the realm, but in the context of dynastic security it is worth remarking that Catherine Parr's widowhood had lasted less than three months when Sudeley married her, and that both before that marriage and after her own death he attempted to press his suit with the Princesses Mary and Elizabeth.[5]

The Earl of Warwick now took full advantage of Somerset's growing unpopularity, unfortunate arrogance and alleged weakness in the maintenance of order, and organised a conspiracy against him. A bloodless coup d'état brought down the Lord Protector. After a period of imprisonment he was released but remained suspect and was executed for alleged treason in January 1552; his nephew's diary for the day contains the cold entry that 'the Duke of Somerset had his head cut off upon Tower Hill between eight and nine o'clock in the morning'. The dominance of the Duke of Northumberland (Warwick's new title) over the King was now unchallenged; but within eighteen months the boy was dead. Edward, perhaps suspecting that for him time was running out, persuaded Northumberland to urge the Council that he should reach his majority at the age of sixteen, but even that was to be too late. Mary, visiting him in February 1553, found him in bed with a feverish chill. From this time onwards rumours of his death were persistent. Partially recovered, he presided at a Council meeting. The members, shaken at his wan appearance, were appalled by an outburst in which, displaying some of his father's spirit at frustration of his wishes, he charged them: 'You pluck out my feathers as if I were but a tame falcon – the day will come when I shall pluck out yours!'[6]

By spring or early summer he knew that he might never see that day. By May the desperate Northumberland, who dared not contemplate the accession of Mary to the throne, had resolved on his course of action. For he had not the slightest doubt as to the effect upon his position of the accession of a woman whose Church he had looted, and whose person he had treated with discourtesy; he may well have believed his head as well as his power to be at risk. He therefore persuaded Edward to interfere with his father's order of succession to the throne. This he did on the double grounds of protection of the Protestant faith from the danger of a Roman Catholic regime and of protection of the realm from the potential menace of a woman ruler married to a foreigner. Edward was brought to declare that 'our long sickness hath caused us heavily to think of the conditions and prospects of our realm. Should the Lady Mary or the Lady Elizabeth succeed, she might marry a stranger [i.e. foreigner], and the laws and liberties of England be sacrificed, and religion changed.'[7]

Yet Northumberland's plans went far beyond the exclusion of Mary Tudor in order to safeguard the Protestant religion. Elizabeth also was debarred, on the flimsy pretext that under

```
HENRY VII m. ELIZABETH
(1457–1509)    OF YORK
                (d. 1503)
```

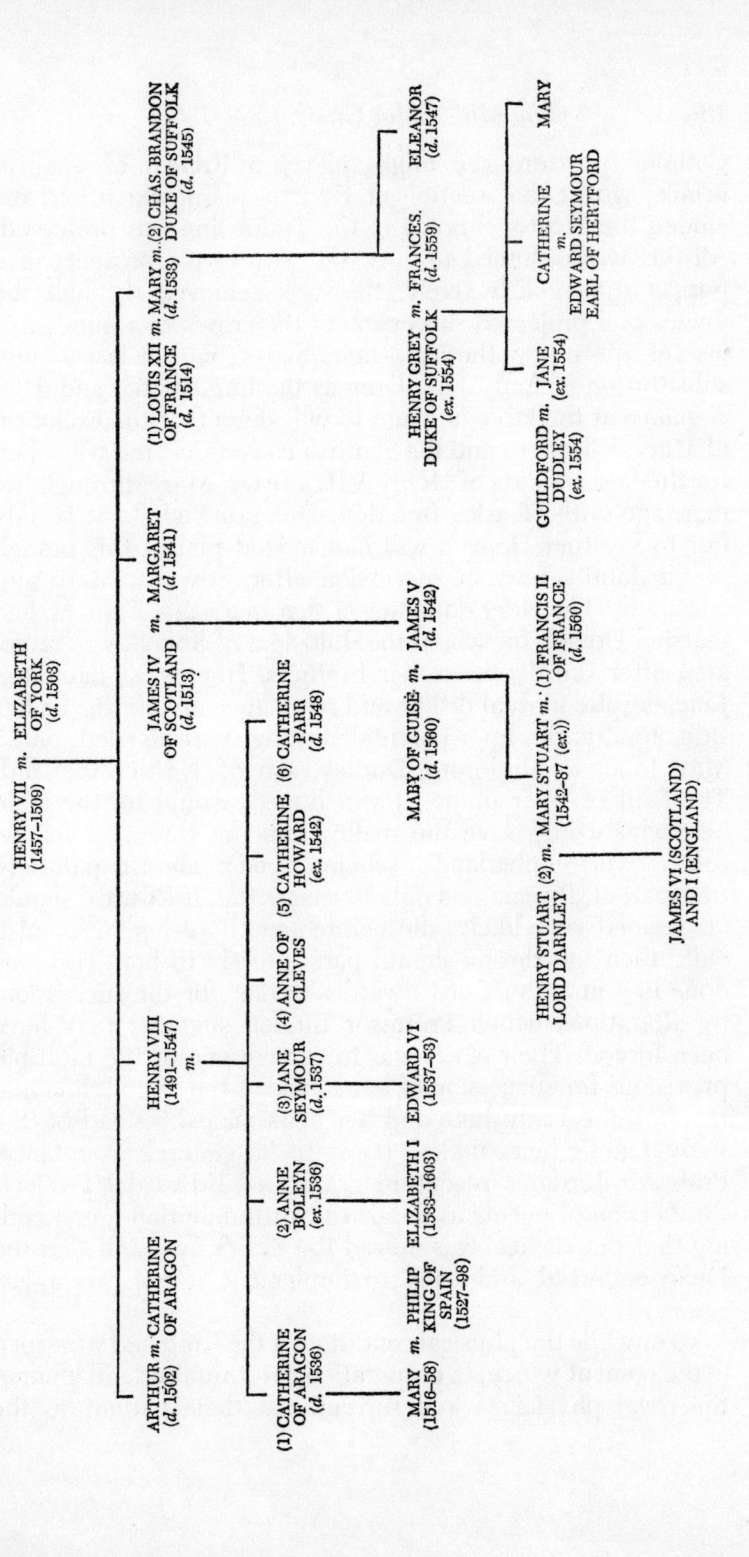

- ARTHUR m. CATHERINE
  (d. 1502)   OF ARAGON
- HENRY VIII
  (1491–1547)
  m.
- MARGARET m. JAMES IV
  (d. 1541)   OF SCOTLAND
              (d. 1513)
- MARY m. (1) LOUIS XII   (2) CHAS. BRANDON
  (d. 1533) OF FRANCE   DUKE OF SUFFOLK
             (d. 1514)   (d. 1545)

Henry VIII's wives:
(1) CATHERINE OF ARAGON (d. 1536)
(2) ANNE BOLEYN (ex. 1536)
(3) JANE SEYMOUR (d. 1537)
(4) ANNE OF CLEVES (d. 1557)
(5) CATHERINE HOWARD (ex. 1542)
(6) CATHERINE PARR (d. 1548)

Children of Henry VIII:
- MARY (1516–58) m. PHILIP KING OF SPAIN (1527–98)
- ELIZABETH I (1533–1603)
- EDWARD VI (1537–53)

James IV & Margaret:
- JAMES V (d. 1542) m. MARY OF GUISE (d. 1560)
  - MARY STUART (1542–87 (ex.)) m. (1) FRANCIS II OF FRANCE (d. 1560)
    m. (2) HENRY STUART LORD DARNLEY
    - JAMES VI (SCOTLAND) AND I (ENGLAND)

Mary & Charles Brandon:
- FRANCES (d. 1559) m. HENRY GREY DUKE OF SUFFOLK (ex. 1554)
  - GUILDFORD DUDLEY (ex. 1554) m. JANE (ex. 1554)
  - CATHERINE m. EDWARD SEYMOUR EARL OF HERTFORD
  - MARY
- ELEANOR (d. 1547)

Catholic pressure she might marry a French or Spanish prince, whilst that section of Henry's plans which had excluded the Scottish branch of the Tudor line was preserved. All this was designed to open the way to the prospect of a puppet queen. Effectively, this was achieved through the device of a projected succession of the crown to a number of (as yet, quite hypothetical) 'heirs males', with a last-minute substitution of Lady Jane Grey as the immediate candidate. A glance at the table on page 15 will show that the exclusion of Mary, Elizabeth and the Scottish cousins left the way open for the descendants of Henry VIII's sister, Mary, through her marriage with Charles Brandon, Duke of Suffolk. It is only fair to say that Henry's will had indeed placed this branch of the family next in succession after Edward, Mary and Elizabeth. The elder daughter of that marriage, Frances, had married Dorset, for whom the dukedom of Suffolk was recreated after the deaths of her brothers. Her eldest daughter, Jane, despite mutual dislike and reluctance (overborne on her side, apparently, by a parental beating) was married, on 25 May 1553, to Guildford Dudley, son of Northumberland. The fruit of their union, it was hoped, would be the male heir who would save the realm from the threat of female rulers. Northumberland's scheme seems almost painfully transparent. It remained only to ensure that if Edward should (as seemed very likely) die before Jane bore her husband a child then the throne should pass directly to her. This was done in a final draft of Edward's 'device' for the succession, by alterations which Professor Bindoff suggests may have been forged. Their effect was to change one of the multiple provisions for succession of heirs male of the Suffolk line into reading 'the Lady Jane and her heirs males' instead of 'the Lady Janes's heirs males'. (Despite its general acceptance, Professor Jordan's recent biography of Edward VI rejects this version of events as unfair to Northumberland, contending that the 'device' was indeed the King's own and that the Duke endorsed and tried to implement it only as a last resort.)[8]

Meanwhile the physical condition of the King had worsened to the point at which, in desperation, Northumberland ignored the royal physicians and surrendered their patient to the reckless expedients of a 'female quack' whose treatments, although ultimately disastrous, produced a short-term rally. Edward now summoned up the resolution and degree of articulacy required to enforce acceptance of his 'device'. Eventually, as the fruit of royal pleading and Northumberland's bullying, over a hundred Councillors or leading personages of the realm signed their acceptance of its terms. Many were loath to do so, including Archbishop Cranmer, who at first 'answered that he might not without perjury, for so much as he was before sworn to my Lady Mary by King Henry's Will', and Edward's own teacher Cheke, who argued that he would 'never distrust God so far in the preservation of his true religion as to disinherit orphans'; but both gave in to persuasion or pressure. Now the artificial stimulus of the 'remedies' inflicted upon Edward gave way before the poisonous effects of their constituents. It remains a moot point as to whether, in the event, the boy died of tuberculosis of the lungs or of (possibly arsenical?) poisoning. He now endured the most dreadful suffering before committing his soul to God at the point of death on 6 July. That death was kept secret for four days while the bitter struggle for the succession commenced. It was to be left to his half-sister Mary, over a month later, to give a full state funeral to the boy who had felt affection for her but had tried none the less to keep her from his throne.[9]

The circumstances in which, despite the careful preparations of Northumberland, sanctioned and given a veneer of legality by the wishes of Edward himself, Mary Tudor succeeded to her inheritance merit the closest consideration. For it may be suggested that her accession to the English throne without widespread bloodshed is perhaps the most significant pointer of the whole mid-century era to the continuity and stability of the Tudor dynasty, as well as the clearest indication of the integration of interest between that dynasty and society. Had Northumberland's project succeeded then the accession of Jane to the Crown might now be (as unjustly) taken for granted as that of Henry Tudor in 1485. At first sight everything seemed in Northumberland's favour. Edward VI had approved his plan; practically every statesman or divine of eminence and influence at the centre of affairs had appended his signature; he held London and had at his disposal what armed forces existed. In terms of *de facto* authority he represented the government of the realm. If rebellion be defined as an armed uprising against established government, then the spontaneous surge of public support for Mary Tudor was a rebellion. Indeed, it is instructive to reflect that it was in effect a *fourth* major rebellion of the mid-Tudor decades (the others being the Rising in the West and Ket's Rebellion in 1549, and Wyatt's Rebellion in 1554; see Chapter 3), and in fact the only successful rising against *de facto* government between 1485 and 1603. It was, in short, a *legitimist* rebellion; in this lies both the reason for and the significance of its success.

One thing only was missing from the almost complete security of Northumberland's position in July 1553 – possession of the person of the Princess Mary. On 4 July both she and Elizabeth received a summons to visit Edward in London. Elizabeth made no move, but Mary actually set out towards the capital. During the night of 6 July she learned, from someone who deliberately breached Northumberland's secrecy, that the boy had died earlier that evening. Immediately she rode north, covering sixty miles to reach Norfolk. In London Bishop Ridley preached a sermon in which he described both Mary and Elizabeth as bastards, and Jane Grey learned that, at the age of sixteen, she was Queen. Northumberland must have been taken aback when the girl whom he had placed on the throne showed ungrateful resolution in declaring that her husband would never be King, but merely a Duke! Ruder shocks were to follow. A force of three hundred men was sent to secure Mary, but the first news received of her was a formal assertion of her right to the throne. Next day, information came that several noblemen had rallied to Mary, together, most significantly, with 'innumerable companies of the common people'.[10]

The significance of this lies more in its indication of popular sympathy for Mary than in terms of military strength. Hatred of Northumberland in East Anglia was the legacy of his suppression of Ket's Rebellion in 1549; but that suppression had demonstrated that spontaneous popular levies, ill-armed and ill-disciplined, were no match for effectively equipped and

The Survival of the Dynasty

resolutely commanded forces. The victor of 1549 was still at hand, but was not easy in mind about leaving London himself in order to capture Mary. When he did so, on 14 July, he seems to have acted at once too soon and too late. Prompt and speedy action, with a small force, might have taken her earlier. But by now the proclamation of Mary in Norwich, on 12 July, and the decision of that city to send her men and arms might indicate a turning of the tide and the prospect of a serious campaign. Northumberland left London with a force of about three thousand and the promise of the Council that they would send him more – a promise that proved as worthless as their fulsome expressions of loyalty. The six ships despatched to intercept any attempt at flight abroad had now put into Yarmouth and declared for Queen Mary, whose forces were augmented by their crews and cannon. Meanwhile the further Northumberland moved from London into the hostile countryside the more difficulty he experienced in retaining the loyalty of what troops he had, especially as it became ever clearer that no reinforcements could be expected en route. It is true that those leaders who resorted to Mary's camp were at first of the lesser nobility, the knights or the gentry; but on this occasion it was they, rather than the greater lords or the 'professional politicians', who seem to have spoken for England.[11]

Back in London the members of the Council began to scent the turn of the tide and the great majority prepared to trim their sails accordingly. Put more harshly, the sinking ship was speedily deserted. On 18 July the Council offered a reward for the arrest of the leader to whom, only four days earlier, it had pledged its loyalty. Next day, to the unrestrained delight of the people, Queen Mary was formally proclaimed. Suffolk, father of the hapless Jane, himself tore down the royal canopy from around his daughter at supper. The wretched Northumberland, hearing the news at Cambridge, proclaimed Mary in the market place. His house of cards had been built without the ace. It collapsed before the irresistible gust of the public will, and did so without violent civil strife. The Earl of Arundel, who had pledged to Northumberland his resolve 'to spend his blood, even at his feet', now came to arrest him. He joined Jane, her husband, and her father, in the Tower. On 3 August, to a tumultuous reception, Queen Mary herself entered London. The historian's deductions from these events are crucial for his judgement of the nature of the Tudor regime; the conclusion drawn by Mary from this overwhelming and bloodless triumph over apparently impossible odds was rather different, but of immense significance for her reign: it was to her, quite literally, an act of God, to whose purposes (as she understood them) her life and policies must now be devoted in the exercise of the power which he had so obviously placed in her hands.[12]

Mary was now thirty-seven years old. Her most notable biographer describes her as 'a small creature, thin and slightly built, with reddish hair, and a complexion which had once been her chief beauty', possessing, incongruously, 'a loud and deep voice, almost like a man's'. Her personality bore the marks of the previous twenty years. At the age of six she had been fleetingly betrothed to the Emperor Charles V, whose son she was one day to marry. In 1525, as Princess of Wales, she had been given her own Council at Ludlow. But from 1527 onwards her father's infatuation for Anne Boleyn, and his redoubled doubts of the validity of his marriage to Catherine, produced an atmosphere of ugly rumours and the deepening humiliation of her mother, which culminated in the events of 1533. After the birth of Elizabeth she was no longer Princess of Wales but 'the Lady Mary, the King's daughter'. In 1534 an Act of Succession formally bastardised her and debarred her from the throne. In face of all this, Mary displayed a stubborn resolution and refused to take an oath to the new succession; but she was now in such despair that she told Chapuys, the imperial ambassador, that her only hope was to die.[13]

Little wonder that the girl, of whom her father declared brutally that 'everyone takes Mary for the bastard she is', toyed with plans of escape abroad. After her mother's death, nearly broken, she was forced to sign a 'confession' in which she accepted royal supremacy in the Church, disavowed the 'Bishop of Rome', and – supreme abasement – declared that 'the marriage heretofore made between his Majesty and my mother... was by God's law and man's law incestuous and unlawful'. It may well be argued in extenuation of the King's apparently vindictive harshness that he was concerned to deprive of any legality what was still a potential focal point of Roman Catholic or foreign-backed opposition to his policies. Yet the impression made upon his victim was also important, for Miss Prescott suggests that 'the scar of her own surrender', the shame of her betrayal of her mother and her mother's Church, marked Mary Tudor for life. Henry recognised his daughter's abject submission by welcoming her once more to court, restoring her household, and even mooting the question of a husband. Among the rumoured bridegrooms were Cromwell, Reginald Pole (her cousin, and a more likely candidate), and then 'a bewildering succession of shadowy suitors' once more including the Emperor Charles, now a widower. Henry had never any real intention of granting Mary to a foreign prince who might revive her obvious claim to succeed to his throne; his daughter well knew that 'while my father lives I shall be only the Lady Mary, the most unhappy lady in Christendom'.[14]

In 1547 her half-brother Edward came to the throne. The tension between their feelings of personal affection and their rival bigotries in religious doctrine increased through his reign. Naturally Mary's enemies suspected her of complicity in the Rising in the West against the First English Prayer Book in 1549. Yet Somerset's moderate policy and Edward's personal inclination concurred in granting Mary a dispensation from the law of uniformity of religious observance, 'for the good affection and brotherly love which we bear towards you [and] in respect of your weakness'. Mary was not among those deluded Catholics who supported Northumberland's plot to overthrow the Lord Protector, discerning clearly that 'the conspiracy against the Protector has envy and ambition only as its motives'. Her fears that the change would worsen the fortunes of Catholicism were justified, and her mind turned once more to schemes of flight. A detailed plan whereby she would escape via Maldon on board a vessel ostensibly trading corn from Flanders, while ships of the Emperor lay off Harwich to escort her, came near to fruition in the summer of 1550. At the last moment haggling over the exact time at which she would dash to the waiting ship and hesitancy on her part, increased by rumour and fear of discovery, let slip the chance. On 14 August the young King's *Chronicle* records a warning of a plot 'to take away the Lady Mary and so to begin an outward war and an inward conspiracy'. The Council's reply to news of this frustrated plan was to make a more determined effort to enforce religious conformity. For the last two years of Edward's reign, Mary's household was denied Mass, although she herself persisted, behind locked doors.[15]

Such was the background of the woman who now came to the English throne. Assessment of her character must avoid the obvious extremes. In regard to personal relationships she was perhaps the kindliest of the Tudor monarchs. Professor Bindoff observes that 'where her own safety and authority were at stake she showed herself the most merciful of her line'. Only two of Northumberland's supporters suffered death with him – an instance of clemency unmatched in Tudor annals. The apparent contradiction between this and the slur of 'Bloody Mary' is striking. Like her half-sister she was doomed to childlessness; but unlike Elizabeth she seems to have shown all the instincts of motherhood. Contemporary comment does not endow her with the reputation for educational attainment and precocity of intellect which attaches to Edward and Elizabeth. We have noted the first-named's disapproval of Mary's fondness for games and gambling and her indulgence in dancing. Miss Prescott finds that 'the root and ground of Mary's character, flawed though it was with faults that her past suffering largely excused, was indeed a plain and humble goodness.... She was no mystic, but she was simply and deeply pious. Her religion did not make her judicious, nothing could do that, since her mind was narrow and by no means acute; but it did make her scrupulous, painstaking, disciplined.' Unfortunately it also made her a fanatic; or perhaps more fairly, her interpretation of the duty which it imposed on her, in the light of her experiences and of the spiritual condition of her realm, made her so. The nationality of her mother and of her bridegroom, together with this element of religious fanaticism, explain the soubriquet 'Spanish Tudor'. Yet she was also her father's daughter, inheriting his resolution and courage, and his ability to appeal to the English people. The bravery displayed by Elizabeth in face of the Spanish Armada was not lacking in Mary in 1553 or again in 1554. Yet, sadly and disastrously, the one supreme characteristic which Henry bequeathed to Elizabeth was denied to Mary: the quality of cool political judgement.[16]

She immediately misinterpreted the circumstances of her accession to the throne. The modern historian may find it clear that 'Mary's triumphant success owed everything to her being King Henry's daughter and very little to her catholic faith'; but to Mary herself winning the throne in despite of all political schemings and military odds pointed a very different moral. It is not surprising that the woman who was to declare that 'I set more by the salvation of my soul than by ten kingdoms' should believe that she had been given charge of a kingdom in order to save the souls of its subjects. The details of her religious policy and its impact will be examined in Chapter 4; our immediate concern is with the effects, upon her personal position and upon the security of the Tudor dynasty, of her joint determination to return her nation to the papal fold and to negotiate a marriage with Philip, son of the Emperor Charles V.[17]

As far as dynastic continuity was concerned, the crucial question in the reign of Edward VI had been whether the boy would live long enough to marry and beget a male heir; the crucial question now, to a country presented at his death with the prospect of no less than seven female heirs apparent and no single male (see table, page 15), was that of the marriage of the Queen. In an era when it was taken for granted that a woman ruler would be weak and subject to guidance the nation would look with anxious eyes at the origin and nature of the support which her consort would bring. For Mary herself the problem was partly resolved by her determination to secure the continuity and stability not only of her line but also of her religion. If reasons of state were not already outweighed in her mind by religious forces, the latter were now heavily reinforced by her personal inclinations. Some few sage counsellors, including Pole, considering her age and the endemic infertility and sickliness of her stock, urged her not to marry. But to Mary the prospect of the succession of a half-sister whose very existence bespoke her mother's shame, her own abasement, and the near-ruin of her faith in England, was abhorrent. Two or perhaps three potential bridegrooms were considered. The candidature of Reginald Pole himself won little support. That of Edward Courtenay, son of the late Marquis of Exeter, released in 1553 from fifteen years' imprisonment in the Tower, was stronger, and may well have satisfied popular wishes and expectations. Yet Mary's Spanish blood, her record of reliance on the support and comfort of Habsburg emissaries through two unhappy decades and the immediate influence of the imperial ambassador Renard directed her hopes elsewhere.

The subject of those thoughts, Prince Philip, expressed his readiness, with some lack of a lover's ardour, in the promise to his father 'to leave it all to your Majesty to dispose as seems fitting'. The French ambassador de Noailles, perceiving the drift of things, urged upon Gardiner the unsuitability of the match, declaring, with prophetic exaggeration, that 'perhaps she would not see him a fortnight in all her life'. The Chancellor himself warned her that 'England would never abide a foreigner, that Courtenay was the only possible marriage for her in England; and that as for Prince Philip the country would not accept him willingly'. On 16 November 1553 a deputation from the House of Commons advised the Queen against the marriage, only to provoke from Mary the hysterical outburst that, if forced to marry against her inclination, 'I will not live three months, and I will bear no children [a superfluous addendum!], and so, Mr Speaker, you will defeat your own ends'. A portrait of Philip by Titian was now despatched to the Queen, with the instruction (again oddly prophetic) that it must be looked at from a distance. But something like panic now filled the English people at the prospect of the marriage, and the portrait's original received from Mary the disquieting instruction to bring his own cooks and doctors. A papal dispensation, required because of the near relationship involved, had been procured, and the terms of the marriage treaty agreed. Mary awaited her bridegroom.[18]

Her happiness was soon shattered by the outbreak of Wyatt's Rebellion: primarily anti-Spanish, secondarily anti-Catholic and supposedly pro-Elizabeth and Courtenay. The support which he mustered brought Wyatt from Kent to London itself. Again, at this crisis point, Mary showed herself a Tudor in making a courageous and successful personal appeal to the loyalty of her London subjects. The near approach of Wyatt occasioned a bedside meeting of the Council between two and three o'clock in the morning, at which Mary – despite the timid counsel of waverers – remained resolute. Her courage and determination were all important, for it would be as correct to say that Wyatt's force disintegrated as that it was defeated (see Chapter 3).[19]

It has been justly observed that in the face of this evidence of national distaste for the match 'a lesser woman would not have dared pursue the marriage; a greater would have realised the folly of it. Mary, with her obstinate courage and her short-sighted judgement, held on'. Her resolution had now a sharper edge. Not now the clemency which had allowed all but three to survive the guilt of Northumberland's attempted coup. Yet another Tudor marriage was 'made in blood'. In the weeks following Wyatt's surrender some scores of the 'meaner sort' taken in arms were hanged on London gibbets. Their deaths were followed by those of Lady Jane Grey, Guildford Dudley, Suffolk, and Wyatt himself. Before his execution the last-named allegedly incriminated Courtenay, the King of France and the Lady Elizabeth in his plot. Although on the scaffold itself he exculpated Courtenay and Elizabeth they were both lodged in the Tower. Gardiner said openly that there would be no peace while Elizabeth lived, but ultimately she was released for lack of evidence.[20]

If this momentary peril to Elizabeth was one 'might-have-been' for the Tudor dynasty, the terms of the articles of marriage between Philip and Mary suggest another. For any son of the marriage would not only have established a near-Spanish dynasty in England and, presumably, have continued acceptance of Roman Catholicism as the official creed, but could also, in certain circumstances, have inherited Burgundy and the Netherlands. These articles were confirmed in April 1554 by Mary's Second Parliament, but a measure permitting the Queen to bequeath her throne by will was defeated while a proposal of Gardiner for a parliamentary disinheritance of Elizabeth came to nothing. Philip himself proved dilatory in crossing to England to see his prospective bride, near ten years his senior, whom he had termed 'our dear and well beloved aunt'. Indeed his father instructed Alva, who was to accompany him: 'Duke, for the love of God see to it that my son behaves in the right manner'. But at last, on a rainy day in July 1554, the couple met at Winchester. Two day later they were wed. Mary fell deeply in love with her bridegroom; but a confidant of Philip described his master as realising 'fully that the marriage was made for no fleshly consideration, but in order to cure the disorders of this country and preserve the Low Countries'.[21]

The impact of this marriage and its consequences upon politics and government, religion and foreign policy will concern us in later chapters. Our immediate interest lies in the dynastic importance of Mary's personal tragedy – her failure to bear a child. For several months, from April 1555 until the end of July when she abandoned hope, the Queen prepared to give birth to a child. The exiled Protestant bishop Ponet alluded to those 'that being desirous of children, procure the midwives to say, they be with child, when their belly is puffed up with dropsy or mole, and having bleared the common people's eyes with processioning, Te deum singing, and bonfire banqueting, use all ceremonies and crying out, whilst another bird's egg is laid in the nest'. This was as unfair as it was savage. Having bitterly deluded herself with false hopes, Mary made no attempt to deceive England with a false heir. At the end of August her husband left for the Netherlands, on a projected short absence which lengthened from weeks into years. Not until March 1557 was Philip to return. He did so for long enough to persuade Mary to declare war against France and then, early in July, left for ever.[22]

These years had witnessed two more efforts to unseat Queen Mary. Although these were not nearly as dangerous as Wyatt's Rebellion the implication in them of the French undoubtedly helped Mary to persuade her Council to the disastrous declaration of war. In January 1558 she once more persuaded herself that she was pregnant. The symptoms may well have been those of her final illness. By the autumn Englishmen – and foreigners, including her calculating husband – were thinking in terms of the succession. Philip's overtures earlier in the year for the betrothal of Elizabeth to a Spanish nominee had, according to Venetian intelligence

The Survival of the Dynasty

sources, provoked from Mary the assertion that Elizabeth 'was neither her sister nor the daughter of ... King Henry ... as she was born of an infamous woman'. Yet in November, as she neared death, the Queen conceded recognition of Elizabeth as her successor. Much has been written of Mary's bigotry and of her lack of political sagacity; yet it is well said that in the last resort, despite her personal distrust of Elizabeth and of all she stood for, despite an almost certain knowledge that Elizabeth's accession to the throne would mean the destruction of all her efforts in the religious sphere, 'Mary Tudor put the integrity of the succession first'. Despite the gravest provocations she had neither destroyed Elizabeth nor prevented her succession to the throne.[23]

It is probably an accurate, if saddening, reflection that it was the death of Mary, as much as the accession of Elizabeth, which was greeted with delight. In some ways Elizabeth came to her inheritance in circumstances more auspicious than Edward or Mary had done: she was at least an adult, while no over-mighty subject attempted to baulk her claim to the throne. Yet a recent study reminds us that 'Elizabeth's accession promised to aggravate the succession question'. Her immediate claim to the throne was not undisputed, while for the future 'past performances indicated that it was not wise to gamble on either the life expectancy or the procreativity of a child of Henry VIII'. This third offspring of that monarch to ascend the throne was now twenty-five years old. She had served an apprenticeship to adversity, danger and intrigue almost as long as that of Mary – and in her case it had lasted almost throughout her life. Declared illegitimate when her mother was disgraced and executed, the infant Elizabeth was precocious enough to notice and to question the change in her style of address from 'Princess' to 'my Lady'. Yet her leading biographer suggests that 'her emotional life, in contrast with Mary's, was unaffected by her mother's misfortunes' – possibly because in her case they were really experienced only in retrospect?[24]

As to her mind, from the age of ten onwards Elizabeth's education came under the guidance of the same school of Cambridge humanists as had provided Edward's tutelage. Especially influential was Cheke's favourite pupil and noted educationist Roger Ascham, who found his pupil eager and intelligent in her studies. These continued into the reign of Edward, but alongside them for the next twelve years ran a schooling of a different type which, if harder and more shrewd, also served to prepare her for her long and successful reign. During her time in the household of Catherine Parr, now married to Sudeley, the latter's rather coarse horseplay with one who was no longer a child evoked the scandalised remonstrance of her governess. Elizabeth left and set up her own household, but Catherine's death in childbed led to renewed talk of marriage with the Admiral, an ambition which contributed to his downfall. There followed for Elizabeth an unpleasant period during which she was suspected of complicity in his schemes; she suffered cross-examination on the actions of certain of her servants, and angrily rebutted the rumour that she was 'with child by my Lord Admiral'. Safely negotiating the first of several such patches of thin ice on to which she strayed, Elizabeth established and maintained a reputation for studious and careful prudence throughout the rest of Edward's reign, and took her place alongside Mary after the failure of Northumberland's conspiracy in 1553.[25]

The concord between the sisters was short-lived. The effect of Mary's religious policy and of her marriage project could only be to turn all Protestant and many patriotic hopes towards the prospective heir to the throne. 'Let Elizabeth's prudence be divine, she could not keep her name from every hot-head's lips; and sisterly affection could not live in such an atmosphere.' Elizabeth's prudence was calculating rather than divine; she experienced a 'conversion' to Roman Catholicism formal enough to satisfy Mary and allay danger, perfunctory enough to assure all zealous Protestants that her head, not her heart, had consented. Mary was not long deceived — we have mentioned her unsuccessful plan to repeal the statutory declaration by which Elizabeth was still her successor. Against this background Elizabeth could hardly escape suspicion of complicity in Wyatt's Rebellion. As to the reality of her implication 'not proven' must remain the verdict: Sir John Neale finds it 'difficult to believe that she was ignorant of the conspiracy'. After two months in the Tower she was released, although kept under strict surveillance for some time. But the failure of Mary to bear a child and the increasing recognition (by Spanish interests as well as by English Protestants) that the accession of her sister was but a matter of time strengthened Elizabeth's position. Two dangers only remained: involvement in some reckless conspiracy, and entrapment into a marriage to serve Spanish diplomacy. She avoided both, and in November 1558 came safely to her throne.[26]

Yet the safety of her tenure of that throne could not be taken for granted. The young Queen was confronted by a complex of problems. These included the existence of a serious rival claimant to her crown, the precarious nature not only of her own recognition but of her country's position in the international field, the legacy of over a decade of religious change and discord, and serious financial and social weaknesses. As to the qualities of personality with which the new monarch faced these problems there is again some conflict of interpretation. What some describe as skilful prudence appears to others as shiftiness, inspired opportunism as lack of principle, a cautious weighing of the odds as dilatory procrastination, cool humanism as shallow religious feelings. In fairness Elizabeth could not but be what circumstances as well as heredity had made her. And where heredity was concerned she seems to have displayed the cool – or cold – political skill, the courage, the flair both for assessment of and for appealing to public opinion which had characterised her father. The charges of vanity, duplicity and vacillation have led to the unkind (and perhaps reckless) assertion that if Elizabeth's undoubted virtues were those of a statesman, her defects were those of her sex.

Elizabeth's sex was at once her weakness and her strength. Once established upon the throne the anxieties of her Councillors and her people reverted to the problems formerly presented by a female accession: the potential strength or weakness of her rule, the influences which would guide her decisions, the choice of a husband, and the question of the succession. That she would be subject to influence and that she would marry in order to perpetuate the Tudor line were hardly questioned. With historian's hindsight it is all too easy to point the contrasts between Elizabeth and Mary, to observe how the former came to terms with her unmarried state as she realised the political and diplomatic ends which it could be made to serve. But to contemporaries it may well have seemed all too likely that the mid-Tudor tragi-comedy of marriage errors had but changed its leading actress, not its nature. In retrospect it may seem clear that Elizabeth was unlikely to forget political expediency in a surge of religious and personal passion as Mary Tudor had done. Events indeed proved that Elizabeth did not choose to exchange a spinster's role which she could use as a queen in her own game of political and international chess for a married state which might convert her to a lesser piece in the strategy of others. Yet to mid-Tudor observers the element of personal passion could not so readily be discounted.

In 1559 the Speaker of the Lower House thought fit to remind his sovereign that

> the Kings of England have never been more careful of any thing, than that the Royal Family might not fail of Issue.... Very lately your sister, Queen Mary, being well in years, married Philip of Spain. If lack of Children use to be inflicted by God as a great Punishment as well upon Royal as private Families; what and how great a Sin may it be, if the Prince voluntarily pluck it upon himself, whereby an infinite heap of Miseries must needs overwhelm the Commonwealth with all Calamities which the mind even dreadeth to remember?

Yet the early hopes of those who looked upon her 'marriage and the fruit thereof as a sure pawn to bind all men's hearts' plummeted when the direction of Elizabeth's marital inclinations became clear. The principal, though not unchallenged, subject of her romantic feelings, Robert Dudley, was already married. Moreover his name and parentage (for he was the son of Northumberland) sufficed to attach to his candidature the keenest suspicion, as reviving all the fears of 1553. Nor was the position improved by the death of his wife, Amy Robsart, in circumstances sufficiently obscure to open the floodgates of gossip. His pretensions to the royal hand met coy, but unmistakable, encouragement. In October 1560 the English ambassador in Paris urged Cecil 'to do all your endeavour to hinder that marriage; for if it take place there is no counsel or advice that can help . . . God and religion will be out of estimation; the Queen discredited, condemned, and neglected, and the country ruined and made prey'. How serious was the danger? Professor MacCaffrey concludes that for a while Elizabeth was 'really tempted to marriage. . . . In the months between summer 1560 and spring 1561 Elizabeth cast off the restraints of duty and convention and gave rein to her feelings in a way which disconcerted and dismayed her advisors. For an interval English affairs were threatened with the fearfully destructive kind of experience which overtook Scotland a few years later, in the wake of the Darnley murder and the Bothwell marriage.' But in the end the head over-ruled the heart.[27]

The dread of an injudicious marriage aggravated a situation which was already sufficiently complicated and precarious to fret Elizabethan statesmen. Alongside the question of Elizabeth's right to occupy the throne of England ran that of the succession to that throne as long as she remained unmarried. In 1561, the revelation that Lady Catherine Grey, sister of the unfortunate Jane and as such the leading contender of the Suffolk line, had been secretly wedded to the Earl of Hertford, son of Somerset, and was shortly to bear his child, provoked from Elizabeth an outburst of fury. Hertford and his bride were sent to the Tower and the validity of the marriage was assailed; a Commission declared the union unlawful and the child was formally bastardised. Vexatious as was this incident, the real threat to Elizabeth came from the Scottish descendants of Margaret, elder sister of Henry VIII. This Stuart branch of the Tudor dynasty had indeed been excluded from the succession by Henry's will. But what if his wishes in this respect could be regarded as part of the complex of decisions bound up with his unjustified repudiation of Catherine of Aragon and illicit liaison with Anne Boleyn? Then to some Catholics they could with equal justice be set on one side along with the bastard Elizabeth. Eyes which scanned such arguments with conviction would turn to Mary Stuart as clearly the legitimate Queen of England.

The eagerness with which her candidature was espoused by the French court and the folly of so much of her own conduct should not blind us to the elements of justice in Mary's case. Professor Levine has pointed out that her purity of descent from Henry VII was beyond dispute, indeed that 'she was his only living descendant whose lineage could not be challenged with a charge of bastardy by alleging a doubtful marriage'. Her cousin Elizabeth, although ultimately tormented by continual plotting into ordering her execution, was to acknowledge Mary's son as the heir to her throne. But the attractions of the accession of the Protestant James which brought about the union of the Crowns of England and Scotland in 1603 did not attach to the candidacy of his mother in 1558. For Mary Stuart represented not only Roman Catholicism but also a Scotland which offered the prospect not of a termination of the old enmity but of English humiliation through the triumph of the 'auld alliance'. To English opinion any loyalty inspired by the element of Tudor blood in Mary's father was far outweighed by fear of the French blood of her mother and her husband. A spokesman in the 1563 Parliament was to declare that even if that body recognised Mary's right to the succession 'our common people and the stones in the streets would rebel against it'.[28]

Nor was the fear hypothetical. For Mary Stuart's father-in-law, Henry II of France, immediately asked the Pope to publish Elizabeth's illegitimacy and to sanction the recognition of Mary which he himself accorded by inducing her to adopt the title and arms of an English monarch. Mary, who had married the French Dauphin in April 1558 (see Chapter 6), was already Queen of Scotland in her own right and soon became Queen of France upon the death of Henry II in July 1559. For a short while a Valois-Stuart monarchy extending from John O'Groats to the Pyrenees seemed a rather tenuous possibility. It grew less likely when Francis II, Mary's husband, died in December 1560. Yet it might be urged that Mary's return to Scotland in August 1561 increased her menace to Elizabeth as a personal rival for the English Crown in that she now appeared to patriotic English Catholics as a claimant in her own right rather than as a pawn in the diplomacy of the traditional enemy, France. As we shall see, Mary found that her Scottish inheritance was very far from untroubled. None the less her return was followed by an attempt to negotiate with Elizabeth to obtain recognition of her right to succeed to the English throne. Elizabeth typically blew hot and cold on this approach. She conceded that 'I for my part know none better nor that myself would prefer to her', but would not commit herself to any formal and overt recognition, and expressed her aversion to this effort 'to require me in my own life to set my winding sheet before my eye'.[29]

Little more than a year later her winding sheet seemed, quite literally, very near. In October 1562 Elizabeth fell ill with smallpox and, at the crisis of the attack, was close to death. There seems little doubt that her death at that time would have been followed by a disputed candidature which, in conjunction with religious tensions and the international interests involved, would almost certainly have led to civil war and possibly invasion. It is not surprising that the Parliament which met in 1563 immediately concerned itself with the question of the succession. It addressed to the Queen a petition whose phraseology has a familiar ring in speaking of

> the great dangers and the unspeakable miseries of civil wars; the perilous intermeddlings of foreign princes with seditious, ambitious, and factious subjects at home; the waste of noble houses; the slaughter of people, subversion of towns, intermission of all things pertaining to the maintenance of the realm, unsurity of all men's possessions, lives and estates; [and the] daily interchanging of attainders and treasons. All these mischiefs and infinite others are most likely and evident if your Majesty should be taken from us without a known heir.

In particular Parliament sought confirmation of the will of Henry VIII or, if that were not possible, clarification of the succession position. But Elizabeth was no readier to yield to their importunities than she had been to those of the Scottish Queen.[30]

She wished to do nothing that would antagonise Mary Stuart, especially in view of the latter's current explorations of the possibilities of a match with Don Carlos, son of Philip II of Spain. Elizabeth's own counter to this was to offer her cousin the hand of Robert Dudley! Unlikely as this may sound it may also suggest that Elizabeth was once more fully in command of herself, and had begun her prolonged development of the matrimonial gambit on the diplomatic chess-board. She had now entered her thirties still unmarried. The succession question was by no means over, the danger from Mary Stuart was to recur in more dangerous circumstances; but the immediate crisis of the Elizabethan reign had been surmounted. Elizabeth had made one thing clear in the Scottish negotiations of 1561: her resolve that 'so long as I live I shall be Queen of England'. The Tudor dynasty was not to survive her; yet, since she was blessed with better health and more political maturity (and perhaps better fortune?) than young Edward or Mary, in the decades that remained that dynasty was to register some of its greatest triumphs.[31]

3 A Crisis of Governance

The ever-present concern about the dynasty itself, whether in terms of its legitimate succession or of its statecraft, was the focal point to which all other aspects of the mid-Tudor crisis must be related – as we shall see immediately in considering the alleged deterioration in quality of government. The assertion that, in an age of essentially monarchical power, the personality and statesmanship of the occupant of the throne would be reflected in the calibre of administration exercised in its name is a truism. Yet this was not the whole story; for when the monarch's personal ability is suspect then the efficiency of the processes and of the officers of government becomes even more crucial. Hence the question of the extent to which the institutions of government continued effectively to perform their functions.

The 'bureaucratic history' of the mid-century decades has been subject to conflicting interpretations, but we should remember that, in what was still a neo-feudal age, events might mean more in terms of the ambition of the 'over-mighty subject' than in those of administrative evolution. What counted, in the last analysis, was power and its exercise. In Tudor England, as far as the mass of the population was concerned, the quality of that exercise largely depended upon understanding and co-operation between the institutions of central authority and their local agents – essentially, although not exclusively, the justices of the peace. The loyalty of the 'political nation' (those whose social and economic standing gave them a presumptive right to influence and leadership – 'a social *elite*' or 'governing class'[1]) not only to the dynasty itself but also to those individuals and institutions that exercised authority in its name was therefore of supreme importance. So too, finally, was the reaction of the governed, of the 'common people' whose docility could not be taken for granted; indeed, the rebellions of this period will claim much of our attention.

That there was some falling-away in quality of governance in mid-Tudor England is agreed; but its extent and the assertion that it may be dated from the fall of Cromwell rather than from the death of Henry VIII have been contested. It is difficult to deny the justice of the 'contrast between the highly successful internal policy' of the 1530s 'and the fumblingly unsuccessful external policy' of the years after 1540. Thereafter we read much of the will and decisions of the King, but little of any coherent purpose. Yet some would attribute the contrast to changing circumstances rather than to Henry's 'dropping the pilot'. Few would dispute the accuracy of the pen-picture of 'a huge, consequential and majestic figure . . . indisputably revered, indeed, in some strange way, loved . . . [who] had raised monarchy to near-idolatry. . . . Thanks above all to Thomas Cromwell, his reign had given England much "good governance". The administrative machine was more efficient and capacious than it had ever been – as was the legal (and this was largely to Wolsey's credit).' But the allusions to his ministers recall the frequent assertion that Henry's mind, for all its aggressive vigour, was not fertile of constructive or original ideas and that most of the fruitful innovations of his reign must be ascribed to Wolsey or to Cromwell. While we must not antedate the death of Henry VIII to 1540, the fall of his greatest minister in that year raises important questions in our present context.[2]

The achievement of Thomas Cromwell is undeniable, but its magnitude and significance have been variously interpreted. Certainly as the King's first minister he was responsible for the crucial legislation of the Reformation Parliament, for considerable administrative reform (in the sphere of finance and in the evolution of the importance of the office of Principal Secretary), and for closer unification of the realm (as in the Act of Union of 1536). Undoubtedly he was a prime mover in carrying through a religious revolution in establishing statutory recognition of the Crown as Head of the Church in England. Professor Elton would go further and discern in the method, objectives and consequences of Cromwell's work revolutionary constitutional implications. Indeed, he emerges as 'the most remarkable revolutionary in English history', under whose guidance 'an attitude to the state that can only be called medieval was ... replaced by one that can only be called modern'. The essential ingredient of this 'Tudor revolution in government' is the establishment of a concept of national sovereignty untrammelled by any competing or limiting authority within or from outside the realm. Moreover the assertion of the omnicompetence of King-in-Parliament as both method and result of enlarging the scope of the state by 'taking over' the Church acquits the minister of any charge of 'despotic' tendencies: 'so far from attempting to build a despotism in England, Thomas Cromwell was that country's first parliamentary statesman'. By contrast with the achievement of these years, the period following 1540 saw the decline or even 'failure of Tudor government' – although assessment of the extent of such deterioration has more recently been qualified.[3]

This stimulating thesis has found its critics as well as its admirers. The former have suggested that it overstates both the personal and the revolutionary elements in the events of the 1530s, in particular that 'the national sovereign state appears more the instrument than the product of the Reformation'. Yet, ironically, Professor Hurstfield has also discerned a turning-point or high-water mark in the extension of the authority of the Crown in an event of the year preceding the fall of Cromwell – but in the context of a very different interpretation of the drift and purpose of his constitutional schemes. In a thought-provoking reopening of the question 'Was there a Tudor despotism after all?' he considers the form and significance of the Statute of Proclamations of 1539 (31 Henry VIII, c. 8). The discrepancy between the apparently sweeping implications of the tone of the preamble and the moderation of the subsequent clauses as enacted leads him to conclude that the object of the original bill was in fact frustrated. While accepting that the statute did not give to Royal Proclamations *per se* the full force of law (thus enabling the Crown to over-ride common law on the one hand and dispense with Parliament on the other) he believes that this may well have been the real purpose of the bill. Indeed both Protector Somerset's repeal of the statute and Gardiner's retrospective comments on its enactment (in 1547) are seen as indicative of contemporary opinion as to its motivation. Thus 'the events of 1539 mark a failure on the part of the government and may well have been the first premonitory signs as far as the King's minister was concerned, that the sands were running out. . . . He was left with an emasculated Statute of Proclamations, unhappy portent of his own crumbling power.' While Professor Elton would not accept the general interpretation, he agrees in identifying 1539 as the year in which Cromwell's power came under serious attack: 'from April 1539 onwards, Cromwell's control of affairs became intermittently precarious, and from the end of the year he had his hands full with attempts to avoid the disaster that in the end overtook him'.[4]

Was it a disaster for the realm as well as for the minister? Did it open the door to administrative deterioration and corruption, to increasingly dangerous factional strife, and to reckless and ruinously mistaken policies? It is clear that Cromwell was not replaced by any single minister of equal eminence. In 1540, almost symbolically, the office of Principal Secretary was divided between Wriothesley and Sadler and lost the exalted rank with which their predecessor had endowed it – although this depression in status was not to be permanent. Other able servants of the Crown were to hand, such as Paget and Petre, who replaced Wriothesley and Sadler as joint Principal Secretaries within a few years and who were to bring much continuity of administrative and conciliar experience to subsequent reigns. It has indeed been suggested that the downfall of Cromwell allowed the status and power of the Privy Council as an institution to emerge with greater clarity: 'never before had it enjoyed such clear and continuous life as a corporate executive, even if it had never before been so ridden with increasingly bitter faction-struggle'. The 'even if' raises the whole question of the calibre of administration and consistency of direction during what have been described as 'the only years in [Henry's] reign when government policy was directly disastrous to the country'. Immediately after the fall of Cromwell,

Gardiner and Norfolk seemed pre-eminent, but by the end of the reign the Howard interest was in ruins and Hertford stood almost unchallenged.[5]

The undoubted fact of Henry's personal dominance in decision-making begs the question of the extent to which the King was becoming increasingly capricious and injudicious in policy as well as harsh and vengeful in temperament. The almost wanton destruction of Cromwell has been adduced as the very clearest evidence of failure of the quality of balanced judgement. It came as the result of personal jealousies and court intrigue, exploiting the charges of heresy and of diplomatic embarrassment, rather than of any closely argued disagreements over policy between King and minister. Within the year Henry was expressing his regrets and his suspicions, berating those advisers who 'upon light pretexts, by false accusations' had 'made him put to death the most faithful servant he ever had'; but it was then too late. Professor Scarisbrick depicts the King as still in control, as master of all the factions at court and in Council, and as revelling in the cut and thrust of complicated international rivalry; yet his final assessment of the effects upon the realm is damning: 'He who had been made the richest King in Christendom ... left it in debt. He who was always ready to parade his paternal care for the commonwealth was guilty of ... a wholesale debasement of English coin, without parallel in English history ... to feed his wars ... Rarely, if ever, have the unawareness and irresponsibility of a king proved more costly of material benefit to his people.' The expense and dubious achievement of his foreign policy, the squandering of confiscated church assets and the missed opportunities of genuine religious and social reform will concern us later. Meanwhile in regard to governmental efficiency it is significant that a detailed consideration of the Court of Wards as 'a microcosm of mid-sixteenth-century administration as a whole' traces the 'corruption and decay of the Henrician system of government' as commencing in the last years of the rule of Henry himself: 'like other Tudor institutions it betrayed marked weaknesses of policy and administration during those last years of Henry VIII's rule as the reins of government began to slip from his hands'.[6]

The relationship between the personalities and the instruments of government, and the question of relative responsibilities for any deterioration in quality of that government, during the decades after 1540, have been subject to sharp conflicts of opinion. Professor Elton, while recognising the prevalence of 'corruption and inefficiency' during the post-Cromwellian era, has now 'come to think that to speak of collapse, or anything remotely like it, is a mistake. What in some ways now impresses me most is the way in which government never lost control despite all the problems facing it', while Dr Penry Williams urges that 'the dependence of the administration upon Cromwell appeared quickly enough in the years after his fall', indeed that 'the decline of the agencies of finance, the collapse of the privy council, and the apparent increase in corruption suggest . . . that the Cromwellian "system" was as vulnerable as the medieval to the accidents of personality. . . . Surely the history of the years 1540–58 suggests . . . that bureaucratic administration flourished when politics were stable, not that stable politics resulted from bureaucratic administration.'[7]

Certainly the importance of administrative considerations, as the end of Henry's reign approached with his son still a minor, was equalled if not exceeded by that of the balance between personalities, or factions, in his entourage, and of the nature and viability of any arrangements by which he attempted to crystallise the position until Edward should come of age. For the ambitions and actions of the over-mighty subject could undermine the smoothest of bureaucratic devices. Worse still, against a background of any uncertainties as to royal succession, the ambitions and rivalries of powerful nobles or the weaknesses or mistaken policies of government might provoke the recurrent nightmare of the Tudor line: rebellion. The events of the period 1547–58 were to justify all these fears. If one suggests as possible criteria of the quality of governance the extent to which the Council remained an instrument for the formulation and enforcement of policies in the interests of the Crown, as distinct from those of individuals, the degree of (relative) efficiency and probity with which the administrative functions of government were discharged, and the success in maintenance of order in the realm and obedient loyalty among the common people, the partial failure of these years is undeniable.

In approaching the troubles of the reign of Edward VI one must recall the enduring validity of the judgement of A. F. Pollard that they must 'be ascribed in the first place not to the feebleness or folly of this or that statesman, nor to the policy which he adopted, but to a constitutional system that required a ruler, crowned and actual, to make it work.... Sovereignty was personal, and it was vested in a child nine years of age. A constitutional fiction was indispensable....' The solution adopted was based upon acceptance and 'interpretation' of the will of Henry VIII. The constitutional validity and even the authenticity of this document have sometimes been questioned; but there is no doubt that at the time it was accepted. It named a Council of Regency, composed of sixteen executors, equal and limited in power. The balance and intention of any conscious distribution of its membership between 'Catholics', 'Protestants' and 'politiques' have been much discussed, but the course of events was decided by three realities: the exclusion of Gardiner, the ambition and determination of Edward Seymour, and the understanding between Seymour and the 'master of practises', William Paget, who had been very close to the dying King and professed to know his intentions. The question, unanswered in the will itself, of the actual working of the executive function of government was resolved (in a breach of its terms) by declaring Seymour to be 'Protector of the realm and Governor of the King's person ... during his minority ... because he was the King's uncle', although he was to act only with the advice and consent of his fellow-executors. The acquiescence which they displayed was soon rewarded by Paget's timely revelation of a list of honours and advancements (and of appropriate grants of land to accompany them) which had been in Henry's mind shortly before his death. Scepticism must be tempered by the fact that Paget himself got nothing – although the Protector had privately agreed to regard him as his chief adviser.[8]

Seymour's undoubted primacy as Lord Protector was now ratified by commissions signed by Edward VI himself during 1547, and Professor Jordan concludes that 'vast and legally almost unfettered power now lodged in Somerset's hands', indeed that 'it required revolutionary forces and colossal and tragic mistakes in judgement on the Lord Protector's part to weaken the structure of power with which he stood seised in late 1548'. As we shall see, these mistakes were duly made – but what of the charge made by those who overthrew Somerset: that his ambition was becoming as unrestrained as his power, that he coveted the Crown itself? While certainty about human motives is rare all the evidence suggests that this charge was wholly unjust. In particular Somerset, unlike his rival Northumberland, was, at the supreme crisis of his fortunes, unwilling to submit the realm to the risk of civil war. Of personal arrogance he was certainly guilty. Moreover he contrived to combine a genuine sympathy with 'Commonwealth' ideals with an almost offensively ostentatious display of the wealth which his career had brought him. Nor was he helped by the personality of his wife, 'a woman of a haughty stomach' whose preoccupation with no fewer than ten children was still not sufficient to prevent her from meddlesome and unpopular interventions into private and political affairs. Pollard's allegedly over-generous assessment of Somerset has been subject to much revision, and it is now quite impossible to miss the seamy thread of personal ambition and greed which runs through much of his career; yet it remains true that impracticable idealism rather than calculating self-interest is the main ground of criticism of his governmental policies. While detailed aspects of these policies will be considered in later chapters, we are here concerned with the general quality of Somerset's rule in terms of efficiency and integrity. In this context it has been suggested that the measure 'For the repeal of certain statutes concerning treasons, felonies, etc.' (I Edw. VI, c. 12) is of fundamental significance as an expression of Somerset's whole philosophy of government, of his tolerance and wish for 'a little more reasonable liberty' than had been the case in the later years of Henry VIII, and of his sympathy with the ideals associated with the 'Commonwealth men'. Somerset's contemporary critics anticipated historians in pointing to the dangers of an impracticably idealist and over-liberal policy, in particular to the fear that a slack hand on the reins might let loose the

A Crisis of Governance

dreaded forces of disorder, faction or anarchy – allegedly endemic, if latent, among the lower orders. Yet an admirer of Somerset might with perhaps equal justice contend that it was the non-co-operation of those of his own order in his benevolent social and economic policies which fomented the troubles of 1549.[9]

Before considering the disastrous climax of Somerset's government we may glance briefly at the personnel and institutions of his rule. The composition of the Council which supported him was, with the exclusion of Gardiner and Wriothesley and one or two minor changes, effectively that of Henry VIII's last years. Its members were distinguished by maturity and experience, many having impressive administrative, diplomatic, military or academic records. Professor MacCaffrey points to the creation by Henry VIII during the last decade of his reign of a body of 'new nobility' distinguished by their worth as royal servants which became, effectively, 'not only the king's executor but also his political heir. It was to them, not to the child Edward, that royal power passed in January 1547.' Concerning this body of men several observations spring to mind: first, despite the immense personal dominance of Somerset they were able, in the crisis of 1549, to depose him without bloodshed; secondly, many of them contrived, with considerable dexterity, to transfer from the cause of Northumberland to that of Mary Tudor in 1553; thirdly, despite their obvious loyalty to the Tudor dynasty, and the considerable continuity of governmental experience and administrative competence which they brought to the perilous mid-century years of that dynasty's weakness, many of them displayed a personal rapacity which fully merits the charge of 'reaping a golden harvest of new titles and embarking on an orgy of political piracy, looting both Church and Crown'. Lands with an estimated capital value of about one and a half million pounds passed from royal to aristocratic possession at the time; in particular, almost forty per cent of all Crown gifts made in the reign of Edward VI went to a relatively small group of peers at the centre of power. Inevitably this raises the charge that the mid-Tudor era was an age of gross corruption. Despite what has been said a word of explanation, if not of mitigation, may be in order; for these men were subject to the maximum of opportunity, pressure and temptation. To put it in its long-term perspective, the emergence and expansion of the duties and powers (social and religious as well as political) of the modern state – a process which was proceeding apace in mid-Tudor England – made its functions ever more important to the ordinary citizen. Those functions were in fact 'exercised by a numerically small sector of the nation ... which controlled the distribution of influence, patronage, the profits of office ... and more jobs sometimes meant more jobbery.... That is why the influence of individuals was important and the quality of government could change with the individuals or group who wielded power.'[10]

Institutionally, it has been suggested that the Privy Council 'came of age during the Edwardian interim, when to a degree it was free of the immense personal authority of the Crown which it had known under Henry VIII and free as well of the paralysing factional divisions which so weakened it under Queen Mary'. Certainly, despite the irksomely personal nature of Somerset's dominance, the use of the administrative device of proclamations backed by King-in-Council reached its peak at this time. Nor did this imply any hostility towards Parliament whose co-operation was sought by Somerset – not always successfully – in the enactment of a substantial body of measures of religious and economic reform. In the implementation, as distinct from enactment or formal promulgation, of policy the local agencies of government were of pre-eminent importance. Expressions of the Council's concern that the justices of the peace were failing to enforce the law rigorously were not peculiar to the mid-century decades, but certainly reached full spate at this time. Ironically, while Somerset's critics were to attribute the disorders of 1549 to his allegedly over-liberal policy and slackness in law enforcement, the leaders of Ket's Rebellion inverted this argument, stating explicitly that a major purpose of their rising was to secure the implementation of legislation and proclamations which the justices of the peace were quite deliberately allowing to go by default.[11]

As far as the Lord Protector himself was concerned, it was his attempts at over-zealous, rather than too lax, administration of certain aspects of the law – especially through the Court of Requests 'for poor men's causes' – that did most to anger many of his colleagues. Moreover, while Somerset apparently displayed little aptitude for the details of routine administration, he took some interest in the completion of one or two reforms projected before the death of Henry VIII. The work of a Commission established in 1546, which included such experienced alministrators as Mildmay, Wriothesley, Paget, Petre and Paulet, to consider the state of the various courts of revenue led to some remodelling of structure by the statute 1 Edw. VI, c. 8, but lax control allowed continued irregularities. Mid-Tudor administration was all too familiar with the precept: 'thou shalt not muzzle the ox when he treadeth out the corn'.

The events of 1549 to which we now turn are of a double significance in our present context: first, as leading to the downfall of the well-meaning though spotted regime of Somerset, and secondly, as marking perhaps the supreme crisis in mid-Tudor government and almost certainly the nadir in relationships between the 'political nation' and the commons of Tudor England. The rebellions of 1549 take on their full meaning not in relation to the immediate, and rather fortuitous, causes of their outbreak, but in the context of the state of endemic riot which existed in so much of England, and in that of long-run social, economic and religious developments. In short, they marked a crisis of society as well as of government. (The fears of government through the summer months of the years 1548 to 1551 suggest a striking, if incongruous, modern parallel.)

Indeed, if we take account of the events of 1553 and 1554, then it is probably true to say that government was confronted by as many serious rebellions in some half-dozen years as it was for the whole of the rest of the Tudor era after the first twelve years of the reign of Henry VII. As we shall see, each outbreak sprang from a different combination of political, personal, regional, religious and social circumstances. Yet consideration of the risings as a group suggest some intriguing points: although such an obvious threat to authority they were in some sense (or at least purported to be) 'conservative' rebellions. They were so very dangerous because – in marked contrast with the Pilgrimage of Grace or the Rising of the Northern Earls – they all took place in southern England near the heart of Tudor power. Each of them reflected also a conjunction of either weakness or rashness at the centre of the national polity with a suggested 'vacuum' of power in the localities. Their nearness to success made them a crisis of government; their whole background was a crisis of society.

The risings of 1549 fulfilled the fears and warnings of Paget (whose own brother, ironically, was involved). His and indeed the whole Council's almost neurotic concern with public order was understandable, for the summer of 1548 had been filled with the rumblings of the discontent which was to erupt in the following year. The problem which their outbreak posed to authority – put bluntly, problems of repression – may be stated in terms of finance, troops and supplies, communications, leadership and confidence. The first of these, already serious enough in view of the Crown's precarious financial position, was made worse by the need to employ large numbers of foreign mercenary troops. The use of such forces was relatively new in England, and the psychological effect of their large-scale employment in order to put down bands of Englishmen should perhaps receive more emphasis; indeed the Council itself conceded that it was 'odious to our people'.[12] Several thousand Italian and German troops were engaged, many drawn from forces raised for the Scottish and Boulogne campaigns but some raised specially when the 'stirs' commenced in the spring of 1549. The fact that they were used in such numbers, despite the preoccupation with the military threat from abroad and the recognition that their employment was abhorent to most Englishmen, gives the clearest possible indication of the Council's fear that the loyalty of the local shire levies could not be taken for granted. The allusion to conflict with Scotland and with France points to another crucially important aspect of the risings: the fact that they came at a time when the international position of England was precarious in both political and military terms. The problem of communications was aggravated by the simultaneous existence of two major rebellions at opposite ends of the country, in the West Country and in

East Anglia, and this in turn made the quality of leadership and of confidence, in the regions affected, even more important.

From April onwards rioting of a more or less serious nature occurred sporadically in almost all the midland and southern counties of England. The Rising in the West had been presaged in April 1548 by the mob murder in Cornwall of Archdeacon William Body, a hated public symbol of religious innovation and of the spoliation of church property which so often accompanied it. Rebellion now burst out at two separate and quite spontaneous flash-points. That at Bodmin need occasion no surprise. That at the small and isolated Devonshire village of Sampford Courtenay, while puzzling at first sight, is doubly symbolic in that the rising both began and ended here, and in that the 'vacuum of power' which the disgrace of the Courtenay family had created in the southwest is suggested as a contributory cause. The overt and basic motivation of the risings was religious (specifically, dislike of the new Prayer Book and forms of worship); but this was undoubtedly mingled with resentment of social and economic grievances and a virulent hatred of 'gentlemen', few of whom participated in the leadership. Dereliction of duty, rather than complicity, was the charge made against the gentry of the West Country, and by late June the two rebel forces had joined at Crediton with the aim of besieging Exeter. Somerset, in view of the troubles nearer London, was understandably reluctant to commit major forces to the far south-west, and seems to have been slow to appreciate the gravity of the position, although Paget (writing from abroad) advocated immediate and stern measures. After an abortive attempt at negotiation Lord Russell was placed in command, but his instructions stopped short of rigorous repression.

Ariving in the west, Russell was as uncertain of his forces, whose unreliability was clearly manifest in their desertion rate, as he was of his orders and his strategy. He contemplated a withdrawal which might well have been disastrous. Fortunately Exeter itself remained loyal, for the ambivalence of its citizens' religious sympathies was less important than their fears of the sack which might follow capitulation. The rebel forces numbered several thousands, but the city stood siege for five weeks. Meanwhile Russell's letters to the Council made it clear that he considered his troops inadequate either for a major engagement or for relief of the city. The Lord Protector and Council replied with promises of limited reinforcements (including Italians and Germans), references to their other troubles, and increasingly impatient suggestions that Russell's forces, properly handled, were already more than adequate for the defeat of the 'tag and rag . . . and the more part unarmed' with which he was faced. At last, towards the end of July, the rebel positions near Exeter were attacked and several bloody engagements followed. Russell still showed hesitation and timidity, his most decisive act apparently being the slaughter of prisoners. Finally on 6 August the city was relieved, just before the arrival of the resolute Sir William Herbert with over a thousand men. Even now, Russell continued to exasperate the Council by wasting ten days in Exeter before moving out to complete the rout of the insurgents. He now had perhaps eight thousand men, many of whom were required for service eleswhere. The last major battle was at Sampford Courtenay on 18 August, but other engagements and the hanging of prisoners (Somerset's instruction that 'sparing the common and mean men ye do execute the heads and chief stirrers of the rebellion' was not always observed) continued until nearly the end of the month. The losses of rebel dead, by battle and by execution, were probably between four and five thousand men; royal forces suffered perhaps one-tenth of these casualties. The disparity probably reflects a difference in arms rather than in courage or resolution – indeed it has been suggested that, tragically, Russell's irresolute leadership encouraged rebel resistance.[13]

The Council's increasingly brusque replies to Russell's querulous demands for reinforcements had reflected their anxiety about the concurrent troubles in the southern and eastern counties, above all, in Norfolk. There is no evidence of any connection or even communication between the Rising in the West and Ket's Rebellion, and a contemporary writer was at pains to stress that they were 'of opinion contrary' as far apart as were their locations (although the difference in causes was not quite so clear-cut). Yet the two had this much in common: the dread inspired in the ranks of responsible society, and the existence of 'a vacuum in local politics' (in Norfolk, the result of the imprisonment of its duke in 1546) which gave them a chance to take hold. Again, the failure of the Norfolk gentry to provide any effective leadership against Ket's rebels, whose ranks very few of them joined, resembled the pattern in the west.[14]

That the essential causes of the spread of the Norfolk Rising were social and economic, and that in so far as the movement had a religious ethos it was Protestant, are undoubted. Yet its outbreak on 6 and 7 July, although symbolic of widespread resentment of alleged economic exploitation by the gentry in that it related to a breaking-down of enclosures, was largely fortuitous. For its leadership derived from what appears to have been almost a competitive exercise in conciliation towards the hedge-breakers by the rival families of Flowerdew and Ket whose enclosures were attacked. Robert Ket assumed the leadership of a mob of rapidly increasing size which moved towards Norwich, breaking down enclosures (including, ironically, some 'poor's enclosures' on the outskirts of the city) and recruiting members as it progressed. Ket set up camp on Mousehold Heath, only two miles east of Norwich, and promptly imposed discipline and organisation upon his followers, now augmented by a stream of individual recruits and by the arrival of at least two other spontaneously insurgent groups. The deliberate choice of a site thus near to one of the largest cities in England was possibly influenced by the degree of encouragement received from sympathisers within its walls. The reluctance of the local gentry to attempt resolute action was paralleled by the efforts of the city authorities to initiate negotiations between the government and the rebel leaders. It cannot be too strongly emphasised that the latter, in turn, were at pains to disclaim any rebellious intent and actually styled themselves 'commissioners of the ... King's Great Camp at Mousehold'.[15]

An offer of royal pardon on condition of dispersal was ignored, and Norwich formally prepared to stand siege. But the number of sympathisers within its defences, and the fact that some of its leading citizens had mixed feelings, explain its relatively easy capture by Ket's men. For the number of artisans and small tradesmen among the rebel ranks makes it clear that the rising was supported by urban as well as rural resentment of grievances. Those ranks now totalled over ten thousand men – a fact which posed problems of supply as well as of discipline. Ket's administrative ability – and large-scale feasting upon the hated sheep – solved the former, while the holding of two services daily (centred on the 'Oak of Reformation') eased the latter. Indeed, the future Archbishop, Matthew Parker, escaped unscathed (if only just!) after preaching to the rebels upon the error of their conduct. Meanwhile the Council had taken no drastic action, partly because of Somerset's sympathy with at least some of the rebels' demands, as shown in the generous offer of pardon, partly because of increasing and distracting commitments elsewhere. At this stage there emerges another odd parallel with events in the west: the appointment of a most unsuitable commander. But whereas Russell seems to have departed from his instructions on the side of excessive caution, the Marquis of Northampton erred in the opposite direction. His entry into Norwich itself, on 30 July, was taken as a direct challenge and the insurgents promptly attacked. After two days' fighting, in which several hundreds were killed, Northampton withdrew and retreated to London.

In August Warwick was summoned from the north to take command of forces now numbering over seven thousand, including many foreign mercenaries. Upon reaching Norwich he made one more attempt at negotiation, but Ket's followers prevented their leader from accepting. On 24 August, therefore, Warwick stormed into the city, crushed resistance, and hanged several score of prisoners. Two days later, possibly because all supplies were now cut off, Ket left his elevated and fortified encampment on Mousehold and did battle at Dussindale. His followers fulfilled the prophecy that the commons would

> ... fill up Dussindale with blood
> Of slaughtered bodies soon;

but the bodies were their own. Having once more rejected an offer of pardon, they stood no chance against Warwick's cavalry and his well-armed and disciplined foot mercenaries. Rebel losses totalled over three thousand men. Despite this blood bath on the field itself, once certain victory was his Warwick was relatively merciful in his treatment of prisoners. He resisted the near-hysterical demands of some of the local gentry, asking rhetorically, 'would they be ploughmen themselves, and harrow their own lands?' Robert Ket and his brother, after trial in London, and some dozen or so followers, were hanged. The combined losses of rebels and loyalists in the Norfolk Rebellion were probably nearly four thousand.[16]

The religious, social and economic context of these tragic events of 1549, which cost the nation about ten thousand dead, will concern us in later chapters. As far as the authority of the Duke of Somerset was concerned their impact was decisive. Not only did his policy stand condemned in the eyes of his peers, but the weakness in government with which he was charged was now quite equalled by that of his own exposed position. For the armed force of which he had stripped himself was now concentrated in the hands of two men who resented and envied his power: Russell, filled with petulant anger at the verbal chastisement of Somerset's letters in July, and Warwick, far more dangerously moved by the drive of resolute ambition.

The story of Somerset's fall, whether read as a study in hubris or in terms of betrayed idealism, has poignantly tragic elements. In relation to discussion of mid-Tudor government, two things of supreme importance stand out: the relative ease with which it was accomplished, because of Somerset's refusal to wage civil war; and the continuity in personnel between his regime and that of his successor. Despite the differences in personality and in circumstances, there is a curious similarity betwen the downfall of Somerset and that of Northumberland in 1553 in that, despite the apparently overwhelming position of power achieved, in the final decisive crisis each stood virtually deserted by the 'political nation'. Briefly, Somerset had forfeited its loyalty by his over-lenient attitude towards the lower orders, by those aspects of his social and economic policy which ran counter to its interests, and by some unfortunate aspects of his personal relationships. He lacked some of the basic essentials of effective statecraft. Professor Jordan, no hostile critic, finds him guilty of 'an almost incredible want of administrative sensitivity'[17] in trying to push through a policy which lacked the essential approval and co-operation of the governing class and (allegedly) justified their worst forebodings by exciting illegal action in those it was designed to help. Somerset's misfortunes and mistakes in personal relations included the behaviour of his brother and then his execution (the Lord Protector let the Act of Attainder run its course; whether he could or should have attempted to save his brother on grounds of policy or of decency has been debated ever since – quite simply, it was a situation in which Somerset could not win); his arrogance within the Council; his assumption of a near-regal status and style of address; and his ostentatious expenditure on building, exemplified in Somerset House itself. The events of 1549 presented his critics with an irresistible case for his removal.

This found its champion in Warwick, a skilful and ruthless intriguer who, despite the friendship of their earlier years, was now bitterly opposed to Somerset in terms both of general policy and of personal interest – the two coinciding when he found his own park ploughed up. The hero of Dussindale returned to London in mid-September and speedily secured the support of those individuals and factions who were, for sometimes different reasons, resentful of the Protector's power. By the end of the month even the overconfident Somerset knew what was afoot and realised his military nakedness. His correspondence makes clear his desperate hope that Russell and Herbert, in the west, would return and prove loyal. On 1 October a royal proclamation charged 'all his loving subjects with all haste to repair to his highness at his majesty's manor of Hampton Court, in most defensible array, with harness and weapons, to defend his most royal person, and his most entirely beloved uncle the Lord Protector, against whom certain hath attempted a most dangerous conspiracy. . . .' Indeed, although his messages to Herbert and Russell met with cold hostility, there is clear evidence that Somerset's general appeal for help met with spontaneous offers of assistance from other quarters. Edward VI recorded in his *Chronicle* how, when his uncle ordered 'people to be raised. People came abundantly to the house.' It seems probable that the Protector could have waged civil war had he so chosen; but, skilled and experienced soldier that he was, Somerset did not need the lesson of the west or of Norfolk to apprise him of the value of such levies in a pitched battle.[18]

Moreover his opponents were not slow to point to his appeals to the commons as yet further proof of the dreadful dangers of Somerset's alleged combination of personal ambition with encouragement of social anarchy. An attempt at negotiation produced the clearest proof of the weakness of his position: his emissary, Petre, one of the few men of stature who had thus far seemed loyal, deserted to the 'London Lords' – as Warwick's supporters, now numbering sixteen, were described. A battle of propaganda, in public broadsheets and in letters, ensued. 8 October proved crucial; on that day appeared 'A proclamation set forth by the state and body of the King's Majesty's Council now assembled at London, containing the very truth of the duke of Somerset's evil government, and false and detestable proceedings', signed by no fewer than nineteen of the twenty-nine Council members. This document accused the Protector of 'malice and evil government... pride, covetousness, and extreme ambition' and of having 'subverted all Laws, Justice and good order of the Realm', deploring the 'division he hath laboured to sow in the Realm, if he might have brought his purpose to pass between the Nobles, the Gentlemen, and the Commons, which must needs if it should continue destroy both parties....' On the same day Somerset heard that Russell and Herbert had brought their troops to within forty miles of Windsor; any doubts as to their attitude were resolved by their letter of 8 October informing Somerset that 'your grace's proclamations and billets put abroad for the raising of the Commons we mislike very much. The wicked and evil disposed persons shall stir as well as the faithful subjects.' Yet, in the last analysis, both sides were as one in 'beseeching almighty god the matter may be so used as no effusion of blood may flow'. Somerset and his few remaining supporters (Cranmer, Paget and Smith) now yielded and Warwick's bloodless coup d'état was complete.[19]

That it was bloodless reflects as much credit on Somerset's humanity as on his belated acumen. The Lord Protector had fallen because of his faults of personality as well as his errors in policy, although it is significant that nine of the twenty-nine articles of complaint drawn up by his enemies were directed at his social and economic policy. But in our present context, the most striking aspect of events is Somerset's recognition that he had forfeited the confidence and support of the Privy Council, that body which, in default of a monarch able to grasp the reality of power, represented both the legality and the continuity of government, and his recognition also that continued resistance on his part might expose the young King to danger and the realm to the terror of civil conflict.

For the rest of the reign the personality and wishes of Warwick were to come to dominate Edward VI himself and the other members of the Council. Yet Warwick's ambition, although more ruthlessly self-seeking than that of his fallen rival, was also far more calculating. He was careful not to repeat Somerset's mistake of excessive ostentation and, while asserting no claim to exercise formal protectorship, tried to establish the legality of what had occurred by a new Commission drafted in the King's name. Almost immediately, he became President of the Council and Lord Admiral. Save from the disgruntled Catholic supporters of his coup – who were quickly disillusioned as to his intentions in religion once his power was firmly established – Warwick encountered little criticism in the early period of his power. For the activities and legislation of the third session of Edward's first Parliament which reassembled on 4 November showed clearly that the policy for which he stood was in full accord with the wishes of the gentry and nobility. Indeed the statute 3 & 4 Edw. VI, c. 5, 'for the punishment of unlawful assemblies and raising of the King's subjects' was as indicative of this philosophy of frightened and oppressive reaction as many of Somerset's early steps had been of his over-sanguine liberalism.

This measure and others equally repressive with which it was associated aroused bitter criticism from 'Commonwealth' idealists such as Latimer, but their cause was ruined. Real liberty of speech within Parliament itself appears to have diminished; William Turner recorded how 'if we spake any thing freely there, we were taken up like butchers' curs, or else were privily met with all, afterward'. Suspicion of any residual loyalty to Somerset's policies (or indeed to Somerset himself) has been suggested in explanation of why, after prorogation in February 1550 this Parliament did not meet again until January 1552. Certainly there is evidence of a wish to influence the composition of Parliament, in by-elections for replacement of deceased members, by ensuring 'that grave and wise men might be elected to supply their places, for the avoiding of the disorder that hath been noted in sundry young men and others of small judgement'. The successive prorogations of the fourth session (which excited comment from foreign observers) during this period of 'Government by Fearful Men' were accompanied by 'obsessive fear of public disorders'. Entries for April 1551 in the young King's *Chronicle* refer to rumours of 'conspiracy' in Essex and in London itself. In the following month Edward noted 'a proclamation made that whosoever found a seditious bill and did not tear and deface it should be partaker of the bill and punished as the maker'. In August the *Chronicle* records how Somerset himself 'taking certain that [there] began a new conspiracy for destruction of the gentlemen at Wokingham two days past, executed them with death for their offence'.[20]

Distrustful of Parliament, and fearful of the commons, Warwick made systematic efforts to consolidate his position within the Council – in instructive contrast with Somerset's neglect of this art of management. Of twelve appointments made to the Council in the next two years, eight or nine were his close supporters. The influence of such as Paget, who proved to be as ready to express frank disapproval of some of Warwick's actions as he had been of those of Somerset, was increasingly counterbalanced by the favouring of such creatures of Warwick as Sir John Gates and Sir Thomas Palmer, whose unquestioning loyalty was to take them with their patron to the scaffold. In October 1551 their master took the title of Duke of Northumberland as one of a batch of honours bestowed upon the ruling junta. Only five days later Somerset was charged with conspiracy and treason. After some months of imprisonment the fallen Lord Protector had been readmitted to the Council, and possibly cherished hopes of regaining influence during an illness of Warwick in the early summer of 1550. It is perhaps worth observing that it is only hindsight that leads us to take for granted the final victory of Warwick and his faction, and recalling Pollard's comment that 'throughout 1550 and 1551 the Council was distracted between the claims of Somerset and those of Warwick'. This tension further weakened government, and foreign observers remarked on the faction struggle as threatening the ruin of the Crown. Finally, since 'the function of leader of the opposition was not recognised in the sixteenth century', the impasse was resolved by the judicial murder of Somerset.[21]

For this final blow Northumberland's jealousy and the fear that his rival was attempting to re-establish his influence among moderate men in the Council provide motive enough. But it is also suggested that Northumberland saw, or professed to see, the personal popularity of Somerset and of his policies as focal points for the endemic discontent and turbulence of the commons which endured, despite the bloodletting of 1549, throughout 1550 and 1551. Any such upsurge of popular sympathy for Somerset was far from wholly shared by his peers. None the less a majority of them rejected the charge of treason, at which 'the people in the hall, supposing that he had been clearly quit, when they see the axe of the Tower put down, made such a shrieking and casting up of caps, that it was heard into the Long Acre beyond Charing Cross'. Their relief was premature. The charge of felony, also a capital offence, was held to be proven – upon doubtful and fabricated evidence. The fullest record of its ludicrous details is set down in Edward's *Chronicle*. The entry for 7 October describes how, allegedly, 'a device was made to call the Earl of Warwick to a banquet with the Marquis of Northhampton and divers other(s) and to cut off their heads'; that for 3 November adds that 'the place where the nobles should have been banqueted and their heads stricken off was the Lord Paget's house....' The attack on Somerset, who was executed on 22 January 1552, was followed by the arrest and fine or execution of several of his most loyal adherents on equally flimsy evidence. Paget, one of the ablest of Edwardian Councillors, was imprisoned. The attempt to smear him with the guilt of conspiracy failed, but he was forced to confess to embezzlement, stripped of office and of honour ('degraded from the Order of the Garter... chiefly because he was no gentleman of blood, neither of father's side nor mother's side'), and heavily fined.[22]

The assault on Paget, whose only real crime was independence of mind, lends weight to the contention that by now Northumberland's 'preoccupation with plots and counter-plots, and the very act of clinging to power, were to absorb almost the whole of the energy and resources of his government'. None the less, despite his concern with consolidation of his own position, with his pursuit to its tragic end of his vendetta with Somerset, with his suppression of all evidence of popular discontent, and finally with his efforts to change the order of succession to the throne, Northumberland's regime was not barren of constructive achievement. For his ministers included men such as Cecil and Mildmay, whose prudent, perhaps time-serving, moderation in political loyalties should not detract from their undoubted administrative skill. Moreover there is some evidence that in the last year or two of his reign Edward VI himself, with increasing maturity, was developing an interest in the problems and the techniques of government. In April 1551 he had prepared his 'Discourse on the Reformation of Abuses in Church and State'. Nor was his interest confined to academic exercises. He drafted suggestions on certain aspects of policy, economic and financial, for consideration by the Parliament which assembled in January 1552. In November of the same year the imperial ambassador reported that Edward had 'begun to be present at the Council and to attend to certain affairs himself'.[23]

The royal interest in the structure and functions of central government, especially in its conciliar and financial aspects, was given added stimulus by the discovery in 1552 of large-scale embezzlement in the Court of Wards (responsible for administration of estates of minors). Meanwhile, in the Court of Augmentations (established to manage the huge monastic acquisitions of 1535–40), Sir Walter Mildmay was urging the need for a general reform. Accordingly in March 1552 a Commission, including Mildmay as its really expert member, was established to examine 'the states of all his Majesty's Courts of Revenue'. Its enquiries took eight months and its recommendations included the merging of the revenue courts which, it was hoped, would both save expense and facilitate the stricter accounting procedures which were quite essential to eliminate wastage and corruption. Statutes of March 1553 (7 Edw. VI, c. 1 & 2) commenced the actual work of reform, cut short by Edward's death; their provisions in fact were re-enacted by the First Parliament of Queen Mary, who implemented the recommendations in part.[24]

Rather wider in their implications – although there is considerable divergence of interpretation as to their exact significance – were 'Certain articles devised and delivered by the King's Majesty for the quicker, better, and more orderly dispatch of causes by His Majesty's Privy Council', prepared for consideration in January 1553. The scheme projected the establishment of an order of priorities in the selection and timing of business brought before the Council, together with the possible delegation of lengthy enquiries to a sub-committee instructed to report back, in order to ensure speedier attention to essential matters of policy. One reading of events sees this within the context of 'Edward's gradual assumption of power and of the administrative control of his government' as 'perhaps his most important administrative action'. Yet another regards the proposal as a second stage in the attempt to reorganise the Council's procedure by effectively establishing committees of the Council in the previous year, but, more circumspect, finds it 'impossible to say whether the idea for the new plan, as opposed to the draft of the articles to put it into effect, was a product of Edward's or of Petre's brain, or a ruse of Northumberland's to deceive Edward into thinking he now held the reins'. A far more critical interpretation of these efforts to 'rationalise' Council procedure and to resolve the problems posed by its unwieldy size (now grown to forty in number) by resorting to committees concludes that 'these dangerous reforms would have substituted faction rule for that of a responsible and universally competent Privy Council, but Edward VI died before they could become effective'.[25]

Meanwhile a Second Parliament of the reign was summoned for 1 March. Whatever the extent or the results of Northumberland's attempts to influence the composition of this body, it proved to be the shortest-lived Parliament in Tudor history and was dissolved on 31 March. By now the shadow of his death lay upon the King, and that of its implications upon Northumberland. Indeed Professor Jordan attributes the first composition of the 'Device' for altering the succession to the throne to January or February 1553, and its origin to the mind and wishes of Edward VI himself. He credits Northumberland with having 'organised no conspiracy until at the end he embraced Edward's own unconstitutional and grossly illegal undertaking'.[26] Despite the massive erudition of his biography of Edward VI one must observe that most Tudor historians would find this verdict over-kind to Northumberland. It also seems a verdict not shared by the Duke's contemporaries. The dramatic events of the summer of 1553 have already been discussed. In our present context it is sufficient to stress the widespread abhorrence at the patent illegality of the scheme and, above all, the significance of its bloodless failure and the avoidance of civil war. The evidence of public identification of peaceful and orderly rule with the continuity of the Tudor dynasty seems very clear.

There is thus a tragic irony in the fact that, while the surge of public feeling which placed Mary upon the English throne is perhaps the most dramatic testimony of the loyalty which the Tudors inspired, the events of her six years' reign were to mark the nadir of the fortunes of that dynasty in terms both of achievement and of popularity. Certainly many of the projected fears of her father – a reversal of his religious policy, foreign intervention, factions at court, weak governance and rebellion – materialised. Yet the gloom was not unrelieved: the immediate danger of rebellion fed by economic and social grievances receded; the financial policies of government itself improved, if only marginally; the machinery of government endured.

In regard to the central function of government, the determination and execution of policy, the key is once more to be found in the personality of the monarch. For despite (or perhaps as a result of) the reversal of fortunes which led to Mary's accession the outstanding fact about the advisers upon whom she depended for support is the continuity of personnel with those of the previous regime. Professor

Lehmberg remarks that 'amazingly few governmental changes accompanied the religious revolution. Mary's Council included as many of Edward VI's councillors – a dozen – as of her own adherents, and at lower levels the continuity of the civil service was greater still.'[27] But this is not really surprising. For, by definition, those who were close personal supporters of Mary were characterised by fidelity rather than by political and administrative experience. In addition, a number of Henrician councillors were recalled. Yet Mary's understandable attempt to secure broad-based advice and support accorded ill with the limitations of her own statecraft; she lacked the ability and the will to follow a cool and circumspect policy, and the decisions (especially in religious and foreign affairs) which she was to make exacerbated faction. Faction was invited by the very size of the Council: in the Queen's apparent wish to get everyone on her side its number had, by September 1553, increased to nearly fifty. Since Mary herself lacked the skill and judgement needed to control, reconcile or subdue faction the situation was potentially disastrous.

Nor did the position improve during her reign. In November 1554 Renard, the imperial ambassador, wrote to Charles V that 'the limitation of the Council's membership is a somewhat invidious though necessary step'; yet later in the same month he confessed that 'the reduction of the excessive number of councillors... has proved impossible to achieve ... for it created too much bad feeling between the old and recent members of the Privy Council' – in particular, some of those excluded 'consider themselves to be as deserving as those who, as they say, rebelled against and resisted the Queen'. It is difficult not to sympathise with Mary, torn between the obligations of personal loyalty and recognition of the harsh truth that the ablest and most experienced politicians and administrators were those who, in the phrase of the times, smacked of the willow not the oak. By February 1555 Renard was complaining that 'the split in the Council has increased rather than diminished; the two factions no longer consult together; some councillors transact no business; Paget, seeing that he is out of favour with the Queen and most of the Council, is often in the King's [i.e. Philip's] apartments'. By March 'neither Arundel nor Paget attended because of their enmity for the chancellor [Gardiner] and other councillors. When the chancellor reaches a decision, the others immediately endeavour to defeat it.' Three years later Renard's successor, Count Feria, listed Pembroke, Arundel, Paget and Petre as among 'leading members of the Council, and I am highly displeased with all of them.... The Privy Council has so many members that it seems no one has been left out.' This highly coloured picture finds confirmation in the fact that 'the queen herself alleged that she spent her days shouting at her council and all with no result'. The rivalry of feuding cliques (of which Gardiner, until his death, and Paget were the centres) was complicated by the intervention and intrigue of the rival ambassadors (see Chapter 6); indeed it has recently been suggested that 'if Mary ever had a chief minister, Renard has the best claim to the title'. Yet Professor Mackie urges that 'behind the contendings may be detected a slow growth in constitutional machinery' and finds in the projects for reduction in size, and the concept of an 'inner council' or committee, evidence that 'one of the basic ideas of the cabinet system was already germinating'. As we shall see later, it has also been asserted that one may discern the emergence of a 'parliamentary opposition' in the reign of Mary. But on a shorter time-scale our immediate concern is with the crucial problem of the maintenance of unity and stability of government in face of bitter disagreements over policy within the Council and within the country as a whole.[28]

For the reign of Mary Tudor has been described as a 'permanent crisis' in the sense that fundamental disagreements regarding policy, within the political nation, were never absent. Dr D. M. Loades sees Wyatt's Rebellion as but one (although admittedly the most dramatic and threatening) expression of an endemic malaise of the gentry with the whole tenor of Marian government and policies, rather than as a rising with a coherent and avowedly Protestant ethos. 'Wyatt's failure was neither a beginning nor an end, but rather the acutest phase in a crisis which continued with fluctuating intensity from the autumn of 1553 to the autumn of 1558.' In terms of an overt threat to authority it was a climax; yet the climax proved to be false in that there ensued no easing of tension or cessation of plotting. The motivations of the rebellion itself were anti-Spanish, anti-papal, and anti-clerical rather than, in any conscious way, doctrinally Protestant. 'Wyatt's rising ... was primarily a political movement, designed to bring about a change in the secular and international policy of the government.'[29]

The religious and diplomatic context of the revolt will concern us later; meanwhile it is not easy to answer the question of how near it came to securing the downfall of the Marian regime. It was certainly the more dangerous because of all Tudor risings it was the nearest to London itself. The forces mustered by Wyatt were smaller in number than those which rose in either of the rebellions of 1549. Yet Professor Bindoff observes that, despite their ultimate failure, 'they had come nearer to unseating a Tudor sovereign than any others before or after them'. What occurred was but part of a projected scheme for risings in Devon, Leicestershire and Herefordshire; indeed Wyatt was to claim that 'though I bear the name, I was but the iiiith or vth man' in the conspiracy. The comparative success of his attempt (despite its partial and premature nature) has been ascribed to the leadership and organisational skill which he displayed, to the deliberate avoidance of precisely expressed aims, which enabled him to appeal to as wide a spectrum of opinion as possible, and to the hesitancy and lack of weight of the Council's efforts at military suppression. Perhaps as significant as the vagueness of the stated aims of the rebellion is the number who stood aside and awaited the outcome. Wyatt's first proclamation was careful to 'seek no harm to the Queen, but better counsel and Councillors'.[30]

The defeat of one rebel contingent was more than counterbalanced by the desertion to Wyatt's ranks of a force of five hundred 'Whitecoats' sent from London to oppose him, with the symbolic (and perhaps pre-arranged) cry of 'We are all Englishmen!' None the less the force at Wyatt's disposal when he reached Southwark on 3 February was only about three thousand strong – apparently less than one-tenth of that mustered by the 'Pilgrims of Grace' in 1536. It was also much smaller than the rebel forces of 1549; it is possible that, despite the very different circumstances and motivations of this rising, the bloody lessons of 1549 had not been lost on many who might have been expected to compose the rank and file. If it be true that the government's ineptitude presented Wyatt with a splendid opportunity, it is equally true that the sources and the strength of his active support were too limited to enable him to clinch his advantage.

In the event a great deal depended upon the resolution of the Queen herself, upon the loyalties of London and upon the element of chance. Mary wisely rejected the advice of Gardiner to retreat to Windsor, advice which would almost certainly have cost her the Crown. She staked all on London and on the loyalty of those around her. In fact the fear of treason from within posed a graver menace than the threat, in strictly military terms, from without. Cardinal Pole's pessimistic conclusion 'that Wyatt was ultimately repulsed rather through fear of a sack than from any antipathy to his cause' echoes the appeal of a royal proclamation of 1 February which, denouncing Wyatt as 'a most arrogant, horrible, and vile traitor' alluded to his alleged design 'himself to have the custody of her grace and the Tower' and asked rhetorically 'what is this but tyrannously to reign himself and chiefly to sack her grace's city of London to the undoing of all her citizens thereof?' After waiting on the south bank of the Thames, in the vain hope that the gates of London Bridge would be opened to him, Wyatt finally marched his troops up-river, crossed it at Kingston, and then brought them back to the city through Knightsbridge, by now 'partly feeble and faint, having received small sustenance since their coming out of Southwark'. The confused contemporary records of events in London itself agree in conveying an impression of a knife-edge balance of loyalties and fears which a relatively minor engagement might easily resolve into complete collapse for either side. For the apparent deadlock was one of irresolution, rather than one of large, determined, and deeply committed forces. At one point Fleet Street witnessed the bizarre spectacle of the forces of one side passing those of the other on the opposite side of the road 'without any whit saying to them'. The bloodshed, when it finally occurred, was on a relatively small scale; combined losses were about sixty or seventy lives. The evidence supports the recent judgement that 'most men were in standing water between loyalty to the Queen and dislike of her policies.... The rebellion was not defeated, but simply collapsed as soon as its unopposed progress ceased.... The real crisis was one of authority.'[31]

Some obvious contrasts with the events of 1549 suggest themselves, including the apparent paradox that, although the physical menace to government (in terms of number of rebels under arms) was nothing like so serious, yet this rising was nearer to achieving success. The explanation may lie not only in the proximity of the seat of the rebellion to London but also in the fact that it was perhaps not seen quite so clearly by the political nation as a threat to authority itself, in the sense of 1549, but as a quarrel within its own ranks. Ket's Rebellion had forced them to unite for the task of suppression because they felt the whole social order to be threatened; Wyatt's Rebellion revealed an uneasy division within those ranks, and only loyalty to the Tudor dynasty (strained almost, but not quite, to breaking point), combined with the normal sixteenth-century abhorrence of all rebellion against an anointed sovereign, and an undoubted element of sheer chance, 'papered over the cracks'. In this context it is significant that a recent study of the rising urges the need for revision of the once-accepted picture of wholesale and savage infliction of punishment upon the rank and file while the gently-born received lenient treatment. Apparently the total number of executions was well under a hundred, and the gentry suffered, proportionately, as heavily as the commons.[32] What remains true is that many in the upper ranks of society were averse to an over-rigorous identification and punishment of guilt, for the very good reason that they had much to fear.

Conspiracy and rumour of conspiracy were ever present for the rest of Mary's reign. Although, with the exception of the Dudley Conspiracy and the Stafford attempt at Scarborough Castle, the plots were individually insignificant, their number was such that the imperial ambassador likened the forces of opposition to a hydra. Their collective impact, in terms of anxiety and administrative preoccupation, was a constant strain upon the resources of government. Yet perhaps as important, at least in perspective, is the evidence of what is seen by some historians as the emergence of a constitutional opposition to the government and its policies – an opposition conducted in and through Parliament. Sir John Neale finds 'no evidence that for her first two parliaments Mary Tudor made any official attempt to influence the elections'; the surge of loyalty which had swept her to the throne was not yet spent. But under the double strain of the Spanish marriage and the projected return to Rome that loyalty ceased to extend to royal policies. In her letters to the Sheriffs concerning the elections to her Third Parliament the Queen found it necessary 'to will and command you that . . . ye now on our behalf admonish such our good loving subjects as by order of our writs should . . . choose knights, citizens and burgesses to repair . . . to this our Parliament, to be . . . of the wise, grave and Catholic sort, such as indeed mean the true honour of God, with the prosperity of the commonwealth'.[33]

According to one contemporary source the subsequent session of Parliament was presented with a governmental proposal to re-impose an old ruling against the election of non-resident members (in an attempt to curb the growing recalcitrance of the Commons by checking the invasion of borough seats by independent-minded and factious country gentry); but this was countered and defeated by an opposition proposal to turn it into a 'Place Bill' by 'prohibiting the election of any stipendiary, pensioner, or official, or of any person deriving profit in any other way from the king or royal council'. Repetition, in the circular letters preceding the election of the autumn of 1555, of pleas for the choice of members 'of the wise, grave and Catholic sort' had such lack of success that the Queen herself complained of the 'many violent opposition members' who were returned. Indeed Professor E. H. Harbison believes it possible that 'the elections of 1555 witnessed the earliest concerted attempt of an opposition group to capture control of Parliament in Tudor history . . .The opposition of some hundred members formed a remarkably well disciplined and suspiciously well organised parliamentary faction, possessed of unusually shrewd leadership.' Meanwhile, the departure of Philip and Renard (who had both left in August) and the death of Gardiner in November seriously weakened the quality of leadership available to the

Crown. This Parliament, which was without doubt the most unruly and obstructive of Mary's reign, met against a background of widespread discontent: dislike of the Crown's political and religious courses was exacerbated by social and economic factors, for the harvest had been poor and prices of food and of fuel were rising steeply.[34]

The Crown's financial and religious proposals met with opposition. In particular the bill to renounce its rights to clerical first-fruits and tenths and to restore these to the Papacy raised in members' minds the uneasy questions of how the gap in royal revenue would be filled and of possible implications for lay impropriators. The bill was hard fought and only passed the Commons, on 3 December, after a scene of 'great disputes and contention in the Lower House, from day break, when they met, until 3 p.m., during which time the doors were closed, no one being allowed egress either to eat or for any other purpose....' A bill directed against those who had fled abroad for reasons of religion met with even more resolute resistance. Perceiving that supporters of the bill, in face of imminent defeat, wished to adjourn the debate, Sir Anthony Kingston (who was later to be implicated in the Dudley Conspiracy) seized the keys and locked the doors of the Chamber and demanded a division, with the result that a majority of the House defeated the bill. The obvious and striking resemblance between this and the forcible restraint of the Speaker in 1629, and indeed between the whole pattern of demeanour of this House of Commons and that of the 1620s, have been observed. It has thus been suggested that 'there was, indeed, a degree of organisation about the parliamentary opposition in 1555, which, though in some ways a flash in the pan, marks a significant stage in the evolution of the House of Commons'.[35]

Yet it is now perhaps time to reflect upon the justice of Conrad Russell's comment that many of the 'difficulties of Mary's reign are normally seen with historical hindsight, and are therefore greatly exaggerated.... It therefore becomes dangerously easy to portray the reign as if it consisted of nothing but opposition. Much discussion of the reign is uncomfortably near the verdict of *1066 and All That*.' He suggests that in fact much of Mary's government, especially in financial and economic affairs 'was quietly efficient', and even that, 'after Edward's reign, the impression is of a government in good working order'. It is true that research into administrative history (particularly its financial aspect) has demonstrated that reaction and sterility were not all-embracing characteristics of this reign. Yet the record of financial recovery, or even progress, reminds us of the element of continuity at an administrative level which was so significant in the mid-Tudor era. This continuity was perhaps exemplified in the career of Sir William Paulet, Marquis of Winchester, which, uninterrupted by changes of monarch, of faction or of religion, was one of the longest records of service as a finance officer of the Crown in English history. The name of Paulet, who was Master of the Court of Wards for a generation, has been associated with that of Mildmay in regard to the improvements in financial administration which straddled the end of Edward's reign and the commencement of Mary's. As a result 'the average annual receipts from wardships rose markedly during Mary's reign' and the Court of Wards retained its independence when, as a result of the work of Paulet, Mildmay and their colleagues, several of the more recent financial courts were absorbed by the Exchequer. In conclusion, although it may seem harsh to attribute to Mary the basic responsibility for the mistakes of religious and foreign policy of her reign, yet to deny her all credit for what positive achievement may be discerned, it is probably true that the latter may be ascribed to the continuity of service of skilled administrators rather than to any substantive contribution of the Queen herself.[36]

The assertion, regarding the accession of Elizabeth, that 'politically, as well as ecclesiastically, the new reign was a new regime'[37] is directed specifically to the contrast between Mary's antagonising of the gentry and Elizabeth's enlistment of their loyalty. But it may fairly be extended to other aspects of political and constitutional affairs – notably, to the superior judgement and statecraft of the new Queen herself, to her selection of and relations with her Council, and to her management of Parliament. We have already remarked the similarities between the inheritance of Elizabeth and that of Henry VII; there may be some merit in suggesting also that in type and quality of statecraft Elizabeth was as much the grand-daughter of Henry VII as she was the daughter of Henry VIII. The difficulties which confronted her need not be laboured – even if many would now modify the characterisation of the period 1540–1558 as eighteen years of bad government. In considering her success in tackling them – clearly if not conclusively evident by about 1563 – three aspects of governance claim our attention: the calibre of the monarch herself; her selection of ministers; and her relations with Parliament.

It is true that any tendency towards an uncritical admiration of every action of Elizabeth has been much tempered by recent studies. Yet recognition of a certain intuitive skill – above all, in the supremely important sphere of public relations – remains. It is fair to add that royal ability was often aided by royal luck, and also (in striking contrast with Edward VI and with Mary) that time was on her side; a combination of these factors sometimes made hesitant procrastination appear in retrospect like shrewd foresight. The Queen's abilities extended to her choice of advisers, although in regard to the members of her Council the most striking feature is once more the element of continuity – perhaps the biggest surprise was the omission of that 'master of practises', Paget. In the person of Cecil this continuity from the mid-century extended through the greater part of her reign. Indeed it has been urged that 'Cecil took up where Cromwell left off' in that 'the failure of Tudor government between 1540 and 1558 was redeemed by Elizabeth's council without major administrative reforms and merely by putting fresh energy and drive into the existing institutions'. Yet Cecil did not 'take up' completely or assuredly in 1558; the resurgence of favour of Robert Dudley from the summer of 1561 onward 'seemed to portend a season of royal irresponsibility and to threaten political anarchy.... However, by the summer of 1563 something like a balance had been struck between the rivals.' In regard to the most important institution of government, the Council itself, Elizabeth soon made it clear that she would not repeat one of her sister's fundamental mistakes. The Queen expressed her intention to limit the number of Councillors, since she considered that 'a multitude doth make

A Crisis of Governance

rather discord and confusion than good counsel'. Most certainly Elizabeth avoided the disastrous Marian pattern of an unwieldy Council rendered almost impotent by wrangling factions. During the first decade or so of her reign the actual attendance at Council (whose full membership never exceeded twenty) was apparently between five and eleven.[38]

The Queen's own caution and innate conservatism accorded well with the mood of the nation after the tumultuous mid-century years. Indeed G. P. Gooch once suggested that 'the accession of Elizabeth was the signal for the cessation of political thinking'. Yet this would seem to apply more particularly to the strain of critical social speculation which had found expression against the background of change, uncertainty and crisis of the Edwardian and Marian era. The view that 'the politics of Elizabeth's first decade seem on analysis to present a time of contradiction and ambiguity' must be related to the context first of those uneasy romantic inclinations which we noted in Chapter 2, and secondly to the problems of formulating the religious settlement. The resolution of the religious issue involved the co-operation of that other supremely important institution, Parliament. Sir John Neale has observed that 'however troublesome Elizabethan parliaments might be, their loyalty never wavered',[39] it is tempting to add that they were seldom other than troublesome. Both the intervals between and the shortness of sessions lend weight to the contention that the Queen viewed them as necessary evils. None the less, if it is true that the major points of friction between Elizabeth and her early Parliaments – the questions of marriage and succession and of the nature of the religious settlement – closely resemble those of her sister's reign, it is equally clear that her handling of those problems, both in its manner and in its direction, was better calculated to inspire confidence and co-operation. Parliament found Elizabeth's evasions on the first of these issues exasperating: but this was preferable to Mary's headlong rush to a disastrous misalliance. In religion many of the members of the Parliaments of 1559 and 1563 wished to go further along the Protestant road than did the Queen; yet Elizabeth's refusal to go with them did not cause the sense of outrage that was awakened by Mary's wholesale reversal of earlier policies and blinkered rejection of national opinion. In the long run the nature and the enactment of the settlement confirmed the parliamentary right of participation in religious affairs which seemed to derive from the events of the mid-century.

The Queen's decision in April 1563 to prorogue rather than to dissolve the Parliament has been taken as indicative of her optimism for the future. In terms of the hoped-for cessation of the importunities of 'ginger groups' it was misplaced; in terms of royal confidence that she could in the last resort manage the members as a whole it was justified. In her management Elizabeth displayed not only those personal qualities which contrasted so sharply with the shortcomings of her unfortunate sister, but also the shrewd judgement which directed her councillors into participating in, and guiding, parliamentary business – the abandonment of which was to be a major cause of Stuart disaster. By 1563, while many problems remained, at monarchical, conciliar and parliamentary levels, the Tudor regime had survived its mid-century testing-time and the stage was set for what has been described as an age of 'consolidation rather than invention ... preservation rather than revolution'.[40]

4 The Crisis in Religion

It is perhaps in the sphere of religion that we shall find the most complicated and contentious aspects of the mid-Tudor crisis. On the one hand, despite the suggestion that it was in some sense 'unique', the evolution of the Reformation in England cannot be isolated from its European context; on the other, the tug-of-war between 'Protestantism' and 'Catholicism' in England reflected not only a genuine debate in theology but also the contingency of complex and changing political, dynastic, personal and diplomatic influences. It was these, rather than any doctrinal originality, that gave a distinctive character to the evolution of the Church in England. The implicit questioning of relationships between Church and State (although the word 'State' itself was rarely used before the mid-century) or Church and society, of responsibility for enforcement of religious orthodoxy, and of the very nature and derivation of religious truth itself, was common to much of western Europe.

It has been justly observed that 'the Protestant Reformation cannot be dismissed as an adjustment of relations between sovereigns and churches'.[1] Certainly the problem of the implied power struggle, particularly in jurisdictional and financial terms, stretched back into the Middle Ages, but so too did that of the tension between the orthodox teachings of the Catholic Church and the recurrent outbreaks of doctrinal heresy. The Reformation in England cannot be considered apart from the deeper tides of religious feeling which swept over much of Europe. The events of the mid-Tudor period constituted a major and indeed decisive crisis of religious allegiance for the great part of the people of England. Yet historians seem to concur in regarding the English Reformation as in some way a special case, as unique in its evolution and in its results. It is contended, with some justice, that the course taken in the management of religious affairs – even where this involved a complete reversal of direction – emerged always from the wishes and decisions of the Crown, which sought political and economic as often as spiritual objectives. Some would conclude that, in face of these changes, the mass of the population remained surprisingly quiescent.

Such an outline is in danger of becoming a caricature. English Protestantism was not a by-product of Henry VIII's 'divorce case' or of Thomas Cromwell's constitutional achievements. It may have formed an alliance (sometimes uneasy and always but partly content) with the Henrician 'break with Rome', but it antedated it. The populace were not all or always singularly quiescent. Moreover, although the crisis may have had definitive long-term results in regard to the basic religious allegiance, or even prejudices, of the English nation, the form which the religious settlement would ultimately take (in retrospect so deceptively inevitable) can have been anything but clear at the time. The course of events is shot through with 'might-have-beens', and the most crucial of these were personal and dynastic. What if the 'young Josiah' of the Protestants (Edward VI) had outlived his biblical namesake or if his half-sister 'Deborah' (Elizabeth I) had not equalled the longevity of hers? Is it not presumptuous to write off the reign of Mary Tudor as an aberrant, inevitably sterile, interlude and to assert that, had she pursued her aim more cautiously or even, alternatively, had the discomfort in her womb betokened the longed-for child and not her death, the cause of (Roman) Catholicism in England was none the less inevitably lost? Precisely because the influence of the Crown upon the direction of religious policy was so overwhelmingly important the changes in beliefs and motivations of each Tudor monarch to mount the throne were potentially determinative for the nation as a whole. Moreover one may suggest that the relationship between the royal wishes and the nature of what became accepted religious orthodoxy was not mechanically authoritative: one might well reformulate the attribution of religious quiescence to the English people by predicating a quite genuine tendency for dynastic loyalty to affect and colour religious allegiance.

Yet it is equally important to remember that the original impetus to religious change did not come from the Crown. Preoccupation with dynastic and political considerations must not obscure the emergence of a genuinely religious movement during the 1520s. In its criticism of the existing Catholic order one may discern irreverent and sceptical anti-clericalism, residual Lollardy and the influx of 'Lutheran' influences from the continent. The first expressed itself in often scurrilous attacks upon the clergy (with Wolsey as scapegoat in chief), and the second in the claim that 'Wycliffe begat Hus, who begat Luther, who begat truth'. Beyond doubt, fourteenth-century Lollardy had indeed anticipated many of the basic tenets of Lutheran Protestantism: appeal to the Bible as the source of religious truth; rejection of transubstantiation; criticism of misuse of church wealth; appeal to the 'godly prince'. Lollardy, with its proletarian character, had been driven underground in the fifteenth century, yet what Foxe described as 'the secret multitude of true professors' remained to anticipate and to welcome Lutheran ideas. The inspiration of early Tudor heresy was overwhelmingly Wycliffe until it merged with Lutheranism in the 1530s.[2]

Meanwhile the focus of Lutheran influence among Cambridge theologians during the 1520s was the White Horse Inn (nicknamed 'Little Germany'). Indeed a list of those associated with Cambridge at this time – including Tyndale, Frith, Barnes, Latimer, Ridley and Cranmer – reads like a martyr-roll of the English Reformation. Of outstanding significance among the first generation of English Protestants was William Tyndale, as a populariser of Lutheran (and sometimes Zwinglian) views and as a translator of the Scriptures. Many Englishmen first encountered the writings of Luther in Tyndale's barely paraphrased or literally translated version. Yet Tyndale was no mechanical hack but a theologian in his own right, with a creative and sometimes provocative contribution of his own to make. Even more important was his work upon the Scriptures; Professor Rupp observes that 'we cannot understand the first decade of the

English Reformation unless we recognise that the edition of the English New Testament was its supreme event'. Despite his betrayal and martyrdom in exile in 1536 Tyndale's influence remained permanent. Meanwhile a fellow-exile, John Frith, had returned to England where, after suffering the indignity of being put in the stocks as a vagabond, he was betrayed to More (with whom he had engaged in a pamphlet controversy), arrested, and condemned to the stake in 1533. Frith's views on Communion were Zwinglian rather than Lutheran, but he was no zealot and in some respects endured martyrdom for the principle of freedom of conscience. It is important to realise that in their persecution and condemnation of such men Wolsey, More and Henry VIII himself were as one; while doctrinal Protestantism gave support to the Henrician break with Rome and was encouraged by its potential implications, its origins owed nothing to the Crown and its extension occurred in the teeth of official opposition.[3]

The legislation of the 'Reformation Parliament' neither began nor ended the process of religious change, and it seems fair to observe that in the England of 1539 although the papal cause seemed vanquished, exactly what had replaced it – in terms both of the ultimate source of ecclesiastical authority and of the precise code of belief which would be enforced – was far from clear. As yet both short-term doubts and long-term implications were masked by the imperious will of Henry VIII. His death was to make them plain. To look first at jurisdictional aspects, whether one chooses to regard the sovereign nation state as the instrument or as the product of the Reformation in England certain consequences of the actions of the Crown, or more specifically of King-in-Parliament, during the decade prior to 1539 seem clear. They had (in English law) extinguished papal authority over the Church in England, subordinated the clergy of that body to the Crown, thrust out any possible intrusion of international ecclesiastical organisations by the suppression of the regular religious orders, and (effectively) annexed ecclesiastical possessions for disposal by the royal will. Yet there surely remained two questions of supreme importance: first, where lay the final and definitive authority in matters ecclesiastical within the English realm; and, secondly, was that authority endowed not only with the right to appoint and discipline clergy and generally to manage church affairs, but also with an original or autonomous power to determine the doctrine of the Church in England? The short-term answer to both questions is implied in the description of the Henrician religious settlement as 'caesaro-papal'. Yet, as has been said, this glossed over rather than resolved the basic issues. In the long run there remained the question (even if the irrevocability of the expulsion of Roman power be conceded) of whether King *solus* or King-in-Parliament was supreme in control of the English Church in jurisdictional and, perhaps even more important, doctrinal matters.

Alongside this problem – conceptually separate but practically inseparable – lay that of the content of the code of belief which the Church in England accepted and looked to see enforced. What Henry VIII had accomplished in the 1530s has been variously described as 'a political, legal and expropriatory Reformation', as 'dynastic, anticlerical, and national in character', and as 'schism without heresy'. The growth of Protestantism in England had taken place against the wishes of the monarch whose *Defence of the Seven Sacraments* had, at an earlier date, won bestowal of the title 'Defender of the Faith'. It is essential to distinguish between the jurisdictional and administrative revolution against papal power which the King and Cromwell carried through, and the emergence of doctrinal Protestantism. Yet this is not to imply a total lack of connection. Henry may have disapproved of and even persecuted what he regarded as heresy, but, inevitably, much of his policy facilitated its development. For many of the forces which enlisted beneath the anti-papal banner and would endorse (and even suffer persecution at the hands of) royal authority in matters religious, would never rest content with a merely jurisdictional revolution. Meanwhile, Professor Dickens observes that it is misleading to think of a 'Protestant-versus-Catholic struggle' in clear-cut terms, for the 1530s had 'remained, doctrinally speaking, an indecisive period of argument and uncertainty'.[4]

Against this background the extent to which the doctrine

and the liturgy of the Church in England were subject to change depended largely upon the wishes of the King himself. Henry's own approach to problems of authority and of dogma was essentially personal (some would say idiosyncratic) and rather fitful in its interest and evolution. For some evolution there was – zig-zag though its progress may have been. If the King was not deeply religious in that sense of questing self-examination which would have won the approval of his more Protestant supporters neither was he content uncritically to accept the established corpus of Catholic orthodoxy. He did not lay claim – at least explicitly – to the ultimate spiritual authority, to the *potestas ordinis*. Yet he was quite ready to apply his own intelligence, backed by the elements of an education in theology, to correct the errors of heretical subjects on the one hand and to arbitrate between the 'Catholic' and the 'Protestant' bishops on the other. His views on specific issues of theology present an at first sight bewildering mixture of conservatism and radicalism. One may even suggest (though the idea would have horrified the King himself) that in his belief in his ability to discern and pronounce religious truth Henry cast himself as much in the role of England's Luther as in that of England's Pope. Professor Scarisbrick has traced, through Henry's writings and in particular through his comments and corrections concerning the *Bishops' Book* of 1537 and the *King's Book* of 1543, the amalgam of the traditional and the novel which characterised the royal approach to such aspects of doctrine as the nature of the seven sacraments or justification by faith alone. Rigorous theology seems to have been absent; but it may well be true that Henry's *ad hoc* amalgam reflected the feelings of very many of his subjects – although he would warmly have rejected any idea of solving religious problems by taking the nation's pulse.[5]

The royal annotations to the *Bishops' Book* (made after not before publication) make it clear that Henry thought it too Protestant. Cranmer objected that the insertion of the two italicised words in the following passage on justification by faith alone completely changed its meaning: the contrite sinner may hope for forgiveness 'not *only* for the worthiness of any merit or work done by the penitent but *chiefly* for the only merits of the blood and passion of our saviour Christ'. It is possible that the rather lax way in which he had given the more Protestant bishops their head in this publication, or perhaps the 'Ten Articles' of 1536 which 'undoubtedly show a degree of Lutheran influence', had marked the peak of Protestant fortunes. Certainly the publication of the 'Six Articles' in 1539, significantly in the form of a parliamentary statute (31 Henry VIII, c. 14), was a victory for the Catholic cause and was seen as such by the Protestant bishops Latimer and Shaxton who resigned their sees, and by Cranmer who sent his wife home to Germany. For if the nature of justification was one touchstone of Catholic or of Protestant allegiance, that of the Mass or Communion was the other. The first of the Six Articles explicitly decreed that there 'is present really, under the form of bread and wine, the natural body and blood of our Saviour Jesus Christ', under penalty for disbelief of being adjudged 'guilty of heresy and burned'. Communion in one kind only, celibacy of clergy and observance of vows of chastity, validity of private masses and auricular confession were the other five articles of faith, denial of which was subject to punishment, ultimately, by 'a felon's death'.[6]

Yet despite the Protestant dismay occasioned by this statute, followed as it was by the end of current negotiations with Lutheran states in Germany and then, in 1540, by the executions of Barnes and Cromwell (events which led older historians to attach the term 'Catholic reaction' to the later years of Henry's reign), it marked neither the beginning of a period of clear doctrinal retrogression nor the end of the Catholic-Protestant 'tug-of-war'. It has been pointed out that 'only six persons suffered death under it' and that it 'did not put an end to the theological ferment of the Henrician regime'. (Indeed, the judicial murder, by Act of Attainder, of Barnes, Jerome and Garret, on unspecified charges of extreme heresy of which they were almost certainly not guilty, only two days after that of Cromwell, must be seen as much as part of the plot against the minister as in any religious context.) If the *King's Book* of 1543 contained doctrine which was 'in large part traditional, orthodox, and sometimes pointedly anti-Lutheran', the Protestant cause could draw solace from the continued eminence of Cranmer, and encouragement from the appearance in 1544 of his English Litany, followed in 1545 by royal authorisation of an English Primer or Prayer Book. Yet, if debate continued, it is probably true to describe the year 1539 (which had, after all, been marked by the appearance of the 'Great Bible' in English as well as by the Six Articles) as establishing the equilibrium position of the Henrician 'Catholic Church'. The suggestion that 'England's *doctrinal* evolution was largely halted in 1540' is an accurate assessment, particularly in regard to *official* pronouncements.[7]

The fact that the doctrinal evolution of several of the more Protestant bishops had not yet ceased, together with the range of the theological spectrum composed by the views of those who none the less remained within the bounds of the Henrician establishment, were soon made clear after 1547. Events of the next ten or twelve years revealed not only the doctrinal divergences between and within the Catholic and Protestant groups, but also the difficulties and inconsistencies of their positions in regard to the nature and exercise of ecclesiastical authority. If Elizabeth I was to inherit a nation whose subjects, by and large, had been chastened by experience of both extremes in religion, she was also to face the fact that many of the questions which during her father's reign had remained unanswered because often unasked, had by now been all too thoroughly debated. Yet this was to be a gradual process. Just as the unresolved problems of the period before 1547 had been pushed aside by the dominant will of the King, so now between that date and 1553 the inconsistencies and lacunae of the Protestant position were glossed over by the assumption that the Godly Prince saw, and enforced, the Scriptural truth that must be plain to all right-thinking men. Since the Protestants had, with few exceptions, taught non-resistance and had waited upon the day when the Lord would indeed 'open the King of England's eyes' they might now fairly claim to have entered upon their inheritance. Yet not far into the future lay the problem of the intransigence of such as Hooper, who would urge that those eyes were still not opened widely enough, to be followed by that of the Marian succession which would transform the whole position.

Protestant hopes were surely based upon the education and personality of the young King, upon the known sympathies of some of the most influential bishops, and upon the dominance of Edward Seymour. Professor Jordan has recently suggested that 'Edward was no bigot; his interest in the Church was principally administrative; and a relatively slight proportion of his writings and of his personal interventions were concerned with religious matters.' Indeed, in 1552 Bernard Gilpin complained bitterly that 'I am come this day to preach to the king, and to those which be in authority under him. I am very sorry they should be absent. I am the more sorry for that other preachers before me complain much of their absence. . . . I will speak to their seats, as if they were present.' Yet there is no doubt that Edward was devoutly Protestant in his personal faith. The incident in his coronation procession when the boy ordered that the three swords borne before him should yield precedence to 'the Bible, the sword of the spirit' must have given joyful confirmation to the hopes of those who welcomed the 'godly imp' as another 'young Josiah'. Edward himself, in his 'Discourse on the Reformation of Abuses in Church and State', was to define the ecclesiastical content of 'the governance of this realm' as consisting in 'setting forth the word of God, continuing the people in prayer, and the discipline' – priorities which some would say betokened Zwinglian or even Calvinist influences.[8]

Equal encouragement may have been derived from the person of the Archbishop of Canterbury. Twice married (his second bride a niece of Andreas Osiander, a prominent Lutheran divine), Cranmer had endured constant attacks from Catholic ecclesiastics in the previous reign. The favour of Henry VIII, and Cranmer's own reluctance to avow or even to formulate certain unorthodox aspects of his doctrinal evolution (a reluctance ascribed by critics to time-serving timidity, and by admirers to a sincere and logical obedience to God-given royal power), preserved him in safety until the accession of Edward VI liberated his ideas from any restraints of mere prudence. Equally ready for a 'forward' movement was one of his chaplains, Nicholas Ridley, who had emulated his patron's discretion in concealing his doctrinal progress, and who became Bishop of Rochester in September 1547. By April 1550, when he was promoted to the See of London, he was recognised as a leading advocate of doctrinal reform. Alongside him in the records of Protestant hagiography, or indeed in pride of place if contemporary preaching repute is the criterion, we find his fellow-martyr Hugh Latimer. Latimer, whose career had been far more controversial, now emerged from the prison to which his beliefs had brought him in 1546, but refused all offers to return to the episcopate. None the less he exercised very great influence throughout the reign. Yet the existence of a very real ground-swell in the direction of Protestant reform of the doctrine and the ritual of the Church does not imply a movement with clear and agreed aims. Controversy was to appear within the Protestant ranks – personified in Hooper, later Bishop of Gloucester. The form and significance of the Communion Service, and the functions, attributes and vestments of the priesthood, were among the crucial topics of debate.

The key to the immediate course of events lay in the power and the personality of Somerset, who was effectively 'the first Protestant to enjoy independent control of the State'. It is worth recalling that the double blow of Henry VIII's deliberate omission from the Regency Council of Stephen Gardiner, Bishop of Winchester, and of the downfall of the Howards immediately before that monarch's death, had gravely weakened the Catholic cause and facilitated the Protector's course of action. The steps taken in the first year of the new reign attest the moderate but sincere Protestantism of Somerset, who corresponded on friendly terms with Calvin, and the liberalism of attitude already noted. The first Edwardian legislation to reach the statute book was an Act (1 Edw. VI, c. 1) 'against Revilers, and for Receiving in Both Kinds'. The title bespeaks the tight-rope which the cause of moderate reform had to walk: it was essential to dissociate such reform from scurrilous anti-clericalism and from the 'heretical' beliefs of the more 'radical' or Anabaptist factions. The statute recognised the need of 'some bridle of fear' upon those tongues which would 'deprave, despise, or condemn the said most blessed sacrament' and imposed penalties of fine and imprisonment. At the same time it declared for reversion to the use of 'the Apostles and of the primitive Church' in 'that the said blessed sacrament should be ministered to all Christian people under both kinds of bread and wine'. The general liberalism of Somerset's approach found expression in the repeal of the statute of Six Articles, of the medieval *De Haeretico Comburendo*, and of the strict Henrician restrictions upon printing, reading and teaching of the Scriptures. The Protector's tendencies towards what was later to be called 'Erastianism' (broadly defined as State direction of Church affairs) led to a decision, short-lived in effect, to appoint bishops directly by royal letters patent, and also to further confiscation of Church property. The statute dissolving chantries (1 Edw. VI, c. 14) attacked such institutions as provisions for maintaining 'superstition and errors', 'blindness and ignorance', and in particular 'vain opinions of purgatory'; but there is little doubt that the chantry endowments were another object of this measure.[9]

Throughout 1548 Cranmer moved methodically towards the introduction of Protestant reforms into the Church: prayers and services in English were introduced, removal of 'abused' or idolatrous images was enjoined, and by the autumn he was completing his English Prayer Book. This work, adopted by Parliament in the first Edwardian Act of Uniformity as the sole legal form of worship from June 1549, has been justly characterised as a 'master-piece of compromise, even of studied ambiguity'. While it avoided specific denial of Catholic doctrine and stressed the need to 'hold the Catholic faith', such phrases as 'all our doings without charity are nothing worth', 'that we have no power of ourselves to help ourselves', and the communicants' confession that 'we do not presume to come to this thy table (oh merciful lord) trusting in our own righteousness' appealed to Protestant hearts. The phraseology used in delivering the Sacrament, in both kinds, to the communicant was of crucial import: 'the body of our Lord Jesus Christ which was given for thee, preserve thy body and soul unto everlasting life.... The blood of our Lord Jesus Christ which was shed for thee, preserve thy body and soul unto everlasting life'. 'For while one modern commentator believes that this formula 'admits of a Lutheran and possibly even a Calvinist interpretation', no less a person than Gardiner announced from the Tower (to which he had been consigned as a result of his opposition to the measures of 1548) that he would accept a wording which clearly implied a belief in transubstantiation. Edward's *Chronicle* records how, in June 1550, the Bishop of Winchester informed a visiting group of Councillors that 'I, having deliberately seen the Book of Common Prayer, although I would not have made it so myself, yet I find such things in it as satisfy my conscience and therefore both I will execute it myself and also see other my parishioners to do it.'[10]

The Act of Uniformity (2 and 3 Edw. VI, c. 1), expressing a wish for 'a uniform quiet and godly order' decreed 'the one and uniform rite and order in such common prayer and rites and external ceremonies to be used throughout'. A graduated scale of punishments was enacted for successive offences, either in obstinately refusing to implement the rites laid down, or in being guilty of 'derogation, depraving, or despising of the same book', or of interrupting the officially established rites. As to public reaction, it has been suggested that the book pleased no one – offending the conservatives who thought it too radical, and the reformers who thought it too conservative. Such a verdict seems too sweeping. Certainly the vast majority of the clergy complied with the not over severe injunctions of the Act of Uniformity, while as far as concerns the laity (whose involvement in doctrinal controversy is often less fervent than historians of religion sometimes infer) the introduction of services in English was probably the really striking innovation. It is true that the rising in the West, a major crisis of the summer of 1549, was motivated very largely by antipathy towards the changes in religion. Yet the rebels' description of the new Prayer Book as 'but like a Christmas game' and the declaration that 'we Cornishmen (whereof certain of us understand no English) utterly refuse this new English' suggest fairly localised causes. The inclusion in the rebels' 'Articles' of demands for the restoration of the Latin Mass, with Communion in one kind only, and of the penalties of the Six

Articles, together with the prohibition of the English Bible, seems conclusive enough in its implication. But there is no absolute reason to accept these views as any more representative of overall opinion than the association of a moderately Protestant religious ethos with the contemporaneous rebellion in Norfolk.[11]

None the less we may well believe that much 'middle of the road' opinion was alienated, on grounds that were partly traditional and partly instinctive, by some other aspects of Edwardian Protestantism. The proposal of 1547 that priests should be allowed to marry, although passing through both Convocation and Commons, met with such opposition in the Lords that it did not reach the statute book until February 1549. The spectacle of so much pillage of church property under the guise of religious reformation evoked some shamefaced breast-beating among the ranks of the Protestants themselves. Mounting Catholic resentment could not but have been exacerbated by a spate of Protestant pamphleteering, especially during 1548, much of it characterised by a coarseness and scurrility extreme even by sixteenth-century standards. Certainly this feeling had risen to such a pitch that Warwick could exploit it in his plot to overthrow Somerset. While Mary Tudor was not deceived as to Warwick's motives, several leading Catholics, including Wriothesley, were induced to co-operate in his coup.

Their miscalculation was soon made clear as Warwick continued, or rather accelerated, the 'forward' policy in religion. Ironically, his motives for so doing were not nearly as sincere as those behind the more moderate innovations of his fallen rival. Three influences seem fairly definite: the well-known sympathies of the young King, with whom it was essential for Warwick to win favour; the inclinations of the majority of his fellow-councillors, whose support he must retain; and the opportunities for personal gain afforded by a policy of further 'reform'. Thus Professor L. B. Smith has characterised the ecclesiastical aspect of Northumberland's regime as compounded of 'a strange union of religious fanaticism and economic avarice': the former symbolised by Hooper and Knox, the latter by those who climbed onto the lucrative bandwaggon. If, therefore, it is true that 'the English reforming party succeeded between 1550 and 1553 in doing all that a German or Swiss city had done', it is only in the sense of determination of the official doctrine of the Church. Few contrasts are more instructive than that between the ecstatic praises with which many leading Protestants greeted Warwick's continuance of 'reform' and the more perceptive, disillusioned comments of a few years later, when Knox was to deplore 'that a young and innocent King be deceived by crafty, covetous, wicked and ungodly counsellors'. If the Protestant reformers were given their head in the field of dogma, their protests against continued plunder of church possessions went quite unheeded. Ridley, in prison awaiting martyrdom in 1555, looked back and reflected sadly that 'our magistrates did abuse, to their own worldly gain, both God's gospel and the ministers of the same'. Many ecclesiastical appointments were made conditional upon acceptance of a 'rearrangement' of the lands or revenue involved, with 'superfluities' siphoned off to court favourites; a project for the wholesale impoverishment of the See of Durham, following the deprivation of Bishop Tunstall, was halted only by the fall of Northumberland himself. As late as 1552–3 no less than ten thousand pounds worth of church plate was confiscated as 'superfluous'.[12]

The first ecclesiastical scheme to appear after Warwick's coup, Cranmer's Ordinal of March 1550 concerning the functions and installation of the clergy, had been enough to confirm the futility of Catholic hopes. Although moderate in its innovations it led to the imprisonment and eventual deprivation of Bishop Heath of Worcester who rejected it. He and Bonner, Bishop of London, who had been swept aside late in 1549, were soon joined, in virtual if not yet legal deprivation, by other Catholics including Gardiner himself. Of their Protestant successors, Ridley, Ponet, Scory and Hooper, the last-named exemplifies both the divisions within the ranks of the reformers and the importance of foreign influences upon this stage of the English Reformation. Hooper had spent much of his exile during the later years of the reign of Henry VIII in Strassburg and Zurich; indeed he had not returned to England until 1549. A period as Somerset's chaplain was soon followed by the offer of the See of

Gloucester in April 1550, but Hooper's logical deductions from the Zwinglian emphasis upon the definitive authority of the Scriptures led to his rejection of the traditional vestments. Both Cranmer (who alluded scathingly to 'some [who] be so new-fangled that they would innovate all things') and Ridley were angered by what they regarded as factious bigotry, and Hooper was even imprisoned for a short while. Finally, in March 1551, he accepted consecration in vestments, after which his obdurate scriptural intransigence was fully equalled by the unremitting zeal of his exercise of all his diocesan duties – more especially those he conceived of as fulfilling the social conscience of the Church.[13]

Meanwhile in the early summer of 1550 Ridley, Bishop of London, while deploring the radicalism of Hooper, had himself been implementing changes in regard to the mode of celebration of Communion. His instructions to the clergy of his diocese to substitute for the altar 'the Lord's board after the form of an honest table', and to eschew any adoration of the elements employed, may perhaps be described as expressing his determination to make of each member of the congregation a 'participant communicant' rather than a passive witness of a re-enacted sacrifice from which vicarious spiritual benefit might be derived. Wriothesley's *Chronicle* records how, at Easter 1551, 'the Bishop of London altered the Lord's table that stood where the high altar was, and he removed the table beneath the steps into the midst of the upper choir in Paul's, and set the ends east and west, the priest standing in the midst at the communion on the south side of the board. . . .' By this time Cranmer and Ridley were considering a further revision of the Prayer Book and, in particular, of the ritual of the Communion Service. It is perhaps in this context that it is most appropriate to consider the question of the extent and impact of foreign influence upon the course of the English Reformation, for such influence almost certainly reached its peak at this time.[14]

Inevitably, since England produced no religious leader of the international repute of Luther, Zwingli or Calvin, and did not become the centre of a proselytising religious ethos, there is a temptation to interpret her doctrinal evolution as a reflection of foreign experience. This is to over-simplify.

Certainly much of the writing of Tyndale, at an early stage of the English Reformation, has been described as barely-paraphrased Luther, while thirty years later the debt of Hooper and Knox to the Swiss Reformers need not be laboured. Yet alongside these facts we must recall the existence in England of residual Lollardy, with roots stretching back to the fourteenth century, eager to receive the impact of continental Protestantism, and remember also the existence of several English religious leaders of at least the second rank whose doctrinal development had an organic vitality of its own, reflecting foreign influence indeed, but not in merely mechanical fashion.

Professor Dugmore sees 'the great eucharistic debate which raged among the Reformers of the sixteenth century [as] but a continuation of that which engrossed the medieval Schoolmen', interpreting the evolution of the beliefs of Ridley and Cranmer within this historical context rather than as an anglicised but largely automatic reflection of contemporary Lutheran, Zwinglian and Calvinist developments. While conceding the importance of the presence in England of religious refugees from Europe, described as 'Zwinglians almost to a man', he stresses that 'Ridley, and the other non-papist Catholics' were neither Zwinglian nor Lutheran, setting them within the tradition of Reformed Catholicism and tracing the formative influence in the eucharistic beliefs of Ridley, and through him of Cranmer, to the medieval theology of Ratramn. Dr P. N. Brooks, while suggesting that Professor Dugmore has 'consciously depreciated all Continental influence', concurs in certain of his conclusions; notably, that Cranmer's eucharistic progress was closely influenced by the guidance of Ridley, and that 'there can be no reasonable doubt that [Ridley's] decision came after a careful study of Ratramn's' work. Moreover Cranmer himself was at pains to protest that his teaching on the Sacrament was that of 'the true catholic faith which the Scripture teacheth, and the universal Church of Christ hath ever believed from the beginning'. Conceding that it is still 'essential to conceive of the English Reformation as Act II of a Continental drama already played out on a different stage' and that one must not undervalue 'the dominant in-

The Crisis in Religion

tellectual climates of Cranmer's day', Dr Brooks stresses that 'the importance of Bucer in the eucharistic *cause célèbre* is immeasurable' in that he came nearest to achieving a consensus. Indeed, by the mid-century the 'true presence' doctrine was 'the common possession of Bucer, Melanchthon, Bullinger and Calvin'.[15]

In an English context we must be careful not to overemphasise the influence of Wittenberg, Zurich or Geneva at the expense of that of Strassburg – increasingly recognised as a major centre of international Protestant influence. In 1549 events forced Bucer to flee the city to exile in England and to a chair at Cambridge. He died in February 1551, but had already been consulted by Cranmer in drafting the Ordinal of 1550 and had produced a lengthy and influential critique of the First English Prayer Book. Significantly, there is some evidence as to his close friendship at Cambridge with Matthew Parker, the future Elizabethan Archbishop of Canterbury. If the influence of Bucer typifies the search for a position of concord, that of the Scotsman John Knox personifies the more aggressive rigidities of the Calvinist position in its 'uncompromising zeal and measureless invective'. Returning from a spell as French galley-slave (see page 161) which was perhaps the most dramatic episode in his vivid career, Knox was retained as a preacher by the Privy Council from 1549 onwards. This patronage did not deter his dour Calvinism from personal criticism of the highest in the land if their conduct fell short of his ideals.[16]

Despite the reality of continental influences the Second English Prayer Book which appeared in 1552 was no more a slavish copy of foreign than it was of English precedents. As might be expected, its most crucial innovations concerned the celebration of what had formerly been the Mass, a term which now disappeared entirely. Some scholars have described it as rather Zwinglian in its phraseology for the rite of the Eucharist, and as 'a perfect vehicle for those Swiss doctrines which taught that the eucharist was primarily a memorial of a sacrifice and that the gift was a purely spiritual gift received by the heart and not the hand'. (It is as well to remember that some theologians would reject any inference that Zwingli himself conceived of the Communion

Service as a merely commemorative rite.) But Professor Dickens points out that while 'the words of administration could indeed be taken to imply no more than a commemorative rite, and a receptionist view of the Presence . . . they do not directly contradict Ridley's "Ratramnian" view, which Cranmer had accepted in 1546 and later claimed never to have discarded'. The form of words employed: 'Take and eat this, in remembrance that Christ died for thee, and feed on him in thy heart by faith, with thanksgiving', while clearly having moved away from the more Catholic tone of the First English Prayer Book seems, at least to a lay mind, to have left ample scope for a belief in a 'spiritual' or 'true presence' in the Eucharist. Such a view receives added weight from the refusal of Cranmer, despite Knox's protests, to delete the instruction that communicants should kneel. None the less the formal substitution of a communion table, as foreshadowed in Ridley's London reforms, instead of the altar as the place of celebration marked the breaking of any real link with pre-Reformational ritual.[17]

The pleas of Knox found more response from the Privy Council, which proceeded, on its own authority, to insert the notorious 'Black Rubric', which explained that

> lest yet the same kneeling might be thought or taken otherwise, we do declare that it is not meant thereby, that any adoration is done, or ought to be done, either unto the Sacramental bread or wine there bodily received, or unto any real and essential presence there being of Christ's natural flesh and blood. For as concerning the Sacramental bread and wine, they remain still in their very natural substances, and therefore may not be adored, for that were Idolatry to be abhorred of all faithful Christians.

This action has been taken as indicative not only of the drift of theological pressures at the centre of power, but also of a significant shift in the balance of ecclesiastical authority. It has been suggested that Convocation was increasingly ineffective during the reign of Edward VI, and was not even formally consulted on many really vital decisions, the liturgical and doctrinal reforms being effectively the fruits of the Privy Council's exercise of royal supremacy which 'attempted to reduce the church, as an institution, to the level of a governmental ministry of religion'.[18]

Observance of the forms of the Second English Prayer Book – by laity as well as by clergy – was prescribed by the Second Edwardian Act of Uniformity (5 & 6 Edw. VI, c. 1). Its sanctions were much stricter than those of its predecessor, extending to the threat of 'imprisonment during his or their lives' for a third offence of attendance at 'any other manner or form of . . . administration of the sacraments'. Since the new liturgy was to be implemented on 1 November 1552 its life was destined to be short, yet in the long run it was to form the enduring basis of Anglican ritual. Meanwhile Cranmer was occupied with a projected reform of canon law and with the formal codification of the beliefs of the Church. The first proved abortive, but the latter emerged as the Forty-two Articles, which received royal assent in June 1553, less than a month before Edward's death. These Articles were as specifically anti-Catholic at one end of the religious spectrum as they were anti-Anabaptist at the other. The combination of beliefs preserved has been not unfairly characterised as placing 'Calvinist Articles alongside a Catholic liturgy.' Catholic doctrines of purgatory, image-reverence and the sacrificial nature of the Mass were denounced. Article Seventeen declared that 'predestination to life is the ever-lasting purpose of God [from] before the foundations of the world [for] those whom he hath chosen'. This quite explicit Calvinism may well reflect the influence of such as Knox – who sat on a committee of six to which, at one stage, the Council entrusted discussion of the draft articles. Certainly Professor Dickens believes that the perhaps deliberate and ambiguous imprecision of Article Twenty-nine (on the Eucharist) 'savours more of compromise between Cranmer and his committee rivals [the Hooper-Knox group] than of a real consensus of minds'. Undoubtedly the Forty-two Articles, while resting upon a sometimes uneasy compromise, mark the most 'Calvinist' position reached by the 'Anglican' Church; yet a modified version, the Thirty-nine Articles, was to provide the basis of its later evolution.[19]

The assertion that no fewer than eighteen of the Articles bear traces of the contemporary dread of Anabaptism points to another important aspect of religious developments in the reign of Edward VI. Anabaptism (literally, re-baptism of consenting adults, symbolising a conscious 'conversion'), 'radical' or 'sectarian' Protestantism – for the word 'Anabaptist' was often used as a conveniently frightening 'umbrella' term of abuse – was no new phenomenon in England. A proclamation of March 1535, declaring that 'of late many strangers . . . are arrived and come into this realm', had ordered Anabaptists to depart within twelve days, under pain of death. Indeed, in May and June of that year about twenty-five 'Dutch Anabaptists' had been tried, and fourteen of them were burnt at the stake. Sporadic pursuit of offenders occurred during the next decade. Yet Anabaptist activity in England almost certainly reached its peak under Edward VI. Hooper in 1550 (as if to illustrate that there were extremes beyond extremes) described Kent and Essex as 'troubled with the frenzy of the anabaptists more than any other part of the kingdom'. A year later the introduction to a translation of an anti-Anabaptist tract by Bullinger (Zwingli's successor at Zurich) warned that 'these Libertines and Anabaptists, are running in hugger mugger, among the simple and ignorant people'. In the last months of the reign the Council again commanded Cranmer to suppress unlawful sects in Kent. The 'radicals' were feared by Protestant and Catholic alike, not only because of allegedly monstrous doctrinal heresy but also because of the potential political and social implications of their beliefs (see page 145). Of the two who were condemned to the fire during Edward's reign the one, 'Joan of Kent', was 'burned for holding that Christ was not incarnate of the Virgin Mary' while the other is described as 'a certain Aryan [i.e. anti-Trinitarian] of the Strangers, a Dutchman'. Anabaptists and other radicals were accused, often quite wrongly, of seeking scriptural justification for what was 'but a carnal and fleshly liberty' and licence to defy 'temporal rulers and magistrates'. The martyrdoms referred to indicate that the forbearance of the Edwardian regime was not without limits, but its comparative liberalism may well have encouraged proliferation of radical groups. Yet the claim sometimes made that most of the Marian martyrs were drawn from the ranks of 'these radical

The Crisis in Religion

sectaries' has apparently little documentary justification; Dr I. B. Horst's recent study of this topic finds some indication of 'a high incidence of anabaptism' but believes the estimate of two-thirds much exaggerated.[20]

The oft-posed question of the extent to which England in 1553 was a Protestant realm is difficult to answer with any confidence. The problem of definition is as intractable as that of interpretation of the evidence. Certainly the basic doctrines of the English Church and the members of its upper clergy were avowedly Protestant; so were most members of the 'political establishment', although many of their number contrived to display chameleon-like dexterity in matching personal faith with political advantage. But what of the ordinary people? Far less concerned with theological niceties than the debates of their learned contemporaries might suggest, it is probably true that the strain of endemic anti-clericalism and hence of anti-Catholicism of earlier decades was now tempered by that of the cynical disillusion evoked by the spectacle of pillage of church wealth under the guise of Protestant reform. Particularly revealing is the shrewd realism of the diagnosis made by Paget (writing in 1549, admittedly in the context of the socio-political implications of religious trends) of a situation in which 'the use of the old religion is forbidden by a law, and the use of the new is not yet printed in the stomachs of the eleven of twelve parts in the realm'.[21] Its phraseology is a salutary reminder of the fact that with the ordinary man custom and usage are apt to weigh more heavily than doctrinal logic. It would seem perverse to deny that, despite the spectacle of the greed of politicians and of the intransigence of tactless zealots, Protestantism had made great headway in the England of Edward VI. While any attempt at quantitative assessment is fruitless, the significance of regional differentiation seems clear; the events of 1554–8 make it difficult to question the reality and sincerity of Protestantism in London and the south-east. Yet considered overall it is unlikely that in 1553 a large proportion of the English nation was either fervently Protestant or fervently Catholic.

Thus Mary Tudor came to the throne neither because nor in spite of any strongly established ground-swell of English religious opinion. Her accession must be attributed to the ingrained belief in legitimacy which the Tudors had established, to an element of personal sympathy for Mary herself, strongly reinforced by revulsion against the blatant self-seeking of Northumberland, and in the last resort, most ironically, to an upsurge of legitimate support in one of the most Protestant parts of the country, East Anglia. The absence of a clear-cut appreciation of the religious, as distinct from dynastic, implications of events is exemplified in the 'Epistle of Poor Pratte' to one Gilbert Potter, a tapster whose assertion of the right of Mary to the throne had been punished by the cutting off of his ears in the pillory: its author brackets the fear that 'the gospel shall be plucked away' with the warning that, in punishment, 'God will take from us the virtuous lady Mary, our lawful queen, and send such a cruel Pharaoh, as the ragged bear [the bear and ragged staff was the traditional emblem of Warwick] to rule us.'[22]

The vast majority of Englishmen probably believed that Mary would, essentially, restore the religious settlement of her father. In an age unused to the spectacle of monarchical abnegation of authority and power once gained, the expectation of a return to Catholic doctrine and ritual would not necessarily have implied abandonment of the caesaro-papal authority with which Henry VIII had endowed the English Crown. Nor is it safe to assume that any return to a policy of 'Anglo-Catholicism' would have been foredoomed to failure. Dr Loades has urged that 'the royal supremacy was deeply rooted in law, in vested interests, and in habitual attitudes of mind. By comparison, doctrinal protestantism was a very delicate plant, forced by the super-heated atmosphere of the previous reign.'[23] (None the less whether rooted in doctrinal precision or not, the sincerity of conviction of several hundred Protestants was to prove hardy enough to endure the flames of martyrdom.) Again, as so often before, we shall find the key to much of what happened in the personality of the monarch. Mary's Catholicism and the whole drift and nature of her policy must be related as closely to her personal background and to contemporary political and diplomatic factors as to any analysis of England's

The Crisis in Religion

doctrinal evolution. Mary failed at least as much because she was a 'Spanish' Tudor as she did because she was a 'Roman' Catholic.

The depth of the new Queen's religious convictions has already been observed; sadly, the faith which had shone so steadfastly through long adversity now hardened with her acquisition of power into a pitiless fanaticism. The Queen was immediately confronted with a religio-constitutional conundrum. Although in canon law the religious changes of the two preceding reigns were illegal, for the time being at least they were binding upon Mary as sovereign of England. Whether she liked it or not her accession to the throne made her 'Supreme Head' of the Church in England. Indeed, the first steps taken to modify the religious settlement derived their validity in English law from that title which she held in consequence of statutes as yet unrepealed. The Queen obtained secret papal dispensations for continuing to use the title, added the words 'just and licit' to her coronation oath to uphold the laws of the realm, and assured a papal emissary that 'it was first necessary to repeal and annul by Act of Parliament many perverse laws made by those who ruled before her'. Meanwhile the exiled Reginald Pole, whom the Pope had created Legate for England, wrote to urge that 'God has given the sceptre and the sword into her majesty's hands for no other reason than that ribaldry and disobedience to the holy laws may be punished ... it is not enough that she should honour God, she must compel her subjects to do likewise and punish the disobedient in virtue of the authority she has received from God.'[24]

Mary's first steps were cautious enough. A proclamation of 18 August, while deploring 'diversity of opinions in questions of religion', prohibiting unlawful preaching or publications on doctrinal matters, and asserting that the Queen 'cannot now hide that religion which God and the world knoweth she hath ever professed from her infancy', declared that 'her highness mindeth not to compel any of her said subjects thereunto until such time as further order by common assent may be taken therein' and advised her subjects to live in 'Christian charity, leaving those new-found devilish terms of papist or heretic.'[25] Most of the leading

Protestant divines were imprisoned on charges of sedition or of breaking the peace, and immigrant Protestants were ordered to quit the realm. Those English Protestants who chose to accompany them were not impeded. Indeed, Miss C. H. Garrett's study of the Marian exiles goes so far as to conclude that 'the so-called "flight" of 1554 was not a flight but a migration', that Protestant rejection of 'the policy of tact and clemency which Gardiner adopted' led him to encourage emigration, 'looking to rid the realm of a seditious element which threatened its stability'.[26] The Queen proceeded to cut through legal niceties in the deprivation and replacement of a number of Protestant bishops, but several of these were but yielding up their Sees to Catholics whom they themselves had dispossessed. In October, by 1 Mary c. 2, the Edwardian religious settlement was repealed, and it was enacted that 'all such divine service and administration of sacraments as were most commonly used . . . in the last year of the reign of our late Sovereign Lord King Henry VIII shall be, from and after the twentieth day of December . . . used and frequented throughout the whole realm of England'.

It is probably true to say that a majority of the English nation would have been fairly content with a stabilisation of this position. Yet the fact that, after 'marvellous dispute', over a quarter of the House of Commons voted against repealing the Edwardian legislation, while a proposal to abolish the royal supremacy had to be abandoned, should have sufficed to indicate to any monarch endowed with reasonable political acumen that in terms of popular acceptance the limit had been reached. Although Wyatt's Rebellion in January 1554 was basically a secular and political movement, in retrospect both Catholic and Protestant propagandist interpreted it in religious terms. The projected Spanish marriage, which had triggered off the rising, had obvious potential religious implications. In short, the religious problems of Mary's determination upon eventual disavowal of the royal supremacy and the pursuit of Catholic doctrinal restoration became increasingly difficult to disentangle from those of national and international politics. Each of them, unpopular *per se*, exacerbated the unpopularity of the others. Whether or not as a reaction against the evidence of national distaste, Mary's own religious intransigence hardened in 1554. A proclamation of 4 March, announcing and rehearsing injunctions to the bishops, prescribed rigorous enforcement of all 'canons and ecclesiastical laws heretofore in the time of King Henry VIII used within this realm'. In particular, vigilant 'repressing of heresies', rejection from among the clergy of any one 'being a sacramentary' (broadly speaking, any holding neo-Zwinglian or more extreme interpretations of Communion) and deprivation of married clergy were stressed.[27]

Wriothesley's *Chronicle* records one incident which attests a growing ugliness of mood 'Sunday the 8 of April was a villainous fact done in Cheape early ere day. A dead cat having a cloth like a vestment of the priest at mass with a cross on it afore, and another behind put on it; the crown of the cat shorne, a piece of paper like a singing cake put between the forefeet of the said cat bound together', and the whole hanging from a gallows. The Second Parliament of the reign, in session at the time (it sat from April to May of 1554), although giving its consent to the Spanish marriage (see page 170), rejected Gardiner's proposals to re-enact anti-heresy legislation, including the Six Articles. Most significantly, the opposition has been described as deriving some of its strength and leadership from 'Henricians' such as Paget as well as from zealous doctrinal Protestantism. Gardiner himself thought it appropriate to write to Cardinal Pole some advice on tactics: in particular he should send 'to the Parliament now in session a letter which should treat, in general only, the question of unity in religion, with such moderation that the right of the pope would be rather suggested than expressed in clear words, and even that not so precisely done that they could conclude it [i.e. the restoration of papal jurisdiction] to be imminent'. This letter should also make it known 'to the leaders of the people of this realm that in the reformation which we desire to effect in our native land there is no intention of making any alteration in the possessions and temporal inheritances throughout the realm....'[28]

In November a royal proclamation duly welcomed 'our most trusty and dearest cousin, Reginald Cardinal Pole, ...

legate *de latere'* entrusted by the Papacy with the mission of reuniting the English realm with Rome. His task was made easier by the fact that the Third Parliament of Mary's reign, which met in the same month, proved more compliant than its predecessor. This in turn owed much to the nature of the settlement which it was asked to enact, which bore 'the character of a bargain between Queen Mary and the governing classes'. On the one hand royal supremacy over the Church was abandoned and the way was made clear for severe persecution of heresy; on the other secular interests in the Council and in Parliament (led by Paget) succeeded in blocking any attempt at the restoration of church lands or at large-scale monastic revival.[29]

By the statutes 1 & 2 P. & M., c. 6 & 8 the medieval anti-heresy legislation was reinstituted as from 20 January 1555, while all the anti-papal legislation of the years after 1529 was repealed and the realm submitted to Rome. After a preamble which deplored that 'much false and erroneous doctrine hath been taught... since the 20th year of King Henry the Eighth', 'the Lords spiritual and temporal and the Commons assembled' went on to declare themselves 'very sorry and repentant of the schism and disobedience committed in this realm' and to request 'that we may as children repentant be received into the bosom and unity of Christ's Church ... in unity and perfect obedience to the See Apostolic'. But the contrition of the 'children repentant' did not extend as far as to include the restoration of the fruits of sin – the confiscations of church property of previous reigns. Royal mediation with the Pope was requested 'so as all persons having sufficient conveyance of the said lands and hereditaments, goods and chattels, as is aforesaid by the common laws, acts, or statutes of this realm, may without scruple of conscience enjoy them, ... clear from all dangers of the censures of the Church'. Significantly the statute was formally entitled 'An Act for repealing all statutes, articles and provisions against the see Apostolic of Rome ... and also for the establishment of all spiritual and ecclesiastical possessions and hereditaments conveyed to the laity.' Pope Julius III had realised that this sour-tasting half-loaf was, in the circumstances, preferable to the alternative of no bread. William Turner, Dean of Wells under Edward VI, now in exile, expressed the bitterness of the Protestant reaction in his pamphlet *The Huntyng of the Romyshe Wolfe*: the 'Romish Fox' addresses one of the chief architects of the reunion with the Papacy.

> Gardiner my Son which with weeping tears,
> Cut once away quite the tips of mine ears,
> Hath taken for me, of late such pain:
> That they are grown and healed again.[30]

On 30 November 1554 Cardinal Pole, exercising his legatine authority, pronounced the English realm as reconciled with the See of Rome. But his enthusiastic orations to Parliament, to both houses of Convocation and to the citizens of London, endeavouring to awaken a religious and indeed a social conscience in a Catholic context, made little tangible impact. It has been justly said that 'preoccupation with the apprehension and punishment of heretics was to divert a great deal of ecclesiastical energy into negative channels.... The Marian church was thus far more concerned with the few who defied it than with the many who ignored it.' Indeed in a wider context 'the Marian reaction betrays an intellectual and religious sterility uncharacteristic of the Catholic Reformation then enlivening so many parts of Europe'. Despite her protestations and talk of renunciation of church lands in the possession of the Crown, Mary was able to restore only some half dozen religious houses, with a total number of about one hundred monks; appeals for the establishment of charitable and educational projects, in regard to which Pole drew unfavourable comparisons between England and Italy, met with little response or success.[31]

The anti-heresy legislation was implemented with ruthless speed. Within a month of its becoming effective several leading Protestants, including Hooper, had been tried, condemned and burnt. The imperial ambassador, Renard, in his account of the first martyrdom, that of John Rogers on 4 February 1555, warned Philip that 'the haste with which the bishops have proceeded in this matter may well cause a revolt'. The sneer directed at Rogers during his examination: 'Thou wilt not burn in this gear when it cometh to the purpose', was unflinchingly given the lie by his fortitude at Smithfield.

Five days later Hooper embraced the stake at Gloucester with the cry of 'Welcome to the Cross of Christ! welcome everlasting life.' The comment of a moralising Catholic sermon that 'it moveth many minds, to see an heretic constant and to die' proved true in a quite unintended sense. For reasons which are not quite clear action against the three who were to be known as the 'Oxford martyrs', Latimer, Ridley and Cranmer, was delayed. In prison the first two showed the utmost courage. Latimer, despite the infirmity of age, conceded that 'the wise men of the world can find shifts to avoid the cross' but was resolved not to recant nor to shrink from bearing witness through martyrdom. Ridley, equally resolute but more combative in character, launched a typically bitter denunciation of Rome in a farewell letter: 'The see is the seat of Satan; and the bishop of the same ... is antichrist himself indeed ... This see at this day is ... the whore of Babylon ... the mother of fornications and of the abominations upon the earth.' It was for Ridley's reprieve that an unavailing offer of ten thousand pounds was made by a distant and Catholic kinsman. The text of the sermon preached prior to their joint execution, 'If I yield my body to the fire to be burned, and have not charity, I shall gain nothing thereby', was amply countered by Latimer's exhortation that 'We shall this day light such a candle, by God's grace, in England, as I trust shall never be put out.'[32]

Cranmer displayed a more wavering and irresolute fortitude. The extent to which his weakening must be attributed to an ebbing courage rather than to a genuine, almost instinctive, tendency to bow the knee to an anointed monarch, the degree to which fear became rationalised into consistency of submission to royal order, must ever remain the subject of conjecture. He signed a number of recantations, the most unequivocal conceding that: 'I, Thomas Cranmer, doctor in divinity, do submit myself to the catholic church of Christ, and to the pope, supreme head of the same church, and unto the king and the queen's majesties, and unto all their laws and ordinances.' Despite this submission he was degraded of his offices on 14 February 1556. It is clear that, from whatever motive, both the Queen and Cardinal Pole were determined upon his execution while Gardiner, who might have urged a more politic course, was dead. Certainly their instinct for revenge proved disastrous for their purposes: from the last ordeal a broken and discredited prisoner emerged as a triumphant martyr for the Protestant cause. At what stage Cranmer's resolution returned can never be known, for he signed additional recantations after he knew that he was to die, the last version on 18 March, only three days before his execution. Indeed he produced a transcript of his proposed speech at the stake (avowing the belief that Christ 'is really and substantially contained in the blessed sacrament of the altar') which, to their later intense embarrassment, the Catholics sent to the printers in advance so that it appeared within a day or so of his death. Cranmer's vacillation lasted until the day of martyrdom, on the morning of which he handed over additional signed copies of his recantation while bearing concealed on his person a Protestant draft of his final speech. In the service immediately preceding execution he astonished and appalled his Catholic hearers by switching from the expected version to a defiant avowal of his Protestant faith. He was stopped but then 'went eagerly out of the church and ran towards the stake, with [Catholic confessors] running beside him, trying desperately to persuade him to recant again before he died'. Significantly his declaration included not only a denunciation of the Pope as 'Christ's enemy and Antichrist, with all his false doctrine' and a reiteration of his own teaching on the Sacrament, but also the assertion that 'I here renounce and refuse ... things written by my own hand, contrary to the truth ... for fear of death, to save my life if it might be; and forasmuch as my hand offended, writing contrary to my heart, my hand shall first be punished therefore; for, may I come to the fire, it shall be first burned.' Hundreds of people witnessed what has been justly described as the extraordinary access of strength with which he fulfilled this pledge. The Queen might reflect that this justified her determination not to spare Cranmer's life for what she believed to be a feigned recantation; yet a more merciful decision would have inflicted far more harm on the Protestant cause.[33]

Not all prominent Protestants were eager to face martyrdom, perhaps the most notable case of submission being that of Sir John Cheke, former tutor of Prince Edward, in 1556. Some fled abroad, like Ponet, or contrived to live in safe if sometimes quavering obscurity, as did a future Archbishop of Canterbury, Matthew Parker. Yet, as they themselves would have put it, the example of those who suffered for their faith sufficed to purge their cause of the dross attached to it by the tawdrier aspects of Edwardian Protestantism. That example was followed by about two hundred and eighty fellow-martyrs. Their occupational and regional distribution is of some interest. The fact that the great preponderance of the victims were drawn from the poorer classes, and included in their ranks more than fifty women, might seem to lend weight to the contention that many of the martyrs were Anabaptists. Yet the available evidence does not support this. The alternative of flight (regularly advised by Latimer and Ridley as scripturally permissible, unlike recantation) was obviously more practicable for the relatively well-to-do, as is confirmed by a detailed analysis of the eight hundred or so who went into exile. The regional distribution is striking, and almost certainly reflects more than the tighter enforcement of anti-heresy laws in and near the capital city. About two hundred and thirty executions occurred to the south and east of a line drawn (roughly) from the Wash to Portsmouth.[34]

Whose was the responsibility for a policy which, however justifiable by contemporary European standards, undoubtedly repelled the vast majority of Englishmen? Professor Dickens' study of the sources has left 'a distinct impression that the urge to severity came from the Queen herself', while Mary's sympathetic biographer, Miss Prescott, cites a case in August 1558 when she rebuked the Sheriff of Hampshire for halting the execution of a heretic who recanted at the first touch of the flame. In truth it needs no subtleties of psychology to predicate a connection between the Queen's bitterness at her personal unhappiness, her childlessness and the general failure of her policies, and her lack of mercy towards those whom she genuinely believed to be leading others to damnation. The names of Gardiner, Bonner and Pole have also been associated with the policy, and the martyrologist Foxe identified the first-named as its initiator. But Dr Loades, in a recent monograph devoted to these events, credits Gardiner with sufficient acumen and elasticity of mind to have abandoned it once he had realised its 'boomerang' effect. Moreover Gardiner died in November 1555. As Bishop of London, Bonner (one of Foxe's arch-villains) could not avoid wholesale implementation of official policy; yet his reputedly harsh and bullying demeanour has been ascribed both to sadistic zeal and to a genuine wish to frighten his victims into submission and out of martyrdom. Interpretation of the part of Reginald Pole is even more equivocal: one historian finds it 'hard to believe that the gentle and scholarly Cardinal ... could have been enthusiastic for persecution', yet a much more recent assessment attributes 'much of the moral responsibility [to] an academic man as dominated by an idea as Robespierre himself, a rhetorical humanist deficient of the sort of humanity' that is essential for statecraft. There remains the question of the Spaniards. Certainly Renard saw that large-scale persecution was impolitic, notably in that it increased public hostility towards Spain in general and Philip in particular. The suggestion that Philip himself disapproved of the burnings, again if only on the ground of expediency, has been countered with the question as to whether this was not merely dissimulation for public consumption. Undoubtedly Spaniards at Court – confessors who had come over with Philip – participated in the persecution, and to contemporary Englishmen its scale and intensity must have seemed almost conclusively indicative of Spanish direction.[35]

In so far as the persecution may justly be attributed to Spanish influence it is yet another example of the immense significance in religion of the personal wishes of the monarch – in this case including the choice of a bridegroom. In attempting to assess the net effects of the Queen's intransigent policy upon the course of religion in England one must concede that the whole issue was bedevilled by personal, political and national influences. One cannot discount the surmise that Mary's bigotry was coloured by her unfortunate personal history, now deepened by her childless and unhappy marriage. This last and the disastrous war into which it dragged the nation (and which, allegedly, sharply diminished church-going!) intensified and was itself in turn made more odious by the unpopularity of the persecutions. Englishmen were not unused to witnessing brutal public punishments, yet the scale and severity of persecution for this cause were wholly alien to the English tradition. The moderate or even apathetic attitude attributed to English public opinion in regard to doctrinal controversies would of itself lead to a greater sense of shock at the holocaust than might be the case elsewhere. The apparently paradoxical assertion that 'in 1553 England was by no means a Protestant country. It was made more nearly Protestant by the reign of Queen Mary' alludes of course to the revulsion of feeling engendered by the burnings which effectively purified Protestantism by fire while associating Catholicism with cruelty and an unpopular foreign intervention. Yet this line of argument rests upon the assumption of Mary's death at a relatively early age. The supply of Protestant leadership was not inexhaustible; by 1558 most Protestants of stature had either been martyred or were in exile. Renard's anxious forecast in February 1555 of rebellion if the burnings were not checked had not yet been fulfilled despite their intensification, although by 1558 Bonner was urging secret executions to avoid the risk of riot. Moreover a recent work of synthesis suggests that the accepted criticism of Mary for 'failing to discover the Counter-Reformation' or to undertake constructive and educational measures, has been overdone. Conrad Russell points out that many of the Elizabethan Catholics in exile had in fact been trained at Marian Oxford and that 'if Mary had lived another fifteen years she could have had as brilliant a bench of Catholic bishops as any in history of the country'. This is a hypothesis, and there is little evidence of a genuine Catholic religious revival under Mary; Cardinal Pole did not respond to Loyola's invitation to send young Englishmen to train at the colleges in Rome. Yet in the event the bishops who were actually appointed were to display resolute adherence to their faith. There was nothing inevitable about the ultimate victory of Protestantism.[36]

Two other aspects of events deserve mention. First, the significance of the procedure forced upon the Queen in her reversal of so much of Edwardian and Henrician policy. The

The Crisis in Religion

bargain which her Third Parliament exacted as a condition of the return to Rome seems rather shabby in terms of principle; yet the fact that Parliament was able to do this, together with its rejection of at least some of the government's measures (as in the intractable Fourth Parliament's defeat of a proposal to treat refusal of exiles to return as a felony involving confiscation of property), was of immense long-term religious and constitutional importance. Secondly, the number, calibre and places of refuge of the hundreds of Protestant exiles were to be of determinative influence in the religious settlement of the following reign and also of some future political significance. For not only did the doctrinal beliefs of so many of these exiles move still closer to those of Zwingli or Calvin, but some of them also abandoned the doctrine of passive resistance which had been so doggedly maintained in face of Henrician persecution. John Ponet's *Shorte Treatise of politike power* (1556) was quite explicit in its declaration of the duty to depose an ungodly ruler. So was a work by Christopher Goodman, Knox's fellow-exile in Geneva, *How Superior Powers Oght to be Obeyd* (1558). The claim that 'the *Troubles begun at Frankfort* [an account of one of the fiercest debates among the exiles] were to close in civil war' (that is, of the seventeenth century), while overstated, is not without its element of truth. In 1642 the opponents of the Crown reprinted Ponet before any other pamphlet.[37]

Such was the complex legacy which Mary bequeathed to her sister. It is fatally easy in retrospect to take for granted the nature and the success of the religious settlement and policy of Elizabeth I. That settlement has been described as effectively 'pre-determined'. In any literal sense this is obviously incorrect; yet the implication that, given her character and motivations, the degree of freedom of choice open to the new Queen was limited seems valid. In the event her religious settlement was to reflect a tense and uneasy balance between her own religious wishes and the possibilities and pressures inherited from the past. Dr Patrick Collinson suggests that Elizabeth's 'conduct of church affairs was above all an act of statesmanship', and certainly few monarchs can have been endowed with a keener awareness of politics as the art of the possible. Yet Professor Haugaard's recent study of her settlement leaves him 'wholly persuaded that we cannot explain it on the common assumption that she treated religion as a tool of political expediency'. Effectively there was a happy coincidence between the Queen's own basic religious inclinations and the promptings of prudent statecraft. Her whole personal background made it unlikely that she would have any papist tendencies, and many who had longed for her accession now hailed it as the signal for a renewal of Protestant progress. Yet Elizabeth had a genuine distaste for both religious extremes. Indeed while not without sincere religious convictions she displayed little real religious fervour. Perhaps the most significant difference between the royal sisters lay not primarily in their personal views on religious doctrine *per se* but in the standpoints from which they looked at the problems of ecclesiastical statecraft. Mary's was the narrow and perspectiveless vision of the zealot; Elizabeth's was that of the calculating and balanced politician. Mary had looked at political issues through the eyes of a religious fanatic; Elizabeth assessed the problems of religion within a context of political expediency. Mary had believed that God had given her the realm, in near-miraculous fashion, in order to save the souls of her subjects; her sister was more concerned to exact their loyalty in the things of this world. The crucial phrase in Bacon's much-quoted and much-argued description of his Queen as 'not liking to make windows into men's hearts and secret thoughts' is the codicil 'except the abundance of them did overflow into overt and express acts and affirmations ... in impugning and impeaching ... her Majesty's supreme power'.[38]

The problem inherited by Elizabeth was complex. At first sight it seems obvious to describe the realm as sickened by the extremes of the last two reigns and to accept a *via media* as the clearly indicated expression of both royal and national wishes. But this is to short-circuit too many problems. It may well reflect the attitude of public opinion, certainly of the 'uncommitted' majority; but the Queen had the task of establishing and implementing a settlement not by referendum but through Parliament and with the co-operation of the clergy. It has been suggested that the Marian martyrs died in part for their belief that the English Church was an aspect of the English realm and for their consequent rebuttal of any return to papal domination. Yet by token of their very resistance we may discern the emergence of an increasing reluctance to identify the realm in its religious aspects with the personal religious beliefs and wishes of the monarch. Moreover, despite its reversal of direction in regard to doctrine, in one respect the reign of Mary had but confirmed and deepened the conviction nurtured during that of her brother: that Parliament was entitled to enact the fundamentals of any religious settlement. As for the upper clergy, while it is true that Elizabeth's task was made easier by the existence of many vacant Sees, the number of which was increased by the death of no fewer than five bishops during the last six weeks of 1558, the fact that only two of the Marian bishops were to retain their Sees is striking testimony to the judgement of Mary (assisted by Cardinal Pole) in their appointments and also to the magnitude of the problem confronting her successor.

Indeed early in 1559 the Convocation of Canterbury was to assert the full Catholic position on papal supremacy and on dogma, while the bishops present in the Parliament of the same year unanimously voted against every change proposed in ecclesiastical affairs. Faced with this resolution and with the martyr-roll of most of those leading Protestants who had remained in Marian England, Elizabeth perforce had to look to returning exiles for many of her bishops. The Catholic bishop who, in his funeral oration for Queen Mary, had expressed his fear of the 'wolves coming out of Geneva and other places of Germany' had a sure instinct despite the vagueness of his geography. If it is true that the martyrs ensured a reversal of Marian policy, it is equally certain that the exiles pushed that reversal rather further in a Protestant direction than Elizabeth herself would have wished. Yet it is well to remember that her first Archbishop of Canterbury, Matthew Parker, had remained in England in quiet obscurity throughout, as indeed had no fewer than eleven of the twenty-five bishops ultimately appointed. It is perhaps a stimulating overstatement to characterise what took place as 'little less than the surrender of the Church to an émigré government potentially out of touch with the queen's own conservative instincts'. Those instincts have been neatly characterised as 'ritualistic proclivities ... doctrinal indifference'; but that indifference most certainly would not extend to the anti-hierarchical views imbibed by many of the returning Genevan and German exiles.[39]

It seems clear that these counter-pressures, combined with the general uncertainty of her position, persuaded Elizabeth against any hasty and over-definitive settlement. Her title, set forth in the first royal proclamation of her reign, described her as 'Elizabeth by the grace of God Queen of England, France, and Ireland, defender of the faith, etc.', in ironic contrast with that which had announced 'Mary by the grace of God ... defender of the faith, and in earth supreme head of the Church of England.' A proclamation of 15 January 1559 included the phrase 'defender of the true, ancient, and Catholic faith'. It is suggested that the Queen did not intend to frame a full and final settlement in the first session of Parliament in 1559; she wanted to wipe out the Marian legislation and to restore the position obtaining in the first year of the reign of Edward VI, but as yet desired neither a prayer book nor an act of uniformity. But her policy was modified by circumstances. Professor Hurstfield suggests that 'as in other crises of her reign, Elizabeth did not start off with any clear solution in mind but rescued compromise out of a dangerous situation'. The dangers of the position, and the nature and balance of that compromise, derived from the almost complete non-compliance of the Marian upper clergy on the one hand, and the strength of Protestant sympathies and influence on returning émigrés in Parliament (to which she was forced to turn) on the other. Some half-dozen leaders of the former exiles, such as Cox, Grindal and Jewel, soon to become bishops, were in London at the crucial time: 'an unofficial Convocation attached to Parliament, the pressure group of a revolutionary party'. Although most of the Genevan exiles as yet had not returned, it is well to remember that the 'moderation' of the 'Anglican' Frankfurt congregation (which had rejected the explicit Calvinism of Knox) had itself found expression in the adoption of a simplified version of the 1552 Prayer Book. The Lower House of Parliament included 'a vital core of at least twelve and probably sixteen returned exiles', many of the 'crypto-Protestants' of Mary's Parliament of 1555, and in all over one hundred members who may be described as convinced Protestants.[40]

Thus the first and very limited 'bill to restore the supremacy of the Church of England to the Crown of the realm' and (almost certainly) to re-establish Communion in both kinds, introduced to the Commons in early February, emerged from the committee stage a much-extended and explicitly Protestant document – Sir John Neale conjectures that it 'revived the 1552 Prayer Book and re-established the religious structure as it was at the death of Edward VI'. In March the Lords effectively restored it to its previous form, but the Commons' reluctant acceptance was followed not by the expected royal signature but by adjournment of Parliament until 3 April. The reasons for Elizabeth's change of mind are still debated. It has been contended that the international recognition accorded Elizabeth by the terms of the Treaty of Cateau-Cambrésis, news of which reached England on 19 March, emboldened her to take a more positive line and led to a more definitive set of proposals; but one historian has asked the pertinent question: 'Why would the news have thrown Elizabeth into the arms of the eager reformers?' The answer may be that the news, together with the evidence of the extent and depth of feeling in the Lower House of Parliament, encouraged the more Protestant members of her Council (perhaps Cecil, Bacon and Knollys) to urge upon the Queen the safety and the wisdom of a compromise which went some way towards meeting the sweeping demands of the Commons' amendments and counter-proposals. For whatever reason there seems little doubt that, in the event, the settlement came rather more quickly and went significantly further in a Protestant direction than the Queen herself would have wished.[41]

In April 1559 a third and government-sponsored bill was introduced which, restoring the royal supremacy with a change of title which has been variously interpreted as a concession to Catholics and to Calvinists, described the Queen as 'supreme governor as well in all spiritual or ecclesiastical things or causes as temporal', and included an oath to be administered to clergy, judges and others. This measure passed rapidly through the Commons and, despite debate in the Lords and indeed its rejection by all the spiritual peers, reached statutory form as the Act of Supremacy (1 Eliz. I, c. 1) by the end of the month. Professor Dickens has observed that the change in title accorded to the Queen was no mere quibble but reflected realities, for 'Parliament was becoming a co-ordinate power rather than an agent. . . . In effect, it told her to act through ecclesiastical commissioners and it defined rather narrowly their powers.' An 'Act for the Uniformity of common prayer and divine service... and the administration of the sacraments' (1 Eliz. I, c. 2) soon followed. The Book of Common Prayer described therein was the product of another compromise. It went far nearer to that of 1552 than Elizabeth (whose preference was for the version of 1549) would have wished; yet the 'Black Rubric' was deleted, while conciliation in regard to the nature of the Eucharist was attempted by the device of including the wording of both the Edwardian Prayer Books at the crucial point in its celebration. The clergy were to conform upon pain of fine, imprisonment and deprivation, while the Queen's subjects were all to attend church under penalty of a fine of 12d. per absence. Clause XIII decreed 'that such ornaments of the Church and of the ministers shall be retained and be in use, as was in the Church of England, by authority of Parliament, in the second year of the reign of King Edward the Sixth'. This clear indication of the Queen's own tenacity of purpose was to prove contentious. Yet V. J. K. Brook sees it as a tribute to Elizabeth's statecraft in that as far as the majority of her subjects were concerned it represented a well-judged conciliatory measure. We have remarked that to the ordinary church-goer these tangibles were at least as important as finer points of doctrine. 'To maintain clerical vestments and customary ceremonial, even at a reduced level, was the surest way to advertise the continuity of the church in England against Swiss innovation. [Indeed] to have given way about vestments would probably have offended far more than it would have appeased, and would have destroyed all hope of a national church.'[42]

The settlement of 1559 was, in effect, the result of a compromise beween the Queen's own wish for comprehension and the pressures of the returning émigrés. Patrick McGrath describes it as representing 'the highest common denominator among the various Protestant groups'. As such, it glossed over tensions which were never to be completely resolved, and established an equilibrium which at the time must have appeared both provisional and precarious. Yet it was to endure as the permanent basis of the English Church. For the task of its preservation and defence against either extreme, but above all against the immediate danger of a further swing towards Calvinism, Elizabeth's choice as Archbishop of Canterbury was ideal. 'God keep us', wrote Matthew Parker, 'from such visitation as Knox have attempted in Scotland: the people to be orderers of things'. Thus the years between 1559 and 1563 saw a further assertion and definition of the essentials of the Elizabethan compromise, despite the clear evidence of underlying tension. The royal injunctions of 1559 concerning preaching, homilies, instruction of youth, clerical garb and communion reiterated the avoidance of either extreme. Of two proclamations concerning religion in September 1560 the one prohibited destruction of church monuments while the other decreed the deportation of Anabaptists. Regulations promulgated in 1561 took steps to frustrate those who wished to reduce English churches to Helvetic simplicity. The Eleven Articles, issued by the bishops in the same year, foreshadowed the Thirty-nine Articles.[43]

Yet in 1563 the more radical Protestants counter-attacked in the Lower House of Convocation. In aggregate the programme of the 'precisians' (a term which approximates to the later more usual 'Puritan') would have changed the doctrinal, liturgical, and disciplinary basis of the Elizabethan Church. In particular they were determined to get rid of what they termed the 'rags of popery'. In some respects they came near to success: their proposals to abolish crossing at baptism, the necessity of kneeling at Communion and Saints' Days were defeated by a single vote. Professor Haugaard's detailed study of this Convocation recognises its decisions, both negative and positive, as marking a decisive point in the evolution of the Church of England which it 'propelled well past the fateful crossroads. It continued on the route chosen by the queen instead of turning to that proposed by the militant reformers.' The settlement of 1559 was confirmed, and the efforts of the 'precisians' in the Lower House to move further in a Calvinist direction were beaten by the steady opposition of Elizabeth's bishops in the Upper House. Moreover this Convocation produced the basic draft of the Thirty-nine Articles of Religion and may therefore 'justly claim to have made the most significant decisions about doctrinal statements in the history of the Church of England'. This modified version of the Forty-two Articles of 1552 clearly condemned the Catholic doctrines of purgatory and of the Mass, and affirmed the concept of justification by faith and indeed the Calvinist view of predestination. What has been termed the Anglican combination of neo-Catholic liturgy with neo-Calvinist doctrine had been established.[44]

The Queen's hope for a truly comprehensive settlement was doomed to failure: the Catholic Tunstall rejected her compromise as too Protestant while Coverdale, Edwardian Bishop of Exeter, condemned it as not Protestant enough. It is fair to observe that despite all difficulties Elizabeth's immediate task was made somewhat easier by two considerations which in the long-run were not to endure: willingness to accept what was thought of as an interim settlement, and reluctance to adopt a policy of active opposition. The acceptance of compromise by many of the 'precisians' was later justified by Grindal, who described himself and his colleagues as having decided 'not to desert our churches for the sake of a few ceremonies'. Yet the fact that, nearly twenty years later, the Queen felt impelled to inflict virtual suspension of Grindal's powers as Archbishop of Canterbury is eloquent testimony that 'the Puritan problem remained internal, not only to English society but to the English Church itself'. Likewise, although for rather different reasons, the threat to the Elizabethan Church from the Catholic ranks remained quiescent during its early years. Patrick McGrath has suggested that 'Catholics must have greatly exceeded in numbers the small minority of committed Protestants which was imposing its will on the nation, but they were weak in the places that mattered.' Whatever one's views on the first contention, there can be no doubt about the second. For the Marian bishops gave witness of readiness to lose office for their beliefs, not of preparedness to resist, while even their example of principle was followed by very few of the lower clergy in refusing the Oath of Supremacy. Yet if the impact of the Counter-Reformation had not reached England in time to stiffen Catholic resistance to Elizabeth's religious settlement, it was to pose a very real problem in the form of the dedicated missionary priests who came, many to martyrdom, in later decades. It remains true, and is of the utmost importance, that the Queen had secured the precious time she needed to establish and consolidate her settlement before Calvinist patience ran out and Catholic counter-attack commenced in earnest.[45]

The year 1563 did not see the end of two inter-related struggles: that concerning the maintenance or shifting of the existing balance between Crown, Convocation and Parliament in the control of ecclesiastical affairs and religious doctrine; and that to preserve or amend the body of doctrine itself. In regard to the first of these the problems posed by a lay supremacy were not made easier by its exercise by a woman. The differences between the position of Elizabeth and that of Henry VIII are all too clear. The Queen did not exercise the caesaro-papal power of her father; the events of the years between had made of Parliament a would-be partner in this sphere. Claire Cross points out that 'the civil authority could not hide the fact that in the first instance the doctrine and the ritual of the church had been established by act of Parliament'. In regard to doctrine, for the first time in the Tudor era there was some divergence between the official teachings of the Church of England and the personal beliefs and wishes of the monarch. None the less it is a tribute to the statecraft of Elizabeth that the breach was not wider. Now, as in previous reigns, the significance for the course of religion of the personality and skill of the ruler was still very great. The equilibrium established by 1563 – the year of the first English edition of Foxe's *Acts and Monuments* (or *Book of Martyrs*) as well as that of the draft of the Thirty-nine Articles – seemed precariously poised. Yet in the future, despite the continued existence of discontent on either flank, it was to prove the stable and enduring basis of a Church which rooted itself in the loyalties and affections of the English people. In this respect, as in others, the year 1563 may fairly symbolise the end of the mid-Tudor crisis.[46]

5 Economic and Social Problems: the 'Dangerous Corner'

Those aspects of the mid-Tudor crisis which we have thus far examined – dynastic, governmental and political, and religious – were fairly closely inter-related. Each of them very largely reflected the changing personalities and policies of successive monarchs. It is perhaps arguable that the subject of this chapter is somewhat different in that it emerged from underlying, long-term developments in society and the economy as a whole. This premise must not be taken too far: first, because the socio-economic aspects of the crisis cannot completely be isolated from the governmental and religious developments; and, secondly, because the actions of individual rulers played a major part in exacerbating certain features of that crisis, notably that of inflation of prices. In short, although in some respects the economic and social problems of Tudor England were of long gestation, there is ample evidence that these problems reached crisis proportions at the mid-century which marked, in Professor Bindoff's apposite phrase, a 'dangerous corner' in English economic and social history.[1]

The implications of increasing individual freedom and contingent loss of communal security in economic relationships, as production for the market increased its role in both agriculture and industry, were long-term; but they were certainly accentuated by the growing commercialisation of the sixteenth century. The gravity of the problem of unemployment engendered by economic change and dislocation, and by the greater impact of market fluctuations, was increased by another secular, or long-run trend: the growth in population. Yet the problem of poverty thus indicated was worsened by the rise in prices, responsibility for which must be attributed at least in part to the deliberate 'debasement' policy of the Crown as well as to 'real' (as distinct from 'monetary') factors. Nor should the social and economic effects of the dissolution of the monasteries be entirely discounted. The pressures of several of these forces came to a head in the tensions and disorders of 1549 (with their uneasy aftermath), the abrupt cessation of a last reckless spurt of debasement in the 'calling down' of the coinage in 1551, and the textiles slump of the same year. Whether measured in terms of the financial security of the Crown itself (the needs of which for war expenditure were the greatest single cause of debasement), of the stability of the economy, or of the maintenance of a healthy and contented social order, the mid-Tudor decades were an era of crisis – a crisis whose duration may not unfittingly be symbolised by the dissolution of the greater monasteries and the Elizabethan recoinage and Statute of Artificers respectively as its terminal points.

In approaching an economy which was still overwhelmingly rural we may well begin with developments in agriculture. This is the more appropriate in that concern with agrarian discontent was very prominent both in contemporary literature and sermons and in the evidence of governmental action. R. H. Tawney's classic discussion, *The Agrarian Problem in the Sixteenth Century*, written over half a century ago, has been subject to much revision – perhaps too much. It seems to be agreed that the problem of 'enclosures' in Tudor England was overstated by moralising contemporaries and by some older historians. Yet an excessively 'minimising' approach has its own dangers. No one would now contend that a uniform, large-scale process of enclosure swept over England; but it is equally misleading to take aggregate statistics (which are admittedly incomplete) and average them over the country as a whole so as to produce a small percentage figure implying minimal impact. The process of enclosure was unevenly spread in terms of location and of time, and it was regional in its incidence; but for these very reasons its effects were the greater. Above all it reflected farming and marketing realities and a readiness to cut across established patterns of land usage (where necessary) in order to maximise its yield.

Of course a commercialised attitude towards agriculture was not new. But what was new in the late fifteenth and early sixteenth centuries was the reversal of the previous trend in regard to the balance between land, population and market pressures. As a result of the catastrophic plagues of the mid- and late fourteenth century the population of England had fallen from about 3·7 millions in 1348 to about 2·1 millions in 1410. Effectively, the bargaining power of labour increased. So did 'stratification' of the peasantry; indeed as the large-scale estate corn-farming for the market of the high Middle Ages diminished so 'from the late fourteenth century the substantial yeoman farmer . . . was the key man in the countryside'. But from about 1450 onwards a very sharp upsurge in the demand for English wool produced every incentive for enclosure of the waste and conversion of arable to pasture. This in turn caused considerable – if scattered and variable – depopulation. It appears that the great age of enclosure and of 'deserted villages' was between 1450 and 1520, rather than later in the sixteenth century. Yet the Tudor period witnessed three extremely important developments: first, a continued upsurge of population which, starting in the late fifteenth century, once more changed the balance between land and labour; secondly, a steady increase in the pressure of market forces; and, thirdly, the fact that, in response to these forces, 'the lord then returned to play an active part in rural enterprise, a role which many had abdicated in the late fourteenth and fifteenth centuries'.[2]

In retrospect the dilemma of Tudor agriculture seems clear: in general terms the continued expansion in demand for wool and woollen cloth implied continued conversion to pasture, while the expansion of population demanded more extensive and/or intensive and productive cultivation of arable land if pressure upon food supplies and living standards was to be met. Increased responsiveness to marketing influences and the consequent commercial potentialities of the land might lead its owners or occupiers to change its farming pattern. The direction of such change would vary with local geography and marketing circumstances, its impact according to the existing pattern of land occupation and usage. But where such change involved the creation of larger farming units or a reduction in size of labour force then its effect in terms of social dislocation, discontent and even suffering is evident. As we shall see, Tudor commentators were not always guilty of the error attributed to them by some modern historians, that is, exclusive concentration upon sheep-farming 'enclosure' narrowly defined. Yet this was indeed the most striking exemplification of those consequences of more 'rational' farming which evoked the most bitter protest: eviction of the peasant-farmer and unemployment. More intensive production of food, involving some degree of regional specialisation, sometimes took place in response to the needs of a growing population, an increasingly large proportion of which (thanks to the meteoric expansion of London) was composed of town dwellers. Contemporary critics had much to say about the exploitation of the consumer by food producers – especially the 'great graziers'. But where the land was at all suitable for conversion to pastoral farming sheep-rearing presented the classic formula for profitable enterprise: high price of product alongside low labour costs. Dr P. J. Bowden's index shows a rise in the price of wool so rapid, particularly during the 1530s and 1540s, that by 1550 it had reached a figure almost double that of a century earlier. Here was an obvious and powerful motive for enclosure and conversion to pasture.[3]

We may look briefly at the position of those who felt themselves injured by agrarian change and at the practices of which they complained. In regard to the first, security of tenure and availability of legally enforceable safeguards were the crucial issues. Those who held their land as freeholders or on long lease could feel safe. But the vast majority of small or peasant-farmers held their land by 'customary' tenure. Of these, those who possessed a copy of the entry in the records of the manorial court of the terms on which they held their land ('copy-holders') were safer than those who did not. Yet here again much depended upon the terms of such tenure – for instance, upon whether or not the 'entry fine' or 'gressom' which a son had to pay in order to inherit his father's tenure was fixed. The social conscience of the lord and the extent to which he would employ legal chicanery or sometimes plain intimidation to get his way were also important. In many cases an evicted tenant had little remedy under common law, through lack of sufficient documentary evidence of title or lack of the funds needed to fight his case; hence the importance in this context of the development of equity courts, notably the Court of Requests for Poor Men's Causes during this period. Perhaps the sharpest critique of this traditional picture of the peasant-farmer under attack is that of Dr Eric Kerridge, in a closely argued case which is heavily reliant upon legal definitions. He concludes that the more recent analysis of C. M. Gray repeats Tawney's errors in failing to distinguish the legal complexities of the position: 'small wonder that new Gray is but old Tawney writ small'. Small wonder perhaps that in a legal jungle which has allegedly baffled scholars of such eminence the average peasant-farmer of the mid-Tudor era had little chance.[4]

Several methods were open to the landlord wishing to increase the yield from his land. Modern critics have justly characterised 'enclosure' as a 'catch-all' phrase of condemnation. Yet most Tudor commentators were not guilty of such confusion. They were often clear both as to the specific types or aspects of enclosure which they attacked, and as to those other methods of exploiting the land which injured the little man. John Hales, in his instructions to the members of Somerset's Enclosure Commission of 1548–9, defined 'what is meant by this word inclosure. It is not taken where a man doth inclose and hedge in his own proper ground, where no man hath commons ... but it is meant thereby, when any man hath taken away and enclosed any other men's commons, or hath pulled down houses of husbandry, and converted the lands from tillage to pasture.' Enclosure of the commons was obviously harmful to the smaller peasant-farmer; yet even if they remained open he was liable to find himself grazed off them by the over-stocking of the large-scale commercial farmer. Equally harmful was the process known as 'engrossing': the amalgamation of two or more farms, involving the decay of 'houses of husbandry'. Dr Kerridge concedes that 'generally speaking, the enclosure of common-field townships for up-and-down husbandry led to a degree of agricultural depopulation. The proportion of tillage was necessarily reduced from about one-half to a third or even a quarter. The labour force was therefore reduced.'[5]

There were several devices by which the would-be encloser or engrosser might dispossess the peasant-farmer occupant of the land he coveted. Sometimes a lease ran out; sometimes the death of the tenant allowed a revision of rent so exorbitant as to justify the expressive contemporary term 'rack-renting'; sometimes a prohibitively high entry-fine was demanded of the heir to a tenancy. In fairness it must be said, first, that in this inflationary era the existing fixed customary rent payable by the tenant had often fallen behind the real worth of the land; and, secondly, that land hunger or sheer cupidity was not confined to the ranks of the landlords – the preacher Lever rebuked the commonalty, urging that 'it is covetousness in you, that causeth, and engendereth covetousness in them. For, for to get your neighbour's farm, ye will offer and desire them to take bribes, fines, and rents more than they look for, or than you yourselves be well able to pay.'[6]

To what extent was agrarian discontent a major cause of the mid-century social and economic crisis, in particular of the constant fear of riot and of the actual rebellions of 1549? It has been suggested first, that the total of land enclosed for the whole Tudor period was only about three per cent of the whole country, and, secondly, that from the point of view of enclosure strictly defined or of resultant 'deserted villages' the Enclosure Commission of 1548–9 came a generation too late. Yet in terms of real impact an overall figure means little; what counted was the incidence of enclosure in a fairly densely populated open-field arable farming area, and it seems that in some such districts up to thirty per cent of the arable land was newly enclosed. Again the puzzlement of some modern critics at the spate of 'protest literature' during the mid-century period when, it is asserted, comparatively little fresh enclosure was actually under way, would speedily be resolved by studying the content of such literature. For in it enclosure is but one of a list of complaints, including the imposition of extortionate entry-fines, rack-renting, engrossing, and over-stocking of the commons – all this against a general background of land hunger and rising prices. Indeed, one interesting recent interpretation of the position suggests that it was not new enclosures that caused the trouble; 'what was needed was to throw down the old and create new tenancies for the growing population'.[7] The real significance of this wave of protest cannot be dismissed on the basis of admittedly incomplete statistics regarding 'enclosures' alone.

There is ample evidence of governmental concern with the impact of agrarian change and especially with resultant discontent as a potential cause of disorder. Fear of depopulation, diminished food supplies, unemployment and poverty were among the explicit motives of governmental action. Between 1495 and 1563 eight statutes of the realm and a larger number of royal proclamations attempted to prevent or even reverse the process of enclosure and its alleged consequence of depopulation. Throughout the mid-century decades such action was repeatedly urged in sermons and in pamphlet literature, above all those idealists who preached the moral responsibility of government for the 'commonwealth' of all its subjects. A harsher note was sounded in several of the Tudor rebellions – from the Pilgrimage of Grace in 1536 to the Rising of the Northern Earls in 1569 – in that these involved at least a substantial fringe of agrarian discontent. There is little doubt that the late 1540s and early 1550s marked a period of almost endemic riot. The conjunction of the dominant but short-lived influence of the 'Commonwealth' idealists under Somerset with the stark realities of serious social and economic unrest and incipient disorder fully explains what has been described as 'the paradox of government action against enclosures at a date when enclosures was least in evidence'.[8]

The articles of complaint put forward by the leaders of Ket's Rebellion, the most clearly socio-economic uprising of the Tudor period and the culmination of a generation of agrarian discontent in Norfolk, are of prime importance. The term 'enclosure' appears only once, but the list of grievances includes 'rack-renting', the imposition of extortionate fines at the in-going of a new tenant, loss of common rights and over-stocking of the commons themselves by rich lords or gentlemen. All told thirteen of the twenty-seven Articles related to agrarian issues. Moreover the rebels' request that 'Commissioners' should be appointed from their ranks contended that this would enable them 'to redress and reform all such good laws, statutes, proclamations, and all other your proceedings, which hath been hidden by your Justices of your peace... from your poor commons' since 1485. The validity of this allegation of the non-enforcement of legislation which attempted to protect the peasant-farmer's interests has been questioned. Yet it derives some colour from the course of events. For both the principal measures taken by Somerset to check enclosure for sheep-rearing proved abortive. His Enclosure Commission met with difficulties and obstruction in accumulating evidence and was, in any case, swept away by the troubles of 1549 (which it was accused of fomenting) and by the fall of the Protector himself. A statute of 1549 (2 & 3 Edw. VI, c. 30) which ordered a census of and poll tax on all sheep together with a levy on cloth, with the real if unavowed objective of penalising enclosure for sheep-rearing, was never enforced; its formal repeal occurred as early as January 1550.[9]

Northumberland's regime did not rest content with this. For a brief and solitary interlude in the whole of the Tudor era the policy of attempting to discourage enclosure was reversed. By 3 & 4 Edw. VI, c. 3 the medieval Statute of Merton was re-enacted, giving landlords permission to enclose common land, subject to a provision (which met with scathing derision from Latimer's pulpit) that an unspecified 'sufficient' should be left for the tenants. But alongside this, and clearly indicative of uneasy awareness of instinctive public reaction, was placed a statute (3 & 4 Edw. VI, c. 5) which made it felony for twelve or more people to assemble for the purpose of abating rents, breaking down enclosures (whether lawful or not) or enforcing rights of common or rights of way over such enclosures. The anxiety of authority over the threat of insurrection became almost an obsession at this time – perhaps more understandably so in the context of instability and distrust at the centre of government itself. For whatever reason by 1552 it was judged prudent to revert to the traditional policy of preservation of tillage by the enactment of 5 & 6 Edw. VI, c. 5. Therefore this policy was maintained, as in a statute of Mary Tudor's Fourth Parliament (2 & 3 P. & M., c. 2). Cecil, who was concerned in both the measures last mentioned, included in his list of 'good laws' that enacted as 5 Eliz., c. 2, which was hopefully designed to restore to tillage all land which had been enclosed for pasture since the twentieth year of Henry VIII. The term Statute of Artificers which has been attached to the famous enactment of 1563 symbolises a shift in the balance of its clauses towards craft or industrial interests during its passage through Parliament; yet its order of priorities retained agriculture and agricultural labour (especially at harvest time) as the prime concern of the economy.

Whatever the reservations and limitations of available statistics, expression of discontent about agrarian grievances had reached its climax in the protest literature of the mid-century and had helped to bring about a condition of almost endemic tumult in much of England, a condition which frightened authority for some time even after the bloody suppression of Ket's Rebellion. Yet all this assumes its full significance only in the wider context of other aspects of economic development. It has been observed that Ket's Rebellion itself 'was no exclusively agrarian movement. It had a considerable urban element, recruited principally from Norwich and Yarmouth.' Contemporary literature attests the awareness of the danger from unemployed or malcontent urban and industrial workers, a menace to which government was particularly sensitive in the metropolis itself. Anxiety on this score was clearly evident in 1551: a foreign observer's account of the discovery in London of a plot 'to excite the people to revolt' was followed, one week later, by a proclamation which ordered the departure from the city of the 'great number of idle persons and masterless men', in groups of not more than four, travelling at least eight miles per day.[10]

To what extent were such dangers increased by any acceleration of change in the industrial and commercial sector of the economy during the mid-Tudor decades? Some years ago it was suggested that in effect an 'industrial revolution' occurred between 1540 and 1640. The evidence of industrial diversification seems clear, as does that of increased output in several sectors such as mining, metallurgy, ship-building, and production of certain building materials. But the validity of the concept has been questioned, and the thesis, while stimulating, was probably overstated. If we adopt the working definition of an industrial revolution, in its generally accepted sense, as a movement which results in a rapid acceleration of the previous pace of industrial growth to such effect that industry comes to exercise a dominant place in the economy, then the implied criteria were not fully satisfied by what occurred after 1540. None the less in our immediate context it remains true that developments in industry and commerce posed serious problems to government, and that a major crisis in textiles emerged precisely at the mid-century.[11]

The crucial change lay in the expansion of that part of industry which lay outside the scope of gild control and was increasingly free of corporate restrictions in its production for an ever-widening market. Certain industries such as mining and metallurgy by their very nature (scale of production unit, location, type of power employed) had seldom been subjected to gild and corporate town control or to craft workshop scale of production. These now expanded and were joined by newer industries and also by sections of the textile industry which escaped from the town to the countryside. While what has been called the 'text-book fiction' of a system uniformly applicable to all urban and industrial workers had never applied, the gilds had done much to control standards of production and to guarantee a certain measure of social security to their members. Essentially they were geared to a localised, limited and hence relatively inelastic market, which required and could support only small-scale enterprises. Hence the feasibility both of the ideal of community of interest between master and man, and between producer and consumer, and of effective gild control. The widening market, increased employment of capital, greater subdivision of labour and need for more elasticity and enterprise broke down these assumptions: problems of regulation and enforcement became more complex, and the gradual separation of the functions of craftsman and of entrepreneur tended to undermine the former's independence. With the (relative) decline of the gilds went that of certain of the older corporate towns, as industry moved to the countryside in search of part-time labour and freer conditions

– a movement perhaps accelerated by some of the desperate efforts of the gilds to tighten and enforce their restrictive privileges. Space will not permit fuller treatment of the internal and organisational explanations of gild decline, but its basic causes were economic and reflect the expansion of the industrial sector of the economy, the rise in number of industrial wage-earners unprotected from the impact of market supply and demand, and indeed the increased importance of such purely marketing forces despite the constant efforts of central and local authorities to maintain some degree of restraint.

The most important industries in mid-Tudor England were, after textiles: leather, food and drink, building, mining and metallurgy. The finishing trades (such as clothing and shoemaking) were of major significance, while urban life was dominated by distributive activities. In several industries the years after 1540 witnessed expansion or significant innovation, such as the introduction of the blast furnace in iron production. Yet textiles remained dominant, especially in regard to exports, and it was developments in this sphere that were most important in the context of the mid-century crisis. Among these developments the further extension of the domestic system was of cardinal significance. While the organisation of textile production was highly complex and diversified, with regional specialisation in both manner and type of output, it is broadly correct to describe it as dominated by the capitalist clothier or 'putter-out'. For the entrepreneur the domestic or 'cottage' system of production had the supreme advantage of the absence of any heavy commitment to fixed or 'overhead' costs. This made it more inviting to curtail or even cease production (or purchase of the products of others) at any time of slackening demand. The impact upon employment of boom and slump, or of any dislocation in communications, was thus accentuated as part of the same process by which the wage-earner was increasingly replacing the individual craftsman who had worked within the framework of gild protection. It is true that incomes from domestic industrial and from agrarian pursuits were very often complementary, and that the case must not be overstated. Yet the consequences of any marked fall in market demand explain the contemporary 'opinions of many great wise men; which think it better that all our wool were sold over the sea unwrought, than any clothiers should be set awork within the Realm. . . . [For] all these Insurrections do stir by occasion of all these clothiers; for when our clothiers lack vent over sea, there is great multitude of these clothiers idle . . . then they assemble in companies, and murmur for lack of living.' The Council's instructions when Lord Russell was despatched to the west in 1549 included the significant direction for 'seeing that clothiers, dyers, weavers, fullers, and all other artificers be kept occupied, and that all occasions of unlawful assemblies be avoided as much as may be'.[12]

These comments support Professor Ramsey's conclusion that 'private and national prosperity rested on the continuing sale of a single commodity' and that 'the importance of cloth in England's export trade made the health of the industry dangerously dependent on the state of the foreign market'. Historians are now rather sceptical as to the completeness or accuracy of Tudor statistics of cloth exports. In particular the increase in broadcloth exports from London from an annual average of 99,000 in 1542-4 to 119,000 in 1545-7, and 133,000 in 1550, may be misleading as a guide to national aggregates for wool and woollen cloths as a whole. Yet there is no doubt that a boom in such exports occurred towards the end of the reign of Henry VIII, and persisted into that of Edward VI, being accentuated after 1547 by the cumulative effects of successive debasements of the coinage which, through the mechanism of an exchange market which rarely operated in England's favour, made cloth relatively cheap (in terms of precious metal content) to the foreign buyer. Despite some recent qualifications in interpretation the coincidence of the upsurge in exports with a decade of debasement and of the subsequent slump with the 'calling down' of the coinage in 1551 suggests that it would be almost perverse to discount this contributory cause. It seems certain that the boom was partly artificial in its nature: there thus emerged a very real danger of over-production on the one side and of saturation of the market on the other. The two-pronged impact of real and of monetary factors pricked the bubble. Excess production and increasingly shoddy standards had already produced the ingredients of a crisis by 1550. Yet it seems probable that the decision of Northumberland's administration, in July and August of 1551, to 'call down' the value of English coinage by fifty per cent would of itself have had a disastrous effect upon cloth exports in that it drastically increased prices in real terms to the foreign purchaser. It ended all hope of any complete recovery of the Antwerp market, a slump in exports of some fifteen per cent in 1551 being followed by a further fall of about twenty per cent in 1552. Within its own context this is a classic example of the perils of excessive concentration upon one industrial product destined effectively for one market. The object lesson was not lost; in face of what proved to be a lasting recession of the order of twenty-five per cent, deliberate attempts were made to diversify the products of the English textiles industry.[13]

Meanwhile concern about the problems brought by industrial change, expansion and uncertainty had led to a steady increase in attempts at governmental intervention and control. Protection and regulation of the gilds and of the industrial privileges of corporate towns, maintenance of standards of production, care for the interests of the consumer and of the employee, were all suggested as motives and often became the avowed objectives of legislation of one type or another. Considerations of benevolence, security, revenue and national wealth jostled with and sometimes cut across each other. The issue was sometimes further bedevilled by the selfish dog-fights of conflicting pressure groups, as in the celebrated case of the five enactments concerning the leather trades between 1548 and 1558, each of which legislated in a sense opposed to that of its immediate predecessor. While any attempt at discussion of this legislation would be beyond the compass of this book, it is important to stress the effect of the commercial crisis and social disorders of the mid-century in confirming the Tudor belief in the need for governmental control. Determination to tighten such control reached its climax in the Statute of Artificers of 1563. Professor Bindoff has observed that 'few acts of any of Elizabeth's parliaments would, if rigorously enforced, have meant so much to the lives and livelihoods of so many of her subjects: their choice of occupation, terms of training, hours of labour and rates of wages, freedom of movement. All these determinants of the "work, wealth and happiness" of every commoner of the realm were themselves largely determined by 5 Elizabeth caput 4.'[14]

Some two years earlier in her reform of the coinage Elizabeth had taken action to deal with what undoubtedly had been a malignant influence in the mid-Tudor economy. While the causes, nature and impact of the price inflation of the Tudor and early Stuart period are still subject to quite vigorous debate, there is fortunately some measure of agreement as to certain of its aspects in the middle decades of the sixteenth century. The protests of contemporaries that prices were rising with frightening rapidity are quite confirmed by modern statistical research, which points to the contrast with the preceding century or more of relative price stability and to the relative slackening in the rate of increase thereafter until the last decade of the century. Recent studies are agreed that, beginning in the 1520s, prices rose with increasing rapidity, but not with uniformity for all commodities, especially during the 1540s and 1550s. By the 1550s agricultural prices were more than double those of thirty years earlier; industrial prices did not keep pace, but had risen to some seventy per cent above those of the 1530s. The very rapid increases beween 1544 and 1551 coincided with the 'great debasement', but also with three bad harvests at the end of this period. The steep rise in figures for 1556 and 1557 reflect harvest failures, the sharp fall in 1558 a savage epidemic of influenza.

The reader will have noted the allusions to divergences between agricultural and industrial prices, and to the part played by real, as distinct from monetary, influences. Indeed when we move to discussion of the causes of price inflation we enter much more debatable ground; both the limitations in agreed statistics and the differences in their interpretation counsel a cautious approach. The fundamental and traditional monetary interpretation of the increase in prices in mid-Tudor England starts with the assumption that the basis of the exchange value of English money (that is, what it would purchase in terms of goods and services) was intrinsic, in the sense that it depended upon the precious metal content of the coinage. It follows that, other things being equal, the successive 'debasements' (that is, reductions in the proportion of precious metal content in each coin) should drive up prices of goods in terms of 'money of account' (the units in which prices are normally expressed). The era of the 'great debasement' started with that of 1542, although this coinage was not actually issued until 1544. As to the reality of this debasement there is no dispute. It continued sporadically until 1551. Dr C. E. Challis has computed that by July of that year 'the circulation medium had risen to approximately £2·5 million ... or about twice the size it may have been before the Great Debasement began, and in so doing came to consist almost entirely of silver'; meanwhile, the Crown had made a net profit of some £1,285,000 as a result of its control and timing of operations at the mint.[15]

That the making of this profit, in order to meet the military expenditure of the Crown, was the deliberate motive of debasement was made clear in a proclamation of 1551 which frankly recalled how 'the late King ... considering at the beginning of his last wars that great and notable sums of money were requisite ... for the maintenance of the same, did therefore devise to abase and diminish the goodness of the coin. . .'. Dr Challis cites a contemporary calculation of expenditure on the campaigns of 1544 to 1550 at about £3·5 million. Since the net yield of all taxation between 1544 and 1551 was only £976,000, while revenue from rent and sale of Crown lands brought in £1,048,255 between 1544 and 1554, it is clear that a huge gap beween royal income and military expenditure remained. This gap was effectively bridged by the profits on debasement of coinage. The process reached its climax – or perhaps its nadir – in the spring of 1551: coins were to be issued of only three ounce fineness, with the royal mint making a profit of 11s. 8d. on every pound of money.

The collapse of confidence which ensued was checked only by the cessation of this coinage and by a formal devaluation of the value of the money – the shilling to 9d. in July and to 6d. in August of that year.[16]

Yet the confidence of so many mid-Tudor writers in identifying debasement as the prime cause of inflation is not shared by many modern historians. It has been pointed out that prices were rising before the great debasement of the 1540s, and that their increase was uneven and did not closely synchronise with the depreciation in the intrinsic value of the coinage. Thus between 1544 and 1551 the extent of the increase in prices varied from about twenty-five per cent for timber to about a hundred per cent for wheat. Above all the qualification 'other things being equal' simply did not apply. The past two decades have therefore seen a very much greater emphasis upon suggested real causes of price inflation, with pride of place assigned to expansion of population. Briefly it is contended that an expanding population would produce an increased demand (although, it must be observed, not necessarily an effective demand, in the economic sense) for goods. Any increase in the level of prices and price variations as between types of commodity would then depend upon the productivity and elasticity (of supply in response to demand) of the agricultural and industrial sectors of the economy. From the failure of agricultural expansion, whether measured by area or in productivity, to keep pace with that of population there followed land hunger, higher grain prices, surplus labour, lower real wages, and migration from the countryside to the town. Meanwhile the greater elasticity of supply in much of the industrial sector was matched by that of the demand for its products: hence the disparity in prices between agricultural and certain industrial commodities. The argument is convincingly, perhaps misleadingly, neat. Dr R. B. Outhwaite has observed that 'we know precious little about the population of the sixteenth century' and pointed to the danger of substituting population pressure for Spanish treasure (at one time a favourite explanation of price movements in much of Europe in the mid- and late sixteenth century) as an 'omnibus' explanation of a complex process, and of attributing price inflation to the pressures of an expanding population while establishing the latter by the evidence of rising prices.[17]

Another real influence of undoubted if variable impact was the quality of the harvest. Professor W. G. Hoskins has urged that this demands far more emphasis in an economy which was still overwhelmingly rural, with a considerable proportion of subsistence farmers, and in which 'the working-class spent fully 80 to 90 per cent of their incomes upon food and drink'. As far as the mid-Tudor decades are concerned the pattern he depicts is of crucial relevance. Whereas the last decade of the reign of Henry VIII included a number of good harvests which was well above the average, the picture for the next fifteen years is very different. After two good harvests at the start of Edward's reign there followed three bad ones in succession between 1549 and 1551; 'thus half the harvests of this reign left the mass of people short of basic food and drink'. The very fact that they were consecutive aggravated their effects, for desperate hunger sometimes led to partial consumption of the next year's seed-corn, thus tending to perpetuate the sequence until a good summer doubled the yield. 'These three bad harvests in a row were of infinitely greater moment for the mass of English people than the commercial crisis of 1551–2.' What have been well described as 'the dreadful fifties' culminated in the two wretched harvests of 1555 and 1556 and the subsequent famine. This was the background to Ponet's description of 'the people driven of hunger to grind acorns for bread meal, and to drink water in stead of ale', and to the decision of certain towns to establish a permanent grain stock. The harvest of 1558 was abundant, in line with the curious fact that each of the Tudor monarchs came to the throne in a year of good harvest. Indeed even the weather seemed to turn in Elizabeth's favour: there was only one bad harvest between 1563 and 1572. It seems clear that neglect of this important influence can lead the unwary into error; Professor J. D. Gould remarks that 'the harvest failures of 1555 and 1556 would mislead those who place their trust in index numbers into looking for evidence of monetary instability in the middle of Mary's reign'.[18]

Professor F. J. Fisher has investigated another real influence upon both population and prices, the virulent influenza epidemic which raged immediately after 1556. The highly coloured contemporary accounts of its severity are substantiated by a study of wills which suggests 'that for a quinquennium, death rates averaged about 150 per cent above the norm'. Although a possible calculation of a fall of some twenty per cent in England's population would be rather too high, it seems very probable that the impact was sufficient to administer a brief check to the course of demographic advance and the upward surge of prices, and to give a temporary buoyancy to wage rates. In conclusion, prudence suggests a provisional synthesis of the monetary and the real explanations of the 'price revolution' in mid-Tudor England, for the two are not mutually exclusive. As far as the mid-century is concerned, while long-term demographic developments may well have caused the ground-swell of increasing prices, it seems hazardous to dismiss the coincidence of the wave-crests of the 1540s and 1550s with the great debasement and with the immense upsurge in governmental expenditure, especially upon warfare, which accompanied and indeed induced it.[19]

The cumulative nature of the effects of inflation was often clearly grasped by contemporaries, especially the fact that 'all those that live by buying and selling' could escape or exploit its impact while recipients of fixed incomes could not. Heywood developed this point in verse that has a curiously modern echo:

> .... Of all ware sellers each shifteth from harms
> By raising his ware, as other wares appear.
> But all that on their pension (or pence) live mere
> ... Without land to let or ware to sell,
> Wherever they dwell may think they dwell in hell.

The connection between debasement, internal price movements and exchange rates with foreign currency was also realised; although its nature was not always accurately diagnosed, the results in terms of artificially boosted woollens exports, dearer prices of foreign imports and drain of bullion abroad were fully appreciated. The perceptive analysis of William Cholmeley, a 'grocer and one that selleth spices', attributed the disastrously adverse real terms of trade not only to 'the basing of our coin' but also to the wiles of the merchants of Antwerp and to 'the exalting of merchandise of foreign countries' (which, in perhaps the earliest English reference to general European inflation, he assessed as 'in every hundred 200 and 300'!).[20]

Yet, serious as it was, the crisis in foreign exchanges and trade of the early 1550s (the background against which Cholmeley wrote) was not regarded as the most dangerous of the effects of the mid-century inflation. High rents and high food prices, with all their potential social distress and fears, attracted comment of a less analytical and more vehement type. Tudor critics of inflation usually concentrated upon a 'monetary' explanation, and were agreed that 'the naughtiness of the silver was the occasion of dearth of all things in the realm'; but those who introduced 'real' or 'physical' factors did so in the context of a moral homily upon covetousness, directed at the rack-renter, the speculator in land, or the exploiting middleman in food supplies. The belief that it was the duty of government to check such activities lay at the heart of the impassioned plea addressed to Secretary Cecil by Bishop Hooper in 1551: 'For the love and tender mercy of God, persuade and cause some order to be taken upon the price of things, or else the ire of God will shortly punish. All things be here so dear, that the most part of people lacketh, and yet more will lack necessary food. . . . Master Secretary, for the passion of Christ take the fear of God and a bold stomach to speak herein for a redress. . . .'[21]

'The fear of God and a bold stomach' were perhaps more characteristic of Hooper than of Cecil; none the less the concern of those in authority with the alleged causes and the all too manifest impact of high prices was often evident. This concern was not devoid of humanitarian impulse, particularly when ministers had any sympathy with 'Commonwealth' ideals, but it was usually a response to the obvious threat to order and security by unrelieved poverty grown desperate. Unfortunately, as far as one possible major cause of price inflation in mid-century is concerned, the Crown itself was at fault in its irresponsible policy of debasement. Not surprisingly the 'official' explanation of high prices usually found it expedient to ignore this and to give wholehearted support to the popular diagnosis of the responsibility of greedy middlemen. Several dozen statutes of the realm and royal proclamations were specifically concerned to condemn and endeavour to control 'the devilish malice and slight . . . of naughty people injurious to the whole commonwealth . . . especially such as make their gain by buying and selling'. The 'great scarcity and unreasonable prices' particularly of victuals, but also of wool, wood and coal and other commodities, were formally attributed to defective functioning of the open market and to the devices of dealers in contriving shortages and acquiring semi-monopolistic positions. The legislation and proclamations alluded to make persistent but never really effective attempts to curb the freedom of middlemen and to regulate the sale and price of many commodities. Those issued between 1549 and 1551 in particular evince a recurrent dread of food riots. In October 1556 justices of the peace were instructed to exercise powers of search and of forcible marketing.[22]

The crisis in food prices in 1556 and 1557 was most emphatically the result of dreadful harvest failures. Indeed, after the final spate of grossly debased coins in the spring of 1551, cut short by the deflation of July and August, the gadarene progress of debasement was checked. The price level in general remained at the 'plateau' reached in 1551 for some twenty years thereafter. Profesor Gould points to continued stability in 'fineness' of the coinage at the level established in October 1551, and to 'a period of marked overall stability in exchange rates' for the reigns of Mary and the early years of Elizabeth I and concludes that 'the Edwardian and Marian settlement of the coinage thus represented a not too unsatisfactory compromise'. The persistent tendency to cite the 'spike years' of grain prices as evidence of monetary instability in the reign of Queen Mary arises from a confusion of monetary and real influences.[23]

The Elizabethan reform of the coinage carried through between September 1560 and September 1561 was therefore the stabilisation of a previously established though as yet uneasily poised equilibrium, rather than any new departure in policy. It was none the less important for this. Briefly all existing coins, whose degree of baseness varied with date of issue, were called in and replaced by a new coinage, issued at pre-1526 standards of purity. The fact that the Crown made a profit by the exercise was once cited as proof of its brilliant efficiency; but its success has recently been accounted 'a triumph not of cleverness but of ruthlessness and organisation', since in terms of relative hardship imposed it was 'the poor who . . . in effect bore the burden of the operation'. For what Elizabeth did was to call down the base coinage below its intrinsic value, securing from the discrepancy both the expenses of re-minting and a profit for the Crown. A proclamation of June 1561 boasted that the Queen had 'now as it were achieved to the victory and conquest of this hideous monster of the base moneys'. But it was followed in November by another which suggests that the conquest may have meant some hardship to the poor, in conceding that 'there is risen great annoyance amongst the poorer sort of her subjects for lack of small moneys of fine silver'. The restoration of prior standards of silver content in the coinage failed to produce any fall in prices. Whether this should be attributed to a steadily diminishing exchange value of precious metal itself as a result of the increasing influx from the New World is now an open question. However, the twentieth century is no stranger to the phenomenon that processes which allegedly produce an automatic increase in prices seldom function in reverse. For all that, in contrast with the demoralising impact of the course of events in the 1540s and early 1550s the re-coinage was of considerable import in terms of public confidence. It marked the end of what is still regarded, by at least some modern historians, as a major source of the socio-economic crisis of mid-Tudor England.[24]

Few would question the real significance of population growth in this same context. Attempts at quantifying the trend move dangerously near that sector of statistics which has been neatly defined as 'guesstimates', while the title of one well-known and deservedly influential investigation in this field, 'Wage-rates and Prices: Evidence for Population Pressure in the Sixteenth Century', is uneasily reminiscent of the warning on pages 128–9. Yet there is some measure of agreement that a recovery in size of population began towards the end of the fifteenth century. One recent estimate suggests that this renewed growth remained slow until well into the next century, with a figure of 2·3 million for 1522–5, then a sharper rise to 2·8 million for 1545. This upsurge was almost certainly checked by the influenza epidemic after 1556, yet the upward trend was resumed and a total of 3·7 million was reached by 1603. Moreover an increasingly large proportion of this population was town dwelling. The expansion of London, whose inhabitants rose in number from about 60,000 to about 225,000 during the sixteenth century, was admittedly exceptional; yet in itself this was sufficient to sharpen problems of supply and marketing in the most sensitive sector of all, that of foodstuffs. Prices in London rose more rapidly than those elsewhere, the disparity increasing during the 1540s and 1550s, and the fact that the real shortages thus reflected would fall most sharply upon the poorer inhabitants posed problems of public security as well as of public conscience.[25]

Overall this population pressure must have had the most serious effects. To reiterate, a growing population might increase the need for goods but, unless matched by expansion of productive employment, would raise neither output on the one hand nor effective demand on the other. Its impact must therefore be seen in the context of the low level of both productivity and elasticity of the dominant agricultural sector of the economy. It seems to be generally agreed that 'Tudor farming technique was inadequate to raise productivity very much, though enclosure of the open fields made possible some increase in efficiency.' Yet we have noted that, even where practised, rationalisation of agriculture brought its own problems. A larger population meant therefore, for far too many of its numbers, not wider opportunities but higher food prices, a greater incidence of unemployment and possible displacement, and pressure on real wages and living standards. Whatever our interpretation of the relationship between the increase in population and inflated prices, their joint effect is clear. The opinion of older historians such as J. E. T. Rogers and Sir John Clapham that the first half of the sixteenth century more than wiped out the gains in living standards which had been made during the fifteenth (the 'golden age of the English labourer') is confirmed by the evidence of modern statistical research. This suggests that what happened was 'catastrophic . . . there is nothing like it anywhere else in wage-history'. The 1540s and 1550s in particular inflicted 'a traumatic experience' upon the wage-earner. The adjective finds justification in the recent view that the urban labourer may well have suffered a fall in real wages of up to fifty per cent. The conclusion that 'the proportion of meat to bread (in a representative basket of "consumables") must have fallen' confirms contemporary opinion.[26]

Mid-Tudor literature is filled with expressions of the fear that the Englishman's traditionally high standard of living was under attack, in particular that he might be reduced to the wretched diet attributed to the unfortunate foreigner. Some recent comment suggests an element of exaggeration here, and suggests indeed that the sixteenth century witnessed an increase not so much in poverty itself as in public sensitivity on this issue. Yet to most historians the evidence indicates a considerable increase in poverty itself in real terms. Certainly contemporaries were in no doubt about this, and their fears as to the problems which it posed for society were shared by government. To those contributory causes which we have already encountered – such long-term trends as the expansion in population and the price inflation, agricultural and industrial dislocation and unemployment – we must add a very probable deterioration in the traditional sources of charitable relief. Acceleration of change in both the agricultural and industrial sectors of the economy increased the incidence of a type of poverty which was particularly dangerous to law and order in that it was clearly quite outside the medieval tradition of attribution of poverty to natural catastrophe or to 'the will of God'. Moreover these causes of poverty brought its real incidence to a peak at the very time when the former methods of relief – inadequate as they were – broke down. Although the time is long past when the monastic institutions were depicted as having provided something like a nation-wide system for relief of sickness and destitution, it remains true that (particularly in regional instances) the effect of their dissolution cannot entirely be discounted. The significance in this context of Professor W. K. Jordan's conclusion that the amount of private charitable benefactions reached its nadir during the fourth and fifth decades of the century is actually deepened by his refusal to allow for the declining value of money.[27]

Now much of this increased poverty had a particularly dangerous characteristic: that of rootlessness. Here is the element of truth in the description of Tudor England as going in 'terror of the tramp'. There is no doubt that increasing mobility of labour dated from the fourteenth century, but it was almost certainly intensified by the demographic and economic trends of the sixteenth. From about 1520 onwards we meet with more and more allusions to the problem of the wandering beggar or vagabond as a menace to society. It has been urged that their numbers were grossly exaggerated and that the contention that these included a substantial proportion of people of good stock driven by desperation to journey in search of work remains unproven. Yet government, as well as moralising pamphleteers and divines, were in no doubt as to the existence of a very real problem. Admittedly the principal object of dread was the 'sturdy' beggar, the hardened, defiant, professional vagrant, condemned as flying in the face of the inherited medieval concept of the beggar as 'called' by God to genuine adversity as a test of the charity of his fellow-Christians. The professional beggar was thought to resort to feigned illness or deformity in order to gull potential alms-givers, and to be guilty of theft, intimidation and outright violence if all else failed. Against such every respectable – or resolute – man's heart and hand were turned. Yet Becon's expression of regret that society, 'seeing the number of beggars increasing daily more and more, do not only not provide any means to exile and banish this absurdity out of the commonweal, but also suffer them to live comfortless, yea, and many to die' clearly concedes the existence within their ranks of the genuinely needy, and raises wider problems.[28]

Public opinion as a whole and government in particular

were forced to reassess traditional assumptions as to the causes, types and methods of relief of poverty. Poverty did not cease to be related to a context of religious beliefs regarding the ways of providence and the obligations of Christian charity, but was increasingly related to another pattern of ideas about the functioning of the economic and social aspects of society. The emphasis shifted from the concept of poverty as essentially a religious and charitable problem which confronted the individual, to an attempt at analysing the functional causes of poverty within the economic organisation of society and the means of relief as part of the social duties of governance. In an age which conceived of such duties very largely in religio-social terms the transition implied no sudden break with traditional ideas, but was none the less significant for the future. There is much evidence that in this transition the mid-Tudor decades marked the water-shed.

Meanwhile from the standpoint of government itself the problem of unrelieved poverty grown desperate had more immediacy in the context of public order than in the humanitarian appeals of moralists and of 'Commonwealth' idealists. It is possible to trace through the poor law legislation the gradual emergence of a more discriminating approach both in analysis of the causes and in prescriptions for the relief of poverty, as well as that of a more methodical organisation of the means of such relief. Yet the note of repression, although its stridency might vary, was ever present. This had been very clear in the important statute of 1536 (27 Hen. VIII, c. 24). This retained the traditional appeal to the charitable to donate alms for the poor, and made the parish the unit responsible for collecting such alms and for relieving the needy. But charity was not to be indiscriminate: work was to be found for those unemployed who were fit, and vagrants in particular were to be forced to work and punished for idleness – a provision extended to orphan and vagrant children of between five and fourteen years of age.

During the following decades the increasingly humanitarian schemes of idealists and progressive experiments in poor relief by certain local authorities did not go entirely unreflected in certain aspects of parliamentary measures. But the recurrent fear of a threat to law and order found expression in harsh, at times almost savage, phraseology and enactment. A proclamation of 1545 ordered 'ruffians, vagabonds, masterless men, common players, and evil-disposed persons' to the galleys. This was followed two years later by what was undoubtedly the most savage of all Tudor poor laws. This statute (1 Edw. VI, c. 3) continued the Sunday collections for the impotent poor, and extended enforced apprenticeship for the needy young up to twenty-four years of age. But its most controversial clauses decreed that sturdy vagrants should be branded with the letters V and S, and subjected to enforced labour, and ultimately slavery, for repeated offences. The appearance of such a measure under the would-be liberal and paternalistic regime of Somerset has evoked some comment. Professor Elton suggests that it reflected the temper of the House of Commons itself. Dr C. S. L. Davies attributes it to the influence of the 'Commonwealth party', 'of men inclined to reason *a priori*'; yet the impractical extremity of certain of its clauses and the uncharacteristic lack of balance between repression and relief seem to reflect a note of panic rather than of reason. As possible explanations of such panic at this time Dr Davies himself suggests the increased incidence of enclosures or the return from Boulogne of a force of some 48,000 men. At all events, the failure to include machinery for the enforcement of its provisions, and the impracticable ferocity of those provisions themselves, made the act a virtual dead letter. Indeed a statute of 1549 (3 & 4 Edw. VI, c. 16) alluding to previous legislation stated quite clearly that 'the extremity of some whereof have been the occasion that they have not been put in use', and repealed the act so obviously indicated.[29]

A statute passed two years later (5 & 6 Edw. VI, c. 2) redressed the balance. Mayors, clergy and householders were to appoint collectors of alms in church; reluctant givers were to be admonished, if need be by the bishop. The collectors were to distribute alms and compile a book of their needy recipients. An Act of 1555 (2 & 3 P. & M., c. 5) broadly repeated these provisions: weekly collection and distribution of alms within the parish, establishment of a register of impotent needy, provision of employment for the fit, but still conceded that it might be necessary for justices of

Economic and Social Problems

the peace to license some to wear badges and beg, if destitution outstripped the sources of organised relief. These statutes, which attest the repeated concern of government with the problem of poverty and its relief during the middle decades of the century, evolved all the basic principles of the later Elizabethan Poor Law. Together with the issue of repeated proclamations (often, understandably, alluding to the threat of the large number of vagabonds in London itself) they suggest that a crisis of apprehension was reached in the late 1540s and 1550s. Thereafter it seems to have eased although, of course, the Statute of Artificers of 1563 contained many clauses directed to control of labour mobility and prevention of idleness.

The literature, statutes and proclamations and even sermons devoted to poverty and its relief yield abundant evidence of another and more sinister aspect of the problem. Discussion takes on a sharper edge from the belief on one side that its misfortunes were the result of conscienceless exploitation, and on the other that importunate demands for relief but barely disguised a wish to assault the fundamental assumptions of the social order. Thus distress was exacerbated by a rankling hatred of alleged injustice, while repressive instincts were made harsher by fears for the security of the whole hierarchical concept of society and of the rights of property in particular. It is indeed possible to distinguish a crisis of society (in the sense of crucial tensions in social relationships) as well as of the economy in mid-Tudor England.

Before considering contemporary opinion as to the nature of this crisis something should be said about social and occupational groupings and the questions of social mobility. While limitations of knowledge, as well as regional variations, preclude precise estimates, the numerical dominance of those engaged primarily in agriculture is undoubted. Of these an increasing proportion was becoming virtually landless, many of their number engaging in supplementary industrial 'by-employment'. A very detailed recent study of the West Riding of Yorkshire between 1530 and 1546 (which suggests seven occupational/social classifications: nobility and gentry; clergy; professional men; peasantry; craftsmen and manufacturers; merchants and traders; and servants) concludes that of an estimated 20,000 households (or 100,000 people) 'as many as 5,000 households . . . would fall into this category of poorer people . . . probably cottage labourers with little or no land of their own'. This confirms Dr Alan Everitt's suggestion that 'the labouring population probably formed about one-quarter or one-third of the entire population of the countryside' and that its size 'almost certainly expanded, both absolutely and relatively'. Hence the significance of calculations that, in percentage terms, the index of the purchasing power of the wage of an agricultural labourer fell from 80 during the decade 1530–9 to 71 in 1540–9, and to 59 in 1550–9, before rising to 66 for 1560–9 and to 69 for the following decade. Such was the unhappy position of the base of the social pyramid in the mid-Tudor countryside.[30]

In considering the urban situation it is important to remember that, at the outset of our period, only one provincial town had more than 10,000 inhabitants, and little more than a dozen topped 5,000. Professor Hoskins, writing of the 1520s, has pointed first to the dominance, in occupational analysis, of 'three fundamental groups of trades' (wholesale and retail clothing; food and drink; and building) which occupied 'some 35 to 40 per cent of the population'; secondly, to the gross inequality in distribution of wealth – in Coventry two per cent of the taxable population owned forty-five per cent of the taxable wealth, and seven per cent just under two-thirds; and thirdly to the fact that 'fully two-thirds of the urban population . . . lived below or very near the poverty-line, constituting an ever-present menace to the community in years of high food-prices or bad trade'. Dr J. F. Pound's study of Norwich confirms this picture: while at the upper levels of the urban pyramid 'the distributive trades were the wealthiest by far . . . the 570 Norwich wage-earners (just over forty per cent of the taxpayers) owned less than four per cent of the city's wealth'. It has indeed been suggested that as the problem of poverty became more and more acute 'for the later Tudors, as the price-revolution took its course from the 1540s onward, it was above all an urban problem', but also that although 'the social contrast between rich and poor was probably greatest in the towns, ... it would be offset by the greater social mobility there'.[31]

Professor Stone has pointed out that since ninety to ninety-five per cent of the population were below the rank of gentry 'a great deal of horizontal, and even some vertical, mobility within the vast mass of the population goes unrecognised. In such a society one cannot expect there to be very much upward mobility at the lower levels.' Now the fact that in 'the century of mobility' which commenced circa 1540 and which witnessed strongly disruptive forces at work within society there occurred 'a remarkable increase in the number of the upper classes' was all too likely to have exacerbated social tensions at a time when living standards at the very base of the social order were declining. Yet, while in countryside and town alike (and despite the general acceptance of the principle of social hierarchy) increasing resentment of such contrasts and of the incidence of desperate poverty was an acknowledged well-spring of disorder, the aspect of social mobility which engaged most attention among contemporaries concerned the fortunes of those at the upper levels of the social pyramid.[32]

In this they have been followed by modern historians. What has been termed the 'storm over the gentry' has debated the impact of such undoubted realities as increased mobility of land and inflation of prices upon the rise or fall of the gentry and the aristocracy (however defined), during the century preceding 1640. The circumstances and effects of Crown sales of so much former church land have recently been re-assessed. Dr Joyce Youings' study of the dissolution of the monasteries, considering 'its place in historical studies primarily as a revolution in landownership, second only to that which followed the Norman Conquest', confirms the accepted picture of disposal by the Crown throughout the 1540s so that by 1547 well over half the former monastic land had been lost. Further grants or sales under Edward VI and Mary raised the proportion to over three-quarters by 1558. Although the occurrence of some speculative purchase for resale at a profit is generally agreed, Professor Habbakuk's conclusion 'that the land was generally sold at the normal market price', that is twenty years' purchase, still holds, and there is little evidence of 'a "fever of speculation" in monastic property'. As to the social implications of this increasingly fluid land market, Professor Woodward suggests that 'on balance the effect of the great transfer of property was not revolutionary' – except at the expense of the Church. As Dr Smith observes, 'that the nobility or gentry between them controlled a very much greater proportion of the land of England in 1640 than in either 1535 or 1540 has never been doubted; the only question at issue ... was the relative proportions held by the nobility and the gentry as separate categories of landlord. This controversy ... relates to developments after 1558.' Space permits no more than this brief allusion to this debate, which has been much more fruitful in terms of scholarship and insight than in those of definitive and generally agreed conclusions.[33]

Certainly Tudor commentators harboured suspicions about land 'purchased by certain dark augmentation practices' by upstarts who 'have chiefly flourished since the putting down of Abbeys'. For although there were some who were prepared to modify the rigidity of the hierarchical concept of society, the continued general acceptance of its principles was clearly evident in the frequent expressions of concern that those principles were in very real danger. At their very heart lay the Tudor belief that 'Almighty God hath created and appointed all things, in heaven, earth, and waters, in a most excellent and perfect order', so that, in human society, 'every degree of people, in their vocation, calling, and office, hath appointed to them their duty and order'. While the analogy through which this ideal was expressed ranged from that of the human body itself or of the pieces on a chess-board, to that of Shakespeare's well-tuned harp, the lip-service it received was well-nigh universal. The favourite 'hate-figure' was that of the 'upstart' – 'Sir Mathew Muckforth.' Thus Somerset's supporters in the crisis of 1549 seized eagerly on the charge that his enemies in the Council were of base birth: 'come up but late from the dunghill; a sort of them more meet to keep swine than to occupy the offices which they do occupy'.[34]

Through much of contemporary discussion there ran two major and potentially contradictory themes: first, condemnation of those who 'ran out of' their degree or calling, whether it be the upstart who rose too high or the 'gentle-born' whose conduct fell short of the standards of true gentility; second, and far more fundamental, qualification or more rarely condemnation of the ideal itself. The first found expression not only in criticism of individuals but also in a number of statutes which attempted for several reasons to restrict 'excess in apparel'; a statute of 1554 (1 & 2 P. & M., c. 2) was especially concerned with excess in apparel of 'the meaner sort'. Such excess might almost be defined as a sartorial expression of social insubordination. Equally reprehensible, in the eyes of the traditionalist, were those of gentle birth whose conduct reflected the motivations of the market place rather than the idealised ethos of social obligation. Nobility and gentry who so far forgot their vocations as to become graziers, sheepmasters and clothiers, or who were 'not ashamed to sell oxen, sheep, beer, corn, meal, malt, coals and things much viler than these be', forgetting their moral obligations towards their inferiors by enclosing commons or arable land, ejecting husbandmen and racking rents – these felt the lash of the preacher as 'caterpillars of the commonweal' and as bringing the very name of gentleman into disrepute.[35]

Meanwhile the ideal of rigid social stratification was itself the subject of discussion. Some commentators were content to acknowledge and approve of the existence of a category defined by one writer as 'Ungentle Gentle', that is, 'he which is born of a low degree, of a poor stock' but who 'by his virtue, wit, policy, industry, knowledge in laws, valiancy in arms' rises to wealth and power, establishing his line as gentry. It seems obvious that the distinction between 'those which climb to honour by worthiness' and 'the right upstarts' was probably highly subjective, yet recognition of the reality, and in part of the case for, some measure of social mobility was fairly common. Archbishop Cranmer, in the context of a discussion of education, observed that sometimes 'Almighty God raiseth up from the dunghill and setteth ... in high authority', while the propagandist Morison answered the complaints of the 'Pilgrims of Grace' about low-born Councillors by attributing to Henry VIII the wish for 'all his subjects to contend, who may obtain most qualities, most wit, most virtue: and this only to be the way to promotion, and here nobility to consist'. It is difficult to decide upon the sincerity with which this prospect of 'careers open to talent' was advanced. But Morison's insistence that the fruits of such merited self-advancement would be safe only as long as respect for the law was maintained points to an area of common ground with the arguments of the traditionalist. For the real threat to the social order was seen to come not from the prevalence of self-seeking upstarts, nor from the failure of the gentry to fulfil their social obligations, nor even from the speculations of humanists such as Morison or Cheke, who conceded that 'many mean men's children do come honestly up'; it came at a much more fundamental and egalitarian level, and was itself in a tradition which stretched back to Langland's *Piers Plowman* and the Peasants' Revolt of 1381.[36]

For criticism of the upstart, of the gentleman who had forgotten the social commitments of his station, and of the whole hierarchical concept itself found their own common ground in a reiteration of the age-old question:

> ... When Adam dolve and Eve span,
> Who was, in those golden days, a gentleman?

The spokesman for the rebellious flies in Heywood's allegory, who asserted that 'yeomen Flies' might rule as well as 'Spiders gentlemen' was but reflecting the fear expressed in a letter of Protector Somerset that 'a number would rule another while, and direct things as gentlemen have done; and indeed all have conceived a wonderful hate against gentlemen, and taketh them all as their enemies'. There is little doubt that this feeling, which – despite some historians' dislike of the term – it is difficult to define except by the phrase 'class hatred', reached its highest pitch against the background of the distress and uncertainties of the 1540s and 1550s. Cranmer's sermon in 1549 on 'Time of Rebellion' warned that this unreasoning hatred of gentlemen would ruin the kingdom. Well might the Archbishop describe it as unreasoning or Cheke put the question to the 'rabble of Norfolk rebels': 'Why should ye thus hate them?' For the pressures that drove men to rebellion, though they engendered unreasoning passion, were real enough. Those pressures were seldom more cogently expressed than by the early 'Puritan' Crowley, in a pamphlet published in 1551, in which he voiced the poor's infuriated rejection of a future in which 'we must be their slaves and labour till our hearts burst, and then they must have all. . . . No remedy therefore, we must needs fight it out, or else be brought to the like slavery that the French men are in!'[37]

Traditionally criticism of the social order was usually suspected of association with attacks upon established religious teachings: quite simply sedition and doctrinal dissent were thought of as twin aspects of the same basic and damnable heresy. The Lollards had been accused of preaching the abolition of private property and that all possessions should be held in common, and the same charge was now levelled at the more radical Protestants. Many of their utterances were, in fact, but restatements of the traditional Christian precepts of stewardship and charity in disposal of the goods of this world. But they were proscribed by more conservative religious authority as heretical because the bluntness of their expression against a background of social and economic discontent almost invited misinterpretation. The assertion that 'he that is rich, and liveth of his rents, may not use nor spend his goods as he will, but thy goods belong as well unto the poor as to thee', falls all too clearly into this category. For it was feared that, behind the mask of an appeal to Christian charity, there lurked the dreadful holocaust that had been pictured by Sir Thomas More: 'For they shall gather together at last, and assemble themselves in plumps and in great routs, and from asking fall to the taking of their alms themselves, and under pretext of reformation ... shall assay to make new division of every man's land and substance, never ceasing if ye suffer them, till they make all beggars as they be themself, and at last bring all the realm to ruin, and this not without butchery and foul bloody hands.'[38]

There was nothing new about this fear, but it was sharpened by the persistent rumour and occasional reality of social revolt in mid-Tudor England as well as by the recollection of events elsewhere – in particular the Peasants'

Revolt of 1524–5 in Germany, repression of which had cost perhaps a hundred thousand lives, or the tragedy of the Anabaptist seizure and misgovernment of Münster a decade later. The equation of Anabaptism as a whole with the nightmare excesses of Münster was quite unfair; the movement was far more often peaceful than violently apocalyptic, and the community of goods which it sometimes preached applied only to the voluntary 'brethren'. Yet the fact that this was sometimes preached was quite enough. A very recent monograph has 'found no evidence of seditious anabaptism' in England; but as Bullinger explained, 'God opened the eyes of governments by the revolution at Münster, and no one thereafter would trust Anabaptists who claimed to be innocent.' When Frederick the Great and Napoleon Bonaparte identified religious stability as an essential social cement they were but echoing a mid-sixteenth-century commonplace. Starkey feared that religious turmoil would result in 'the ruin of all civil order, and of all good worldly policy, whereof good and true religion is the most stable and sure foundation'. Paget, in his diagnosis of the troubles of 1549, urged that 'society in a realm doth consist and is maintained by means of religion and law', and traced the evils which ensued when 'the use of the old religion is forbidden by a law, and the use of the new is not yet printed in the stomachs of the eleven of twelve parts in the realm'. The significance of the conjunction of economic crisis, social discontent and religious ferment was certainly not lost upon contemporary analysis of the crisis of mid-Tudor society. The dread that, together with a suspected faltering of executive power itself, this might lead to full-scale rebellion not only against governance but against the existing social order explains why for several years after 1549 authority was hypersensitive to any suggestion of the imminence of a peasant jacquerie. It is against this background that we must set Paget's warning to Somerset that 'your pardons have given evil men a boldness to enterprise as they [have done], and cause them to think you dare not meddle with them', and the sharp rebuke of Russell and Herbert (during the crisis of the fall of the Protector) that 'your grace's proclamations and billets put abroad for the rising of the Commons we mislike very much'.[39]

Finally it is hardly surprising that, at this time of acute anxiety lest a culmination of discontents should lead to attacks upon the whole political and social order, the scope of the social and economic responsibilities of government itself should have become an urgent topic of discussion. The crisis of society produced a ferment of debate as to the very nature of that society and the duties of its governance. This was most fully reflected in the writings – and sometimes the careers – of a number of thinkers who are often referred to as the 'Commonwealth men'. At no time were they in any sense a 'party', and it is perhaps more accurate and meaningful to refer to a 'Commonwealth' ideal – an ideal with medieval roots, in its general form the object of almost ubiquitous lip-service, yet also the subject of various and stimulating interpretation. Its religious basis and acceptance of the existing social and political order were almost constant; the variants concerned the extent and the depth of the social obligations of government, and the rationale, methods and objectives of its intervention in the economic process. Within the writings of the 'Commonwealth' tradition there existed an uneasy and unresolved tension. The traditionalists appealed to government as a residuary legatee of the teachings of the Catholic Church on economic and social relationships; these were essentially normative in a moral sense, with stewardship, charity and equity in the use and distribution of this world's goods as primary objectives. Others propounded a forward-looking and utilitarian concept of government as responsible for the creation of a framework within which the individual's urge to extract the maximum selfish benefit from his activities could be harnessed and directed towards the optimum aggregate output for society as a whole.

Any attempt at exploring the suggestions of these men in regard to the policies to be adopted in dealing with the agrarian, industrial and commercial trends of the age would be outside the scope of this book. Many of their projects – for some of which the description as a mid-Tudor equivalent of the ideal of the Welfare State is but little exaggeration – were well in advance of what was considered practicable or desirable by their contemporaries. Moreover the disgrace and fall of Somerset, undoubtedly their most whole-hearted political patron, marked the shattering of the hopes of the most committed idealists, while the riots and repression of 1549–51 were far removed from the social harmony for which they hoped. Yet the middle decade of the century, with its dangerous conjunction of so many constituents of economic and social crisis, also marked a turning-point. Thereafter the stability of the coinage was restored, at least some of the lessons of the cloth export débâcle were grasped, governmental 'paternalism' attempted to encourage output and employment while the means of poor relief became increasingly effective. Certainly not all problems were resolved, but the more frightening tensions seem to have eased. Meanwhile the continuity suggested in the career of Cecil is indicative also of some modification of ideals to conform with 'the art of the possible'. The more idealistic projects of the 'Commonwealth men' did not die; they lay fallow until stirred up once more by the crisis of society in the middle of the seventeenth century. Yet their comparative quiescence in succeeding decades bespeaks the diminished urgency of those problems which had made them the subject of such passionate debate in mid-sixteenth-century England.

6 Foreign Affairs: the 'British Problem'

In the sphere of foreign affairs the middle decades of the Tudor period were doubly critical: first, because the mistakes and weaknesses in policy made more precarious the position both of the dynasty and of the nation over which it ruled; and, secondly, in that – at least in retrospect – these decades signalled a reorientation of English foreign policy. In the context of the mid-Tudor crisis, England's relationships with the foreigner were inextricably linked with the fortunes and security of the dynasty and its succession, with the changes and tensions in religion and indeed with the Crown's financial straits; yet we must remember also that these years were of crucial importance in the context of the long-term evolution of English foreign policy as such.

Early Tudor foreign policy may be characterised as an adaptation of traditional patterns to suit immediate dynastic and commercial interests. The preservation – and to this end the procurement of foreign recognition – of his line, together with a keen eye for the interests of national trade and royal revenue, had been the prime objectives of the diplomacy of Henry VII. In pursuit of these, friendship with the emerging Burgundian/Habsburg/Spanish power complex became, and for long remained, the corner-stone of policy; dynastic recognition, trade with the Netherlands, residual medieval enmity with France – all operated in the same direction (despite such awkward cross-currents as the feud with Margaret of Burgundy). Avoidance of serious military involvement against France and the marriage alliance with Scotland bespeak a shrewd appreciation both of the dangers to Tudor England from the 'auld alliance' and of a possible method of resolving it. The reign of Henry VIII introduced new complications into this late medieval/early Tudor pattern: the zest for foreign adventure and military glory of the King himself, the occasional ministerial willingness to experiment and above all the diplomatic implications of the 'break with Rome'.

A word is necessary about the European situation within which these policies were pursued. We must remember England's weakness, in terms of population, in face of France on the one hand and of the Habsburg complex which had emerged by 1519 on the other. Professor Wernham has observed that 'lack of men and lack of money, and the growth of two great military powers in western Europe, thus forced the Tudors into policies more insular and more defensive than those of their Lancastrian and Plantagenet predecessors'. By the sixteenth century the enmity between Valois and Habsburg had replaced that between France and England as the chief axis about which western European diplomacy revolved. In the early decades northern Italy or the Netherlands were as often as not the cockpits in which this rivalry was fought out. But by the mid-century the position was to change: dynastic weakness, religious dissension, socio-economic crisis, and even a suspicion of a faltering in the stability and resolution of governance, made it all too possible that because of these internal difficulties the British Isles might become both the battle-ground and the prize.[1]

In an age when kingdoms were perhaps still thought of as the possessions of a royal house at least as much as they were considered the political expressions of nationality, the importance of English dynastic troubles is clear. Yet the roots of this aspect of the mid-Tudor crisis lay not only in the obvious dynastic weakness after 1547 but also in the events of the preceding decade or so. During the period following the fall of Wolsey the King himself had taken a much closer personal interest in external relations; Cromwell's control of foreign policy was never equal to that of his late patron. But from the early 1530s onward both the Crown and its minister found dynastic, strategic and commercial considerations in foreign policy complicated by another factor of immense importance – that of religion. For it has been aptly remarked that, after the breach with Rome, 'the Papacy would provide, as it were, an undying Margaret of Burgundy, a permanent and *ex officio* foreign director of any and every anti-Tudor faction'. The foreign policy of Wolsey (whatever one's interpretation of its motives) had done much to loosen the roots of the traditional Anglo-Habsburg entente which had flourished since the early years of Henry VII. The religious changes of the 1530s continued the process and awakened the fear of a Franco-Habsburg rapprochement based on a projected Roman Catholic crusade against England.[2]

The apparent security achieved in 1537, symbolised by the birth of Edward in October, which emboldened Henry to allow the talks with the German Lutherans to collapse, was soon shattered. The death of the Queen within less than a fortnight was a sharp reminder of the fatality which haunted the Tudor line. In the summer of 1538 a conjunction of events revived all Henry's fears: in June James V of Scotland married Mary of Guise (to whom Henry himself had briefly and unsuccessfully paid court); this earnest of a renewed commitment of Scotland to the French alliance coincided very closely in time with the conclusion, under papal mediation, of the Truce of Nice between Charles V and Francis I. In December the Pope published a bull denouncing and deposing Henry VIII and followed this with a formal appeal to the Habsburg, Valois and Stuart monarchs to unite in its military execution. The threat of a Franco-imperial crusade with papal blessing, or indeed of a triple attack, gained added credibility from the despatch of Reginald Pole to exhort the Spaniards and the French, and of Cardinal Beaton on a like errand to Scotland. Professor Scarisbrick describes England as 'seized with war-panic' in the early months of 1539; 'southeast England was in a frenzy of preparation', and the county levies, here and in the north, were mustered and armed. Wriothesley expressed the fear that, in face of a combined assault, England would be 'but a morsel amongst these choppers'.[3]

The two years 'of intense marriage-mongering' in which Henry engaged throughout 1538 and 1539 therefore reflect not only his marital and dynastic determination but also a near-desperate quest for allies amid the growing fear of English isolation. Apparently at least nine candidates were seriously considered. Although the story of the rejection of the English monarch's suit by one of them on the ground that she possessed but one head is apocryphal, that of Henry's proposal for something approximating to a 'beauty parade' for his inspection at Calais is true. It is the more ironic that the upshot was the futile and disastrous Cleves marriage alliance – futile in both marital and diplomatic terms, and disastrous for Thomas Cromwell. The negotiations which led to this sprang from the panic of early and mid-1539, a panic which led also to the wholesale spoliation of monastic property in order to pay for the frantic defence preparations and to the imprisonment and judicial murder inflicted upon relatives of Cardinal Pole. Diplomatic overtures towards the German Protestant League of Schmalkalden ended in mutual recrimination, deepened by the enactment of the Six Articles in June, but the proposal of a marriage alliance with the house of Cleves was pursued and the marriage treaty was concluded in October 1539. Henry's distaste for his bride, whom he none the less married on 6 January 1540, certainly weakened Cromwell's position. It is now thought very probable that the forces of factious conspiracy, exploiting the King's infatuation with Norfolk's niece, Catherine Howard, together with the ruinous charge of heresy, were the primary causes of the downfall of the minister in June, rather than the marital and diplomatic débâcle. It remains true, however, that by this time the evidence of a weakening of the always precarious agreement between France and the Emperor had removed much of the apparent diplomatic necessity for the union into which Henry felt he had been entrapped. The fall of Cromwell was followed by Convocation's annulment of the marriage with Anne of Cleves early in July, and by its replacement by a union with Catherine Howard within a month. Meanwhile at the Diet of Regensburg (July 1541) Charles V attempted to placate at least some of the German Lutherans. Hence the conclusion that 'it was clear enough that the old amity with Spain was England's again for the asking.... Everything was back to normal and England's years of peril were past.'[4]

In so far as this peril derived from any genuine fear of invasion, beneath the mantle of a papal crusade, by a Franco-imperial alliance this was true. Yet the actions of Henry in

Foreign Affairs: the 'British Problem'

what remained of his reign did much to exacerbate if not actually to create the potential dangers to England's international position which reached their climax at the mid-century. Interpretation of the motives and the calibre of these last years of Henrician foreign policy has varied. At least one authority believes, on the evidence of Henry's negotiations with the Emperor at Ratisbon (Regensburg) in 1541, that 'the wars of Henry's last years could be seen as the outcome of careful negotiations to avoid the isolation of 1539/40 rather than as capricious folly'. Few would deny the justice of Professor Elton's verdict that 'hostility to France and the hope of conquering Scotland still dominated his unoriginal mind'; but there is some difference of opinion as to the order of priority, if any, accorded these objectives. Professor Wernham suggests that the recent dangers had shown not only that enmity between Valois and Habsburg was almost a necessary condition of English security, but also 'that there might be times when the continental powers would be strongly tempted to intervene if the domestic situation within the British Isles offered them a good prospect of success'; it was therefore to this 'British problem' that Henry now turned his attention. Professor Scarisbrick 'is doubtful if Henry was ever either capable or guilty of such high statesmanship'. It is still debatable if Henry's Scottish policy should be viewed in conjunction with the assumption of the title 'King of Ireland' in 1541 as part of a conscious attempt at unification of the British Isles, or if it was simply a revival of the attack upon the 'auld alliance', with interest in Scotland essentially subordinate to his major preoccupation with an attack upon France. Perhaps Henry himself was not always over-clear about precise motivations. Certainly the two were not mutually exclusive – unless it be in terms of feasibility. What does seem clear, within our present context, is that, on each front, military victory was counteracted by diplomatic failure, and that a pattern of circumstances emerged in which for Henry's successors internal weakness and the threat of foreign intervention would be even more closely connected.[5]

As far as relations with Scotland are concerned emphasis is usually rightly placed upon the failure to make constructive use of the splendid opportunity presented by the death of James V. Yet that event could hardly have been foreseen, and was (if we accept the story that the Scottish monarch died broken-hearted after the news of the rout of Solway Moss) an indirect result of Henry's aggression. This in turn may partly be attributed to Henry's concern, in the light of his own still delicate succession problem, over the implications of James's claim by blood to the inheritance of the English throne. Indeed Professor G. Donaldson has pointed to the fact that 'from the marriage of Margaret Tudor to James IV in 1503 a union of the crowns was never a remote contingency, for through the whole century, except during the twenty years between the birth of Elizabeth and the death of Edward VI, there was never more than one life between the Scottish line and the English throne'. For some years Henry had despatched emissaries northwards with appropriately avuncular advice as to how the Scottish King might follow his example in mastering the Church and annexing its possessions. Once persuaded to the right side of the religious fence James would then presumably become an ally as he was already a kinsman. These efforts reached their climax in 1540 and 1541. In the summer of 1541 Henry himself for the first time in his reign went north to York in order to meet his nephew, who snubbed him by his failure to arrive. Perhaps the Scottish King also had his fears; his young sons had recently died, and the risk of kidnap may have crossed his mind. At all events the incident was followed by a rapid deterioration in the tone of diplomatic exchanges together with more frequent border incidents. Renewal of Franco-Habsburg conflict in the summer of 1542 was followed in the late autumn by increasingly warlike messages from Henry to his northern commanders. A specific instruction to devastate the borderland in fact arrived after Norfolk had already launched a six-day raid to do just that. A Scottish counter-attack in late November ended in the disaster of Solway Moss. Details of the conflict are not entirely clear, and estimates of the size of the Scottish army range from ten to twenty thousand; but the number of the English force was certainly smaller, perhaps as low as three thousand. In terms of losses only a skirmish (one source puts the number of dead at seven on the English and twenty on the Scottish side), in terms of impact it was a rout; it has indeed been described as 'the most disgraceful field that ever Scotland fought'. The English took hundreds of prisoners, including many leaders, and the ease of the victory appeared to the Scots a national humiliation, the shame of which allegedly killed their King.[6]

Historians are agreed that Henry VIII failed to exploit the opportunity now offered by the spectacle of a six-day-old girl on the Scottish throne, that he 'overplayed the magnificent hand which fate had dealt him' and 'handled a delicate situation with singular ineptitude'. There is some doubt as to the nature of his miscalculations and failures, and in particular as to the relationship between his subsequent Scottish policy and the renewal of war with France. The contention that 'he had never intended to do more than contain the Scots ... his major interest lay elsewhere', is difficult to reconcile with the clear view that 'his mind was set upon control of Scotland rather than on conquests in France'. For whatever reason, Henry now attempted to consolidate military with diplomatic success, thinking perhaps that the weight of advantage in regard to dynastic succession now lay in England's favour. In January 1543 his Scottish captives were 'brought unto the king and sworn to be true, and so was ransomed and sent home again', pledged to act, in effect, as agents of a design to bring the infant Mary to England for betrothal to Prince Edward. But Henry had failed to grasp the tangled complexity of the faction struggle for power within Scotland itself, the depth of Scottish resentment aroused by the proposal to hand over their Queen or the strength of remaining French influence (personified in the Queen Mother, Mary of Guise, and Cardinal Beaton). The attempt at achieving his objectives by diplomacy needed a lighter touch than that which drafted his 'Declaration' of 'the true and right title that the king's most royal Majesty hath to the sovereignty of Scotland'. The Scots refused to send Mary to England, and by the Treaty of Greenwich in July 1543 Henry accepted this rebuff and also dropped his demand that the Scots should renounce their French alliance. Diplomacy by bluster had failed.[7]

Meanwhile England's new treaty of alliance with the

Emperor, concluded in February, had been kept secret until the end of May. But by June Henry felt secure enough to follow up an impossible ultimatum with a declaration of war upon France. If this boldness was based upon a false assessment of the strength of the English position in Scotland, it was soon requited by the resurgence of the French faction in that country. Cardinal Beaton was joined by Arran (heir-presumptive to the Scottish throne should the infant Mary die, and Governor during her minority), and the so-called 'English lords' were forced to submit. In December the Scots Parliament repudiated the agreements with England and renewed the commitment to France. Significantly it also enacted anti-heresy legislation, for the policy of encouraging Protestantism in Scotland as a weapon of political subversion which Henry (no lover of popular Bible-reading) had adopted with some misgiving, had now 'boomeranged'.

Yet despite this shattering of his hopes for an easy subjugation of Scotland the English monarch made a new agreement with Charles V for a large-scale invasion of France in the following June. As a preliminary to this in the spring of 1544 he renewed his policy of direct assault in the north. A. F. Pollard once suggested that 'the campaign was an action for breach of promise, and not a conquest of Scotland'; rarely can a jilting have evoked such savage revenge and widespread misery. Henry's instructions to Hertford, his commander-in-chief, explicitly required a punitive expedition bent upon sack, slaughter and devastation. Hertford's reservations as to the diplomatic and indeed strategic wisdom of such action were brushed aside, and in May he faithfully executed his orders; Edinburgh was sacked and burned, and the English army left a trail of terror as it withdrew. At Dunbar it waited until the inhabitants were abed and then 'in their first sleeps closed in with fire; men, women and children were suffocated and burned'. Scotland was indeed knocked out of the war, but all previous hopes of getting control of that kingdom by diplomatic methods and a union of Crowns were ruined. The verdict that 'Henry VIII's Scottish policy combined right aims with wrong methods' still stands. Indeed it might well be argued that Protector Somerset's later efforts at achieving those aims were vitiated from the start by the actions which he had taken, albeit reluctantly, as Henry's commander.[8]

In mid-July Henry himself sailed for France, after a niggling correspondence with Charles about the allies' projected military tactics, and settled down with an army almost forty thousand strong to besiege Boulogne and Montreuil. He had acquired a number of modern guns but these, although more accurate, were not as hugely impressive as those of earlier times; the defenders of Boulogne were therefore confronted with the spectacle of monster dummy guns with smaller real ones affixed to their backs. In mid-September Boulogne capitulated; the English King inspected and fortified his trophy, won at a dreadful price in terms of men and money, and returned home. But on the very day that Henry had entered the town in triumph his imperial ally had made peace with France at Crépy. This humiliating snub exposed England to the full weight of French attention and the withdrawal of the main force was not free from a note of panic. Despite its impressive achievement in terms of prestige 'the English campaign of 1544 was a muddle even by the generous standards of the times'.[9]

Diplomatic relations with England's late ally deteriorated still further during the winter. Meanwhile persistent border raiding in the north led in late February 1545 to the first Scottish victory for many decades, admittedly in a small-scale engagement at Ancrum Moor. Thus encouraged, and with the Emperor standing aloof while Henry's frantic search for allies among the German Protestant Princes yielded no result, France prepared for a major attack. The siege of Boulogne was renewed, an expeditionary force stood ready for Scotland, and a large fleet made ready to assist a projected main invasion force of fifty thousand men. In short through 'circumstances of [Henry's] own making England now faced a threat greater than that of 1539, greater than any, perhaps, she had known for generations, or would know again until Philip II threatened her. She awaited invasion from three or four quarters by two powers whom she had drawn against herself and whose common cause she had herself largely re-fashioned.'[10]

In face of this threat England mustered all her resources;

one estimate puts the number of men, including militia, kept under arms during the summer of 1545 as high as a hundred and twenty thousand. One night in late July a chain of fires warned the nation that the enemy fleet had been sighted. The manœuvring that took place when the French vessels entered the Solent was marked by the dramatic loss of the *Mary Rose* when she heeled over too sharply with her lower gun-ports still open. But the French attempted only small-scale landings on the Isle of Wight although they also raided and burnt Brighton. Skirmishing continued until mid-August before the French fleet, now hard-hit by disease after a month out of port, sailed off into the Narrow Seas. By early September the immediate threat of invasion was over, and by the end of that month the siege of Boulogne had been slackened. Professor Wernham concludes that although 'there had been no great battle, no spectacular engagement, either by sea or by land...the strength and success of England's resistance, and the national unity behind it, were even more impressive to foreign powers than the preparations of 1538–41 had been'.[11]

None the less the assessment of several contemporary English statesmen of the position in which their country now found itself was anything but sanguine. Gardiner, writing to Paget from the imperial court in November 1545, described how 'we be in war with France and Scotland; we have an enmity with the Bishop of Rome; we have no friendship assured here.... And thus be things entangled. Thus we be in a labyrinth.' Indeed, both he and Norfolk were willing to concede Boulogne in order to meet the overtures of Francis I who professed willingness to abandon the Scots in order to end the war. Gardiner stated bluntly that 'the French King will never have peace without he have Boulogne' and followed this with the sententious but shrewd observation that 'if the King's Majesty [i.e. Henry VIII] thinketh Boulogne so necessary, it is a worldly thing, and then remember this conclusion, that worldly things require other worldly things for their maintenance'. His comment that 'our war is noisome to the wealth of our realm' evinces some grasp of the disastrous financial implications of any continuation of hostilities. This was more sharply expressed in the desperate appeal of

Foreign Affairs: the 'British Problem' 159

Wriothesley, again to Secretary Paget, describing himself as 'at my wits' end how we shall possibly shift for three months following'. Over two million pounds had been poured into the campaigns between 1542 and 1547. To pay for this even an unprecedentedly large burden of taxation (some £650,000) was quite inadequate; it was supplemented by the proceeds of forced loans and benevolences, the profits of a deliberate and conscienceless debasement of the coinage, and the receipts from sales of royal lands (including many of the recent monastic acquisitions) to the value of about £800,000 – the latter much to the detriment of the future financial security of the Crown.[12]

Fortunately the year 1546 saw no major campaigns. The Scots' position had been strengthened by the arrival of French aid, but the cause of the dissident Protestant faction was now advanced by the storming and occupation of St Andrews Castle, which involved the murder of Cardinal Beaton whose body was kept in salt by his assassins. A month later in June the Treaty of Ardres was negotiated with France: England was to hold Boulogne for the space of eight years, at the end of which France could recover it on payment of a large lump sum, while Henry VIII was to receive a French pension during his lifetime; a vague promise of peaceful intentions towards Scotland was included. 'What precisely Henry's diplomatic intentions were during the months which ran from the conclusion of the Anglo-French treaty in June 1546 to his death at the end of the following January only Heaven and Henry know.' Yet in retrospect a balance sheet of the net results of the foreign policy of this decade suggests bankruptcy in diplomatic as well as financial terms. These years (and especially those of serious negotiation with the German Lutheran Princes) had witnessed the steady erosion of any remaining basis of trust for the traditional Anglo-imperial alliance; the establishment of a certain military prestige whose symbol, Boulogne, was likely to prove as dangerous a legacy in financial, military, and diplomatic terms as was to be the French enmity to which its ruinously expensive acquisition had given a keener edge; and a confusion of aims and methods in Scotland which had turned the very real opportunity offered by the death of

James V into the actuality of a yet deeper Scottish hatred of the ancient foe. As to the results within his realm it is difficult to characterise as over-harsh the assertion that 'in order to pursue his futile and ill-conducted wars, the king destroyed the financial independence of the crown and undermined the prosperity of his country'.[13]

The ministers of the boy King Edward VI thus inherited what was already a complex and difficult situation. Both Hertford (soon to be Somerset) and Warwick (later Northumberland) had been most actively engaged in Henry's warfare, on land against Scotland and at sea against France respectively. But new elements of danger were now added by the youth of the King himself, and by the vexed question of the succession to the throne, intertwined as this was with the problem of religion. Just as between 1542 and 1547 dynastic and religious issues in Scotland could never be divorced from their international implications, so now relationships between the children of Henry VIII, and attitudes towards their respective religious policies, were never to be free from the schemings of other European monarchs who wished to manipulate them for their own purposes. Somerset may have inherited his late master's objective of an Anglo-Scottish dynastic marriage; but across the English Channel the new French King, Henry II, saw in the death of Henry VIII prospects very similar to those which that monarch had discerned in the demise of James V. In truth both the European background to English diplomacy and the internal security of England herself (an essential basis for successful foreign policy) had changed for the worse. Charles V, indeed, was deeply engaged in an attempt to settle the religious position in Germany – his apparently overwhelming victory over the Protestant Princes at Mühlberg in 1547 and subsequent imposition of the 'Augsburg Interim' settlement in 1548 being followed only by continued French intrigue and intervention and finally by a renewal of war in 1552. The Emperor was therefore in no position to heed the appeals of the Papacy and of Cardinal Pole to intervene in order to enthrone his cousin, the Princess Mary, who was the legitimate monarch in many Catholic eyes. Nor was Charles so inclined; he was aware that this might be a papal manœuvre to distract his attention from the Council of Trent. In general the Emperor adopted a friendly attitude to the regime of Somerset, accepting his ambassador's belief that both he and his close associate Paget 'regarded peace with the Emperor as the cornerstone of their policy'. But this was to change completely, as we shall see, after Warwick's coup d'état. Meanwhile from the outset Henry II, who succeeded to the throne of Francis I on 31 March 1547, prepared to take advantage of the internal weaknesses or embarrassments of both of France's traditional rivals, and in particular to assert what we may describe as the Franco-Scottish claim to the English monarchy. In short for the next dozen years or so the position was such that 'the interest of England's foreign relations lay less in what she herself did than in what others might do to her'.[14]

Yet England's posture, at the outset of the reign of Edward VI, was anything but defensive. For the Lord Protector, Somerset, prepared to pursue the policy of union with Scotland in furtherance of a genuine vision of a united Britain. Unfortunately to Scottish eyes he still appeared as the commander of the troops which had inflicted such devastation upon their land. Somerset might claim that the Scots were still legally bound by the Treaty of 1543, but for them such legalities had been washed out by the bloodshed of the intervening years. Since he was conscious of the dangerous implications, especially for Boulogne and Calais, of the accession of the ambitious and aggressive Henry II, the question arises of Somerset's wisdom in forcing the Scottish issue. None the less in fairness to him there is some justice in the comment that, although Gardiner might advise the Protector to 'let Scots be Scots, with despair to have them, unless it were by conquest', until the King should come of age, the immediate 'problem was to prevent their becoming French'. For in Scotland itself the French cause, buttressed by a few thousand troops, was becoming more solidly established; at the end of July St Andrews Castle, held by a Protestant and English-subsidised garrison, surrendered to a French naval force. Among those taken for service in the galleys was John Knox. It might therefore be contended that unless all hope of maintaining English influence and of supporting the Protestant cause in Scotland was to be abandoned, Somerset's move from a diplomatic to a military course of action was enforced and also that its timing, a few months after the imperial victory at Mühlberg had given France some food for thought, was not ill-judged.[15]

During August a large land and sea force of over sixteen thousand men was collected, and on September 10 near Edinburgh the somewhat larger but very ill-equipped Scottish army rashly abandoned a commanding position and was shattered. National shame at the débâcle of Solway Moss was now replaced by horror at the toll of dead at Pinkie Clough. Well-equipped, strengthened by mercenaries and by an unusually high proportion of cavalry, and assisted by artillery and by a galley close inshore, the English force left between seven and ten thousand Scottish dead upon the field or along the course of their panic-stricken flight, as against its own loss of perhaps five hundred. Yet once again an overwhelming military victory – this time in real as well as symbolic terms – was followed neither by successful diplomacy nor by Scottish submission. Somerset himself soon departed for London, leaving behind him a policy which included settling English garrisons at selected strong points; what has been termed 'the fragile policy of building strength in Scotland on treason and on purchasable aristocratic support'; and distribution of English Bibles, dissolution of monasteries and encouragement of Protestant preaching. It is true that the progress of the Reformation in Scotland has been seen as a cause 'operating in favour of Anglo-Scottish amity'. But the basic objective of Somerset's campaign, the child Queen, had been moved to the west, while an appeal for help was despatched to France. The Protector's attempts to buy off the French, which went as far in December 1547 as offering the cession of Boulogne for the price named in the Treaty of Ardres in return for a pledge of abandonment of French opposition to an Anglo-Scottish marriage alliance, all failed. His statesmanlike-sounding 'Epistle to the Nobility of Scotland', with its appeal for the creation of one united kingdom, taking the 'old name of Britain again [and] having the sea for wall, the mutual love for garrison, and God for defence', found no echo in Scottish national feeling, which was in no doubt as to the centre of gravity of such an entity and was not appeased by Somerset's description of his approach as that of 'a loving physician . . . to the mistrustful and ignorant patient'. In particular the factious Scots nobility and the French Queen Mother had nothing to gain from such a union. Scottish pride saw the danger from France, which Somerset so emphasised, as far less grave because far more distant.[16]

The French themselves were probably shaken by the scale and decisiveness of the English victory at Pinkie, and in the early summer of 1548 despatched a force of six thousand men to Scotland. In July a Scottish national assembly near Haddington, whose English garrison now found itself besieged, agreed to Henry II's request that their infant Queen should be sent to France. Nor was this merely for safe-keeping; her betrothal to the French Dauphin and the indissoluble union thereafter of the two Crowns were formally agreed. A few weeks later the child set out for France, sailing around the west coast of Ireland and arriving in Brittany in mid-August. This was disastrous for English hopes, yet the position in Scotland was not readily abandoned. Somerset now reiterated the claim to suzerainty, and most of the English strong-points were stubbornly held — the siege of Haddington engaged over five thousand French and about four thousand Scottish troops and excited international interest. French provocations, including raids on Boulogne and the triumphant assertion by Henry II that France and Scotland were now united, were ignored in the hope of keeping English hands free for conflict in the north. Preparations for the campaign of 1549 included the recruitment of large numbers of Italian and German mercenaries, but as we have seen the bulk of these were to be diverted elsewhere in circumstances that were ultimately to prove ruinous to Somerset. As if the troubles of the disastrous summer of 1549 were not enough, in August Henry II, encouraged by the failure of Somerset's desperate overtures to Charles V (seeking the extension of imperial protection to Boulogne, which was not covered by the treaty obligations of 1542), issued a formal declaration of war. Indeed French intrigue was ever ready to take advantage of English internal dissension, and in particular to do its utmost to help procure the downfall of a statesman so dangerous to the Valois cause in Scotland; it had shown interest in the hare-brained schemes of Sudeley as a potential cause of civil war, and again, some two years later, was to urge the speedy execution of Somerset.[17]

Such was the position which Somerset bequeathed to the men who seized power from his hands in October 1549: a war on two fronts, with the doubtful fruits of his own and of Henrician aggression under simultaneous attack, the nation's resources strained to (and financially beyond) the limits, combined with fears for the stability of the whole basis of social and political cohesion and for loyalty within the realm itself. Assessment of the Protector's personal responsibility for what proved to be an untenable position is generally unfavourable. Certainly he had inherited the lines of policy which he pursued. Yet despite the magnanimity of his vision of a united Britain he seemed to have learnt nothing from the mistakes of Henry VIII in his treatment of Scotland. Professor Jordan, no hostile critic, believes that 'Somerset's preoccupation with Scottish affairs and his attitude of almost personal outrage at the revocation of the marriage treaty was obsessive'; at least twenty thousand dead were the price of his mistaken policy which 'laid waste even the historical possibility of union for another half-century'. After the event, it seems painfully clear that, in the context of the international situation, his Scottish policy was recklessly ambitious and gave too many hostages to fortune. Even its military victory was a diplomatic defeat. It ignored the crucial factor of Scottish national pride, the all-but-inevitable reaction of the French whose hostility merely awaited an opportunity, and finally it foundered on the shifting sands of financial bankruptcy and personal disloyalty at home.[18]

His successor in power if not in title, Warwick, faced an extremely dangerous position. The English hold in Scotland had been gravely weakened, and in September Haddington had been evacuated; Boulogne held out, but some of the outer defences had fallen; the financial situation was ruinous. Negotiations with France commenced in January 1550 and by March peace was concluded. Boulogne was handed back to the French for about half of the sum required by the Treaty of Ardres, while England agreed to abandon what few strong-points she still held north of the Scottish border. In some ways the cession of Boulogne was a relief. In financial and military terms it had been a running drain of English resources since its acquisition; in terms of diplomacy its possession by the foreigner had been a festering wound in the side of France, inevitably poisoning any hope of genuine agreement. Understandably in terms of prestige its loss was seen by Englishmen as a blow to national pride. The contemporary allegory, *Philargyrie,* sneered at Warwick as having 'sold for ready gold forts that were builded strong', and it is true that the French, on taking over, were surprised and relieved that the impressive inner fortifications had been surrendered without really being put to the test. Yet Warwick had little alternative, in a position in which the English ambassador could report that the French 'know too well our estate, and thereby think they may ride upon our backs'. Pollard's verdict that 'while it was high-handed at home, the government was cringing abroad' may now seem a little harsh. A kinder judgement states frankly that 'peace at almost any price was the only policy that Somerset's failures left open to his successor'.[19]

There is still the question of what was to be done with the breathing-space so dearly bought in terms of national prestige. Here there is far less ground for exculpation of Warwick. It may well be argued that as his regime took root he came increasingly to regard foreign policy as an adjunct to his own internal ambitions. Peace with France was one thing; that England should become almost a satellite state another. Meanwhile relations with the Emperor became strained to the verge of war, while little real effort was made to refurbish English military strength. The key to much of this is to be found in Warwick's internal policies. In particular his alliance with an increasingly dogmatic strain of Protestantism led to an ever-harsher attitude towards the religious convictions of the Princess Mary, while his personal interests ultimately made him unwilling to contemplate any prospect of her succession to the throne. Inevitably the former friendship with her cousin, Charles V, gave way to acrimony as the whole tenor of Somerset's foreign policy was reversed. Here once more we see the impact of dynastic, religious and personal factors upon the drift of England's foreign policy. The nation was driven into increasingly servile amity with France not primarily from politico-military necessity but in furtherance of Warwick's personal schemes.

It is true that the effects of the 1549 rebellions dictated the abandonment of a really virile policy. 'A government that could not rely upon the county forces and could afford to hire only a limited number of mercenaries . . . could not pursue a strong or independent foreign policy. It could not even feel secure against rebellion and invasion.' Yet the peace of March 1550 had given Warwick the possibility of retrenchment. This he used to secure his own power against any possible internal danger (whether from an insurgent populace or from a personal rival) rather than to build up the national defences against the menace of any external aggressor. 'Bands' of armed men led by a few nobles who were considered trustworthy were established, while the force of 'royal guards' was increased to a thousand men. Yet the troops returning from Boulogne were soon discharged, while garrisons in Irish and border strong-points were reduced. Naval forces also were depleted. Again in fairness it has been observed that the increasingly sophisticated methods and weapons of warfare, and the need to have recourse to continental supplies of expensive equipment which England could not, as yet, produce for herself, made it almost impossible for her in her present financial crisis to adopt a more aggressive stance. But Northumberland's resumption from December 1551 onwards of hiring foreign mercenaries is eloquent testimony of the fact that his fears were mainly directed inwards within the realm. Moreover some at least of the money that might have been employed to restore the country's military security was siphoned off in pensions and grants of land to procure the continued loyalty of Northumberland's supporters.[20]

While any attempt at a clear-headed appraisal of English interests abroad was vitiated by Northumberland's preoccupation with the preservation of his personal ascendancy, the nation's international position was further compromised by the consequences of his 'forward' policy in religion. Unlike the imperial ambassador the Princess Mary had been under no illusion as to the religious implications of the coup d'état of the autumn of 1549, and her fears were soon confirmed. By March 1550 her cousin Charles V found it necessary to submit a formal request that the Privy Council allow her freedom of worship. Not all the bigotry was on one side, for English feelings were aroused by an imperial edict of April 1550 which gave the Inquisition a free hand against *all* heretics in the Netherlands. But one cannot question Professor Jordan's conclusion that 'the diplomatic crisis which dominated much of the period of Northumberland's rule was in part the consequence of the steadily increasing pressure ... on the Princess Mary to secure her conformity in religion'. The *Chronicle* of Edward VI records how, in March 1551, 'the Emperor's ambassador came with [a] short message from his master of [threatened] war ... if I would not suffer his cousin the princess to use her mass'; during August 'certain pinnaces were prepared to see that there should be no conveyance overseas of the Lady Mary secretly done'. Not only was such a project, and imperial involvement therein, real enough (see pages 21–2), but by the autumn of this year only his cumulative misfortunes elsewhere distracted the Emperor from serious consideration of an invasion of England. It is in this wider context of the dynastic and diplomatic implications that the folly of Northumberland's attitude towards Mary is most clearly seen. Mr Secretary Cecil expressed the fear that, in a quarrel concerning 'the Lady Mary ... the majority of our people will be with our adversaries, and it is reasonable to think that although, so long as all is quiet, the Crown can maintain tranquillity, should war break out, they will listen rather to what they will consider the voice of God, calling on them to restore the Papacy, than to the voice of the King'.[21]

Such was the background to the negotiations which led to the Treaty of Angers with France in July 1551. By its terms King Edward resigned all claim to the hand of Mary Stuart and accepted betrothal to a French princess – after squalid haggling over the dowry which reduced England's initial claim of 1,500,000 crowns to 200,000. The French had been encouraged to drive a hard bargain by reports of continued dissension within the Privy Council – for Somerset was quite opposed to this complete reversal of his policies. Northumberland now effectively gave France a free hand in Scotland and a pledge of English neutrality in the event of renewal of conflict with the Emperor. The imminence of such a conflict exposed the essential fatuity of Northumberland's policy. He 'had bought time when he might have had it free and he had bought it in such a way that he could not use it to any good purpose' – for an emboldened renewal of his bullying of the Princess Mary hardly merits this description. In the following year a plea from Charles V for the help to which he was entitled by the terms of the 1542 alliance was refused on technicalities as disingenuous as they were dishonourable. It might be pleaded that this was a requital for his own rebuff of 1549, yet an explicit declaration of the imperial intention to honour treaty obligations had helped to confine French attack to Boulogne, sparing Calais. Northumberland was shrewd enough to ignore French appeals to join them in an anti-Habsburg war, yet England, with no pretence at independence of action, was merely a hamstrung onlooker and not an arbiter. The outcome was a humiliating defeat of the imperial cause in Germany, and this tipped the balance dangerously in favour of France. Charles V's acquiescence in August 1552 in the Treaty of Passau, which virtually conceded religious independence to individual rulers within the Holy Roman Empire, was followed by a speedy attempt at renewal of negotiations with England. The Emperor for his part wished to oppose any further extension of French influence within Britain, while English anxieties over Calais intensified. Yet despite apparent community of interest the renewal of the former Tudor-Habsburg entente, so obvious on national and strategic grounds, could come to nothing as long as Northumberland's internal policies and, for the last few months of the reign, dynastic schemes endured. Thus it was that England's international status and repute diminished as the weakness and futility of her policy became ever more apparent so that 'in four short years [she] became the laughing-stock of Europe'.[22]

The ruin of Northumberland's scheme and the accession of Mary Tudor was therefore of the most profound international as well as dynastic and religious significance. Unlike her brother Edward and her sister Elizabeth the new Queen was herself half-foreign. The Spanish element in her parentage and personality had been confirmed by the years of shared disgrace with her mother, Catherine of Aragon, by the bond of religion and by dependence upon the advice and sympathy of Habsburg ambassadors. It is therefore hardly an exaggeration to describe her foreign policy as an emanation of her Spanish blood and her religious purpose rather than a conscious act of English statecraft; she became 'the one ruler in Tudor history who deliberately outraged – and thereby fostered – the patriotism of her subjects'. To her cousin Charles V the immense upsurge of Tudor loyalty – as unexpected as it was successful – which swept her to the English throne may well have seemed to mark the turning of the tide after the defeats of 1552. Indeed Professor E. H. Harbison credits the imperial ambassador, Renard, with having helped 'to initiate a revolution in the Council which was to prove the determining event in Northumberland's downfall'.[23]

The setback to France of the collapse of this 'client regime' was equally clear. Henry II's continued possession of the Scottish Queen was no longer so potent a threat, in view of the maturity and Catholicism of the new occupant of the English throne, as well as the Habsburg support she might expect. Yet France did not abandon the game. The gambit of exploiting national fears of foreign domination, used with such effect in Scotland against the policies of Henry VIII and Somerset, was now transferred to the English chessboard where French diplomacy made much of the dangers of Spanish patronage. The centre-piece of the Franco-Spanish diplomatic conflict was the duel, at the English Court itself, between the rival ambassadors, Renard and de Noailles of France. In this contest Renard was overwhelmingly victorious. A basically superior strategical position was developed with far more skilful tactics: 'if Noailles, like Gladstone, too often considered Mary as a public institution, Renard, like Disraeli, knew how to please and flatter the woman in the Queen'. But French influence, as we noted in Chapter 3, worked also at a lower and more sinister level: its agents were implicated in much of the treasonable plotting of this reign. Moreover in April 1554 the French hold in Scotland was to be further strengthened when Mary of Guise secured the Regency.[24]

The personal decision of Mary Tudor to commit herself to the Habsburg alliance in the closest possible way by marrying the son of Charles V was received with as much dismay by the French as it was with pleasure by the Emperor – if not by the prospective bridegroom. The day after he learned of the negotiations de Noailles began his efforts to stir up both parliamentary and popular opposition to the match. Petitions and pleas of Parliament and Privy Councillors alike having failed to shift the Queen from her obdurate determination to wed Philip of Spain, certain desperate factions projected a nation-wide plot, which would include the hoped-for assistance of French naval cover against any Habsburg intervention. This plot found premature and partial but none the less frightening expression in Wyatt's Rebellion of February 1554. Significantly several of the captains of the force from London which ruined an early attempt at suppression of the rising by deserting to Wyatt with the patriotic cry of 'We are all Englishmen!' had been suborned by a Scottish agent of de Noailles.[25]

By this time the terms of the marriage alliance had already been decided. Philip was to take the title of King and assist in government; but both the duration and the extent of his powers were limited. He was not to confer offices in Church or State; these, to make doubly sure, were to be filled only by Englishmen. He was to do nothing 'whereby anything be innovate in the state and right, public or private, and in the laws and customs of the said realm of England'. Nor was he to 'lead away the ... Queen out of the borders of her realm, unless she herself desire it', nor take out any ships, guns or jewels. In particular it was asserted 'that the realm of England by occasion of this matrimony shall not directly or indirectly be entangled with the war that now is betwixt' Spain and France. If Mary died childless then all Philip's powers in England died with her; but the provisions for dynastic inheritance should she bear issue suggest an intriguing if tenuous might-have-been in the pattern of international power politics. The eldest son was to inherit England

and the 'Burgundian' possessions in the Netherlands and the Frenche-Comté; moreover if Philip's existing son, Don Carlos, died without issue then all of the Spanish possessions were to pass to the 'Anglo-Spanish' line. Philip's secret protest that he would not, in all circumstances, consider such terms as binding, was matched by English incredulity and suspicion.[26]

Professor Wernham, who emphasises (as did its leaders) the national rather than the religious roots of the rebellion of 1554, suggests that in an important sense 'Wyatt's revolt was different. It was not a protest against war taxation.... It was a protest designed to prevent the adoption of a particular policy, a protest made in advance. It was an attempt to join in the debate about what foreign policy should be. This was something new in English affairs' in that 'public opinion, outside as well as inside Parliament, began to claim a positive part in the shaping of English foreign policy instead of merely protesting at its results'. Some might object that this thought-provoking assessment goes too far; yet it is now abundantly clear that the reign of Mary Tudor marks the turning-point in the fortunes of that Anglo-Habsburg alliance which had for over half a century been the norm of Tudor foreign policy. Certainly in terms of popular feeling this was so. The Queen judged it necessary to issue a proclamation ordering her subjects to greet 'the said most noble prince or any of his train, with courteous, friendly, and gentle entertainment', refraining from such 'cause of strife or contention' as 'taunting words, unseemly countenance'. A contemporary chronicler records how in fact, 'the people, nothing rejoicing, held down their heads sorrowfully', and indeed how 'the day before his coming in, as his retinue and harbingers came riding through London, the boys pelted at them with snowballs', while later, in over-boisterous sport 'the boy who represented the prince of Spain being taken prisoner was hanged, and narrowly escaped strangulation'.[27]

Despite his efforts Philip never achieved popularity, while members of his entourage were accused of personal arrogance. As we have seen, whether justly or not the Spaniard was to be blamed for the wave of religious persecution. Meanwhile if Englishmen were ill-content with Mary's consort Philip himself was far from pleased with his position. The Queen's failure to bear a child frayed the always feeble personal link, while parliamentary blocking of attempts to grant him the full dignities of a crowned King of England deprived his irksome sojourn of the reality of power. In August 1555 he left for the Netherlands. His disillusionment with the fruits of the alliance was shared by English public opinion. Any hope of full participation in the Spanish colonial trade was rebuffed. The 1550s were distinguished by an upsurge of English participation in maritime and colonial adventure; expeditions set out for America, Africa and Russia. Commercial interests were therefore angered by Philip's determination to uphold the Castilian monopoly of trade with Spanish America (and also apparently his neighbour Portugal's monopoly in Africa), as well as by his efforts to support the privileges of his Netherlandish subjects and of the Hanse against the Merchant Adventurers. The growing difficulties of trade with Antwerp, which disposed Englishmen to look elsewhere for their markets, in fact injured more, and more important, elements than those involved in Spanish colonial trade. Nor was resentment assuaged by Philip's readiness to sanction projects for English investigation of the less attractive North-western and North-eastern Passages. In short the traditional basis of co-operation of English and Burgundian commercial interests was still further undermined during these years, presaging the trouble of 1563.

Another event of 1555, the election of Cardinal Caraffa to the papal throne as Paul IV, effectively splintered the tacit assumption upon which much of Marian foreign policy was based: that the interests of the Spanish alliance coincided with those of the Catholic Church. In fact many Privy Councillors had never been convinced of this identification. Gardiner, whose party looked to Rome, had perceived that 'in marrying Philip, the Queen would involve England in everlasting strife with France and invite French intrigue with English heretics'; Paget's group looked first to Brussels and the imperial alliance, and their doubts as to the political wisdom of religious intransigence had been shared by Charles V himself. The potential divergence between Spanish and Roman interests now became reality. For the Neapolitan

Foreign Affairs: the 'British Problem' 173

Pope regarded Philip as a major threat to his political ambitions in Italy, and (ironically) Cardinal Pole as a neo-heretical danger to his bigoted conservatism in doctrine. The fact that he was seventy-nine years old in no way moderated his splenetic zeal in pursuit of his vendettas. In July 1556 a formal alliance was made with France and the efforts of papal diplomacy now nullified English endeavours to preserve a Valois-Habsburg truce. In September Philip's forces invaded the Papal States and he himself was excommunicated. By November the Spanish King was appealing for English help in the impending renewal of conflict in the Netherlands. Receiving no pledge of substantial aid Philip returned to England in March 1557, two months after hostilities commenced, with motives that were all-too-clearly martial rather than marital. The joint pleas of King and Queen had little effect in Council – although Philip's belated offer to open Spanish America to English trade and to resist French influence in Scotland extracted in return a promise of help marginally greater than that to which England was still bound by treaty obligations. But now the position was both complicated and resolved by two further developments. The futility of the Stafford expedition of April 1557 did not diminish the knowledge that it had sailed from a French port, armed and blessed by the French King. A royal proclamation enunciating the reasons for war with France explicitly declared that Henry II had 'supported and furthered' Northumberland's treason, the Wyatt and Dudley conspiracies, and had furnished the Stafford attempt 'with armour, money, munition, and ships, to surprise our castle of Scarborough'. This was the decisive reason for English entry into the war, but in the same month Pope Paul withdrew the authority of Pole as *legatus a latere*, and followed this in June with a recall to Rome – a summons which the Cardinal most wisely disobeyed.[28]

England's formal declaration of war against France in June 1557 was therefore understandable on grounds of national honour in face of the most blatant provocation and of personal motivation in that Mary supported her Spanish husband against his Valois rival, and her closest spiritual ally, who had reconciled the realm to the Catholic Church, against the spite of that Church's titular head. Yet the irony of Mary's position did not escape unnoticed. The thread which had thus far linked all aspects of policy – religious, marital and diplomatic – had been an almost fanatical loyalty to the Church against whose recognised leader the Queen now found herself forced to take up arms. The nation entered the conflict with misgivings rather than with confidence, for many Englishmen perceived that only the folly of the French King had forced them into a war which they did not want in pursuit of an alliance which they no longer relished. The stage seemed set for tragic failure and this duly ensued – although the first action appeared favourable enough. A force of some five thousand troops led by Pembroke, the hero of 1554, left England in July and participated in the Spanish victory at St Quentin in the following month. But Philip neither followed up the success nor rewarded the help. Insolvency exacerbated his habitually dilatory tendencies and allowed the French to regroup their forces. In face of this Philip appropriated certain arms which had been purchased by England, and diverted to his own use a force of three thousand German mercenaries (which Mary had hired for employment on her northern marches) together with the money borrowed for their wages. The troops were needed because Scotland, honouring her French alliance, declared war on England; yet Philip did not keep his own promise to declare war on the Scots. Finally Mary's husband did very little to help defend the last English continental possession, Calais.

The fall of Calais traditionally marks the nadir of Mary's misfortunes. Seen in long-term historical perspective its loss (at some time or other) appears almost inevitable and barely regrettable – for its upkeep in terms of men, money and international ill-will was hardly justified by any real utility to England. In this it resembled Boulogne. Yet this expensive prestige symbol was highly prized, and its loss was as much a national disgrace in English eyes as its capture was a patriotic triumph to the French. Moreover the strategic effect of the loss in one decade of both Calais and Boulogne, bases from which England might seek for control of the Narrow Seas and thus to some extent of Spanish communications

Foreign Affairs: the 'British Problem'

with the Low Countries and French links with Scotland, should not entirely be dismissed. The Queen's reaction was a sense of personal shame, but the blame must be more widely apportioned. Philip showed little concern until it was too late; perhaps both he and the English government believed that St Quentin had secured the position. Obvious French preparations for assault under the command of the Duke of Guise in December 1557 evoked near-panic pleas for help from commanders who were keenly aware of the shortcomings in their defences and in the number, equipment and morale of their garrisons. Yet the Council, with what has been described as 'criminal carelessness', decided that a major attack in the depths of winter was unlikely; indeed the English fleet was laid up. In fairness it must be conceded that the Crown was very short of cash. Parliament had not met since 1555, so that no grant was available from this source to meet the rapid increase in expenditure, and an attempt to meet the deficiency by recourse to a forced loan in November 1557 encountered a widespread and mutinous unwillingness to pay. The French assault on New Year's Day took barely a week to gain its objective, although both Calais itself and Guisnes, which held out until 20 January, were defended with some resolution.[29]

The fact that the Parliament which was summoned to meet on the very day of the fall of Guisnes proceeded in face of this disaster to vote only a niggardly grant of taxation may help to explain why no real effort was made to recapture England's lost ground. It is well to remember that in any case the fear of an attempted invasion of England itself dominated such military preparations as were made. To pay for these the absence of an adequate parliamentary grant drove the government to the expedients of increased tariffs and forced loans. By the summer England felt strong enough to send a few ships to assist in the Spanish victory at Gravelines, but this was counter-balanced by the French seizure of Alderney. In October a truce was signed and the negotiations began which resulted in the general peace of Cateau-Cambrésis. But English interests carried little weight in these negotiations, and they had not gone far when Mary died on 17 November 1558.

In retrospect Mary's ill-starred reign was as disastrous for England's 'old alliance' with the Habsburgs as it was for the 'old religion'. On both of these the Queen had set her heart; to them she brought fanaticism of purpose and inflexibility of policy; and for both of them her blinkered disregard of her subjects' feelings and her country's interests in their uncritical pursuit was to prove disastrous. The seeds of the 'diplomatic revolution' so often ascribed to the reign of Elizabeth were sown and took root in that of her sister, while 'in any attempt to account for that alliance of Protestantism and nationalism which has marked English history since the reign of Elizabeth, the reign of Mary the Catholic must ever be of crucial significance'. It is impossible to withhold our sympathy from this Queen, doomed almost in her inheritance, 'forsaken by her husband and estranged from her people . . . ploughing her cheerless furrow across a stubborn land'. Yet if in the sphere of religion the bigoted ardour of the zealot overcame the merciful instincts of the woman, in that of diplomacy the devotion of the wife prevented a rational political calculation of her country's interests. It is fair to observe that she had inherited a position that was diplomatically and militarily precarious and financially weak, and also that a reversion to the traditional Spanish alliance seemed preferable to Northumberland's near-servile relationship with France. Yet whatever the formal terms of the alliance the complete imbalance in the weight given to Spanish and to English interests, both by Philip himself and by his pathetically loyal spouse, became painfully clear. In the event the Spanish alliance became associated in people's minds with a degree of religious persecution that was alien to English experience, and with the most bitter national disgrace of the century.[30]

Despite the obvious contrasts some interesting parallels emerge between the reign of Mary Tudor and that of her brother Edward. Both were distinguished by diplomatic and military humiliation at the hands of France, although in rather different circumstances; in the reign of Edward the reckless over-extension of national resources by Somerset was followed by Northumberland's cession of Boulogne and personally motivated pro-French policy; in that of Mary the effect of

Foreign Affairs: the 'British Problem'

deliberate subservience to Spain, combined with the weakened state of England's military and naval power, completed the loss of English territory on the continent. Again in both reigns dynastic considerations provide the key to the changing course of diplomacy. Under Somerset this took the form of aggressive pursuit of the union of the Tudor and Stuart lines envisaged by Henry VIII; for Northumberland the impossibility of friendship with the cousin of the Catholic Mary, and then later the attempt to debar that princess from the English throne, determined his course of action; finally, Mary Tudor's Spanish blood and Spanish marriage over-rode all national interests in determination of her foreign policy. In both reigns the fears of Henry VIII were amply justified; contending French and Spanish interests suggested on occasion the possibility that the British Isles might replace Italy as the military as well as diplomatic cockpit of the Valois-Habsburg combat.

The accession of Elizabeth I did nothing to dispel that fear. The enthronement of another female, and one whose claim, except to most English eyes, was clearly suspect, seemed to offer continued scope for foreign intrigue. Furthermore, whereas Mary Tudor's religion like her descent offered no genuine pretext for the intervention of the great Catholic powers, Elizabeth's case was quite different. As to her inheritance the assertion that 'Tudor England was in 1558 at its lowest ebb of weakness and demoralisation' finds ample corroboration in the contemporary analysis of the position: 'The Queen poor, the realm exhausted, the nobility poor and decayed. Want of good captains and soldiers. The people out of order.... Divisions among ourselves. Wars with France and Scotland. The French king bestriding the realm, having one foot in Calais and the other in Scotland. Steadfast enmity but no steadfast friendship abroad.' The aftermath of national disgrace, with the weakness and poverty of the English forces allowing no prospect of redress in military terms, was accompanied by the conduct of peace negotiations in which England counted for little and in which Elizabeth's very recognition as Queen was by no means assured. The interrelated problems of securing such recognition, of establishing a religious settlement whose international as well as internal repercussions could not be ignored, and of treading a tight-rope between the unpopular and disastrous aspects of the Spanish alliance bequeathed by her sister on the one hand, and the dangers implicit in French recognition of Mary Stuart, Queen of Scots, as the rightful Queen of England on the other, all combined to confront Elizabeth with a challenge which demanded a brave heart, a cool head and shrewd judgement.[31]

Elizabeth owed her survival in the short term, and her triumph in the long, in part to her possession of these qualities, in part to the very complexity of the European situation, and in part to good luck – to the emergence of problems within those very states which menaced the independence of her own position in 1558. The Queen's personal ability in the diplomatic arena is widely acknowledged. It rested upon both learning and judgement, and demonstrated an intuitive mastery of its shadier arts of equivocation and duplicity. The problems of the years after 1558 required all these skills. Yet the very intensity of the rivalry between France and Spain and the eagerness of both for the English allegiance made possible the achievement of an admittedly precarious equilibrium by counter-balancing the pressures or threats from either side. The Queen might well have anticipated the resolve expressed much later in the words of the greatest of Elizabethan dramatists: 'out of this nettle, danger, we pluck this flower, safety'. Finally Elizabeth was fortunate in that she came to the English throne at a time when the two great continental powers, war weary after decades of intermittent conflict, were concluding a truce of exhaustion. Each of them would watch eagerly lest the other should strike for the English prize but neither was likely to launch a direct thrust in the immediate future. The conclusion and the terms of the Treaty of Cateau-Cambrésis (April 1559) were thus of considerable importance for England. France kept Calais upon condition of a worthless promise to return it in eight years' time or forfeit 500,000 crowns. Unpalatable as it was to English stomachs this was a recognition of reality, and, as Conyers Read drily remarks, the face-saving condition 'brought peace without too much dishonour'. It may be urged that the peace ended the open conflict between

Spain and France upon which England had so often counted in earlier decades; but in the immediate past England had been dragged into that conflict much to her disadvantage, while for the immediate future a crucial aspect of the settlement was the recognition of English independence as a condition of equilibrium which neither of the major powers could openly assault without renewing large-scale conflict.[32]

Spanish influence at Rome had countered and nullified French efforts to procure a papal declaration that Elizabeth was illegitimate and excommunicate, and helped to secure for the English Queen effective recognition by the Treaty. Indeed Camden asserted that her 'most inward Counsellors' were resolved 'that Amity was to be holden with the Spaniard by any means whatsoever, and the ancient League with the House of Burgundy confirmed'. Yet in fact, as Elizabeth clearly perceived, subservient reliance upon Spain was not the inevitable price of security against France. For the prospect of a Valois-Guise-Stuart bloc stretching from John O'Groats to the Pyrenees was one that Philip dared not contemplate; recalcitrant and unco-operative as Elizabeth might prove, he was committed to her support. The Spanish King, whose agents had paid court to Elizabeth before her sister's death, soon realised that the new Queen had no intention of allowing him to exploit England's weakness. The gauche assertion of his ambassador, Count Feria, that Elizabeth owed her throne to his master met with the tart rejoinder that it derived from her people. His boast that Philip had merely to ask for Elizabeth's hand in marriage was equally wide of the mark; his conditional offer made early in 1559 met with no serious consideration, for the Queen had no intention of becoming a Catholic as he asked. Elizabeth could blow cold on Philip's suit without any real fear that he would stand aside and abandon her to French attack. There seems little doubt that 'the threat that Spain would intervene on her behalf was one of Elizabeth's greatest assets in the perilous early years of the reign', for 'Philip was not a free agent . . . as the rival of France and the ruler of the Netherlands, commercially dependent upon England, he could not afford to desert her'.[33]

All this is not to minimise the gravity of the danger that

'the ancient friendship between France and Scotland . . . looked like turning into a personal union which would put England squarely between the jaws of a nutcracker'. Let it be said that Elizabeth's escape from this predicament owed much to her own coolness and ability but much more to fortune – to the emergence in both France and Scotland of precisely those problems of the succession and calibre of the dynasty, and of religious dissension, which had throughout his reign enabled Henry II to take advantage of English weakness. In 1558 all this lay ahead. Elizabeth's immediate asset, against the background of Valois-Habsburg rivalry, lay in the fact that she herself was such an obvious prize in the field of dynastic marriage, Her immediate danger lay in the recognition which Henry II promptly accorded to his son and daughter-in-law as King and Queen of England, a recognition provocatively symbolised in the use at a dinner given to English representatives at Cateau-Cambrésis of plate which bore the royal arms of England. Ironically, it was at a joust in celebration of the establishment of peace with Spain (in July 1559) that the French King received the mortal wound which set in motion the course of events which eased Elizabeth's position. Yet in the short term the accession of Francis II and his bride, Mary Stuart, seemed destined only to settle the anti-English Guise faction yet more firmly in the saddle both in France and in Scotland.[34]

Events in Scotland were to be the focal point of concern for the next year or so. The reign of Mary Tudor had both diverted English attention from this sphere and postponed any assertion of the 'Stuart-Valois' claim to the English throne; now the accession of Elizabeth reopened the field. Meanwhile the years between 1554 and 1558 had seen important developments within Scotland itself. The years following the seizure of the Regency by the Queen Mother, Mary of Guise, saw the consolidation of French influence to the point at which, in Professor Wernham's judgement, 'Scotland became almost a province of France and the Stuart claim to the English succession became virtually a Valois claim.' Indeed Professor Donaldson maintains that the Franco-Scottish entente became 'so close that it anticipated Winston Churchill's famous offer of 1940 [of complete union between

England and France], because French and Scots enjoyed common nationality', a position confirmed 'by the Scottish parliament in 1558'.[35]

Yet not all the advantages lay with one side; first, as a natural reaction to these trends, Scottish national pride might come to identify French rather than English intervention as the real enemy; secondly, as a result of the Marian persecutions Protestantism was no longer hag-ridden by the suspicion that it was simply the 'religious arm' of English ambitions in Scotland – indeed any genuine progress of the Reformation in Scotland might lead to a significant reorientation of attitudes should religious and national interests become fused. At first the Queen Regent had displayed a politic tolerance in religion, so that some English Protestants found asylum north of the border and the 'reforming' party grew. In December 1557 the 'Lords of the Congregation' swore a covenant to press for church reform. This movement drew its support from a mixture of genuinely religious motivation, increasing resentment of alien overlordship, and the political ambitions of certain nobles. Thus, in this altered context did some of the efforts of Henry VIII and Somerset belatedly bear fruit. But as yet the policy of toleration was so successful that in the very month of the swearing of the covenant the overwhelming majority of those Protestant lords present in the Scottish Parliament voted in favour of the marriage of Mary Stuart to the French Dauphin. As late as 1558 a submission of a formal demand for redress of church abuses and some modification of the form of service did not meet with complete rejection. The rapid change in this position may be traced from the burning (the first for eight years) of a Protestant martyr of over eighty years of age, in April 1558. The reaction of the Protestants to this heartless and gratuitously provocative action (undertaken, to be fair, neither at the instigation nor with the subsequent approval of the Queen Regent) led gradually but inexorably into rebellion. Attitudes hardened further after the accession of Elizabeth, with all its implications, in November of the same year; if Scots Protestants derived encouragement from that event French influence, drawing similar conclusions, counselled a policy of sterner repression. In March 1559 all unauthorised sermons were forbidden, and two months later certain Protestants, including John Knox who had just returned to Scotland, were summoned to answer for their disobedience of this order. The presence of Knox was of immense importance for his biographer describes him as 'the only leader of a popular revolution in the sixteenth century who managed to persuade the nobles to join the revolutionary movement'. After serious Protestant riots in Perth in May, Mary of Guise employed French troops against the rebels. This, together with underlying resentment towards French garrisons in Scottish fortresses and French domination at court, created a religiopolitical situation which offered every opportunity for English counter-pressure.[36]

While Mary Stuart, still in France, might embarrass Elizabeth by appealing to English Roman Catholics, the English Queen could now use the religious issue to weaken her rival's position in Scotland itself. Yet much would depend upon the quality of statecraft with which this opportunity was exploited, and to Elizabeth's credit the contrast both with her father and with Somerset is instructive. For a false move, a presumptuous or over-bold assertion, or a clumsy attempt at obvious 'capture' of this movement under way might ruin all. At all costs the revulsion of Scottish national feeling against French domination must not once more be reversed. It was a situation to which Elizabeth's policy of 'reluctant intervention', which sprang both from the relative weakness of her country's position and from her own innate caution, was therefore ideally suited. In June the Scottish Protestants achieved considerable military success, but an appeal to Cecil in the following month received a carefully noncommittal reply – although he conceded in a private letter that the 'Lords of the Congregation' must be helped 'first with promises, next with money, and last with arms'. Elizabeth would have been less than human if she had not welcomed Mary's difficulties, yet she could hardly condone the spectacle of rebels in arms against their lawful sovereign, and was hardly mollified by Knox's belated declaration that she herself might be another Deborah and thus an exception to the rule asserted in his *First Blast of the Trumpet Against the Monstrous Regiment of Women,* published in Geneva in the previous year. Yet her position was surely far preferable to the quandary of Philip II, as depicted by Sir John Neale: 'He did not want Elizabeth to annex Scotland, and much less France to annex England. Nor did he want the Scots to get away with their revolt and impose their heresy on Scotland.' The Spanish King could therefore do little but wring his hands; at least Elizabeth had some opportunity of fruitful action.[37]

For some time this took the form of guarded encouragement and clandestine subsidies. But news from France of the accession of Mary's husband Francis II helped to sharpen English awareness both of the dangers threatened and of the opportunities offered. For Guise, victor of Calais in 1558 and brother of the Scottish Queen Regent, was now in virtual control. In August 1559 a French expeditionary force prepared for Scotland. In these circumstances it became ever clearer both to the Scots and to Elizabeth that a more forceful English commitment was imperative. In October the Lords of the Congregation, their position now made to appear rather more respectable by the recruitment of the Duke of Châtelherault (otherwise Arran, heir presumptive to the throne, whom Mary of Guise had ousted from the Regency in 1554), declared the Queen Regent deposed. Early in November Elizabeth nerved herself to promise increased financial aid and the interception of French sea-borne reinforcements. An appeal a few weeks later for open and large-scale English intervention was underlined by rumours of a French landing as forerunner of a full invasion force, but Elizabeth refused the risk of formal war. Instead she took the lesser but still substantial gamble of sending a fleet with directions in effect to 'exceed instructions' in attacking any French invasion force.

As was so often to be the case, the Queen's postponement of resolute action in the Micawber-like hope that something would turn up was justified. As they were to do nearly thirty years later, the elements fought for her. In late December the vanguard of the French fleet left port, but although some ships reached Leith others got no further than the Zeeland sand banks; the main force, early in January 1560, got to within sight of the Scottish coast before being shattered by even fiercer storms. The English fleet, providentially delayed by the tempests that had crippled the French, now sailed for the Firth of Forth and, although losing some half dozen vessels en route, proceeded to cut the communications of the garrison of Leith. Thus emboldened, Elizabeth now extended to the Scots her formal protection, and the pledge of an English army, by the Treaty of Berwick on 27 February 1560. This Treaty was at pains to recognise the loyalty of the Scottish nobility to their sovereign and to profess the objective of protecting Scotland's liberties and independence against French annexation – a danger which the secret clauses signed by Mary Stuart in her marriage treaty of 1558 suggest was very real. Indeed the policy of Elizabeth was to disavow any hostility towards France or Scotland or their respective monarchs, exculpated because of their youth. This comes out very clearly in a proclamation of 24 March 1560 which explained that 'her majesty of her good and gracious nature is content to think that the injurious pretense made by the Queen of Scotland to this realm ... hath been bred and issued only out of the hearts of the principals of the house of Guise, to whom the chief governance of the crown of France now of late hath happened'; nor was this faction content to 'intermeddle with the governance of France', they now proceeded to 'enterprise the eviction of the crown of Scotland out of the power of the natural people of the land'.[38]

In due course Philip II protested, naïvely proposing that Spanish troops be sent to Scotland while he mediated a settlement. But by now Elizabeth's position had been further strengthened by the news from France of the Huguenot 'Conspiracy of Amboise' – although Dr N. M. Sutherland finds the charge of English involvement in this incident quite unproven. Despite its failure this demonstrated to the Guise regime that dangers from a factious and Protestant nobility lay nearer home than Scotland. At the end of March an English force of some nine thousand men crossed the border and assisted in the siege of Leith – an action described significantly as 'the War of the Insignia'. In June occurred the death of Mary of Guise, herself the personification of French influence in Scotland, and this was followed in early July by the conclusion of the Treaty of Edinburgh between English and French delegates. Mary Stuart and her husband were to abandon all claim to the English title; French troops were to leave and never return to Scotland whose laws and liberties were guaranteed; Scottish governance was to be in the hands of a Council, from which aliens were excluded, jointly selected by Queen Mary, Parliament, and the Lords of the Congregation. In August the Scottish Parliament adopted a 'Confession of Faith' which made their realm a Protestant state; and Dr Jasper Ridley concludes that 'Scotland had passed into the English zone of influence'. None the less Elizabeth was shrewd enough in the autumn of this year to reject an invitation from the Great Council of Scotland to marry Arran (son of Châtelherault) and displace Mary. As we shall see, Scottish affairs were far from settled: Mary and her husband refused to ratify the Treaty of Edinburgh; friction developed between the 'Lords' and the spiritual leaders of the 'Congregation'; and Scottish Catholicism, in turn, was now freer of the charge of foreign subservience. Yet from an English standpoint the achievement and the good fortune of the events of these years is undeniable. In so far as the danger from Scotland as a subservient ally of France was a major element of the mid-Tudor crisis in foreign affairs, a crucial turning-point had been passed.[39]

Meanwhile by the end of this same year the position within the other member in the 'auld alliance' had also changed to Elizabeth's potential advantage. In December Francis II died of a brain abscess – Calvin's unctuously savage remark that 'He who had pierced the father's eye, struck off the ear of the son' being echoed by Knox's comment that 'as the said King sat at mass, he was suddenly stricken with an aposthume in that deaf ear that never would hear the truth of God'. His death severed the personal link between the French and Scottish Crowns (incidentally shattering any faint hopes of a common heir), and brought to the throne the ten-year-old Charles IX. A mere year or so earlier the Guises had bidden fair to dominate Scotland through the Queen Regent, Mary of Lorraine, and France through her daughter Mary Stuart; they now found themselves struggling to retain their ascendancy in France itself, against the Queen Mother,

Catherine de Medici, on the one hand, and the increasingly menacing Huguenot faction on the other.[40]

In August 1561 Mary Stuart returned to Scotland (her personal reluctance, for she had been in France since the age of six, overcome by disastrously miscalculated Guise persuasion), on the implicit understanding that she would not attempt to overthrow the politico-religious settlement established by the Lords of the Congregation as long as they in turn would allow her freedom of worship. Paradoxical as it may seem, the waning of French influence in Scotland did much to revive the fortunes of Catholicism and the prospects of Mary herself. Within a few years she was to wreck those prospects by 'behaviour [that] suggests not politics but a biological urge that would not be denied'. But in the immediate future she presented Elizabeth with a nice dilemma: was Mary to be recognised as heir-presumptive to her throne, in order to placate the Stuart Queen herself, Scottish pride, and English Catholics, or would such an action crystallise potential factions within England itself and weaken Elizabeth's own security? (See page 32.) Cautious, tentative and distrustful negotiations culminated in May 1562 in a projected meeting at York which never materialised. For by that date attention had been distracted and the issues complicated by dramatic events in France.[41]

Mounting political and religious tension erupted into the first of the Wars of Religion which were to rack France for the next generation. The flashpoint was the massacre by the Duke of Guise of a Huguenot congregation discovered at worship, admittedly illegally, at Vassy in March 1562. The early success of the Guises both in the field and in reasserting control of government revived their former ambitions – now the more dangerous in that the religious implications and the prospect of gaining a client faction within France itself might dispose Philip of Spain to a more favourable attitude towards their cause. The Huguenots in turn renewed the appeal to England which they had first made after the Conspiracy of Amboise. It had then proved abortive; but now Elizabeth, in a stronger position and perhaps reflecting upon the successful backing of the Potestant cause in Scotland, felt bolder. In the event she over-reached herself. Perhaps the major diplomatic lesson of her Scottish adventure had been that England gained most by seeking – or at least appearing to seek – least. The demand now made, to be granted occupation of Le Havre and Dieppe as security for the projected cession of Calais as the price of English help, antagonised all moderate or uncommitted French opinion and embittered the Huguenots themselves. Nor were matters helped by Elizabeth's disingenuous assertion to the Spanish ambassador that her intervention had Calais, and not religion, as its objective. English forces occupied Le Havre in October, but rendered no real assistance to their allies, and the defeat of the Huguenots and capture of their leader Condé in December 1562 was to make the position quite untenable.

Against this background the illness and near-death of the Queen herself in October of the same year (see page 33) had brought home to England just how narrow was the base upon which her stability and security rested. Providentially to English eyes and 'certainly in very good time for Queen Elizabeth's good', it was the Duke of Guise who died, victim of an assassin in February 1563. The death of their great leader weakened the Guise faction and Catherine de Medici regained control. Yet Catherine's return to more moderate and conciliatory religious policies, based upon an understanding with Condé, implied Huguenot co-operation in driving out the foreigner, and by the end of July Le Havre had been abandoned. In so far as Elizabeth's intervention in France had helped to distract attention from Scotland, and had demonstrated to her potential enemies that assistance to 'rebels for religion' was a gambit that more than one could employ, it may be urged that it was not completely fruitless. Yet on balance and certainly in comparison with her achievement in Scotland it must be judged a failure. Elizabeth herself came to terms with reality in the Treaty of Troyes in April 1564, giving up all claim to Calais. Thereafter her policy was more circumspect, employing the weapons of diplomacy and intrigue in preference to military expeditions. Professor Wernham has observed that the abortive French adventure ('it was Dudley's war' wrote Conyers Read) went far towards settling the relative positions of Cecil and the more adventurous Dudley in Elizabeth's counsels.[42]

To contend that all or even most of the problems of Elizabeth's foreign policy had now been solved would be facile and superficial. Mary Stuart was to plague her for another quarter-century; relations with France, unhappily embroiled in no fewer than eight 'Wars of Religion' in the next thirty years, were a constant worry; while Philip II was to change from would-be protector in 1558 to 'master of the Armada' thirty years later. Yet it may be suggested that the immediate and pressing dangers which Elizabeth had inherited from the misfortunes and mistaken policies of the previous twenty years – disastrous enmity with Scotland and the menace of the 'Stuart-Valois' claim to the English throne on the one hand, and the threat of overwhelming Spanish domination of England on the other – had been resisted and reduced. Moreover events in the Netherlands clearly presaged not only a continuing reorientation of Anglo-Spanish relationships but also the emergence of forces which were to hamstring Philip's freedom of action. In 1563 trade with Antwerp, which a combination of financial and commercial and of political and diplomatic influences had rendered increasingly precarious since the early 1550s, was suspended for several months; indeed, a government-sponsored establishment of an alternative mart at Emden was mooted in January 1564. Meanwhile Philip's intransigent religious policy in the Low Countries, which further weakened Anglo-Spanish amity, was to help provoke rebellion later in the decade. With the Revolt of the Netherlands the storm centre of western European international tension was to shift away from the British Isles.

Admittedly an element of good fortune which had been lamentably absent for her predecessors had attended Elizabeth's efforts; yet those efforts, thanks to the Queen herself as well as to her shrewdly chosen advisers, had borne many of the marks of statecraft, and such calculated risks as had been taken deserved success. Professor Wallace MacCaffrey distinguishes between the English intervention in Scotland, which was forced on Elizabeth and her ministers 'by events outside their control yet ended in dazzling success', and the intervention in France, the product of deliberate choice which 'ended in flat failure'. Even if the contrast is not slightly overstated, the lesson of the latter was well learned; for 'with it ended the spirit of adventuresomeness which had characterized the regime up to this point; the years after 1563 were ones of cautious isolationism in foreign affairs'. Meanwhile England's confidence was boosted by the increasing signs of unity at home, so frequently absent under Edward VI and Mary, and by the demonstration at sea and on land of adequate defensive power. To the extent that the mid-Tudor crisis in foreign policy derived from the adoption of rash, short-sighted and ill-judged policies by the Crown or its ministers, exacerbated by polarisation of religious extremes and by the erosion of the financial, economic and social bases of national stability at home, and by the intervention of powerful forces abroad ready and able to exploit these and dynastic weaknesses, we may fairly suggest the year 1563 as marking its termination.[43]

7 Conclusion

At a time when it is so fashionable to stress the elements of continuity in history it is barely necessary to observe that the choice of 1563 as the terminal date of this survey of the mid-Tudor crisis, while given at least symbolic validity by the conjunction of events during that year, is convenient rather than definitive. Certainly the case may seem clearer to historians than it was to contemporaries. In the context of the inherited taint of sickliness in the Tudor stock Elizabeth's illness of 1562 must have presaged yet one more repetition of a familiar and fatal pattern. Nor would their fears have been allayed by the royal plea, believing herself to be near death, that the Council should declare Robert Dudley to be Lord Protector of the realm. The longevity of the Queen which in retrospect solved so many problems could not be taken for granted in 1563. The danger from the rival claimant, Mary Stuart, and the absence of a clear and accepted line of succession to the throne to which Elizabeth's flirtatious indiscretions promised no solution; the threat to the newly established and precariously balanced religious settlement from either side; the somewhat fortuitous improvement in the nation's diplomatic position seemingly put at risk by the Le Havre adventure: none of these would indicate room for royal or ministerial complacency.

Yet if, almost by definition, the longevity and maturing judgement of the Queen were to prove decisive only in the long term, they are also some justification for concluding our study in 1563. For the mid-Tudor crisis was above all a crisis of the dynasty. The last years of an ageing and ailing man, and the reigns of a sickly boy and a short-sighted religious zealot, had built up cumulative problems which by 1558 demanded both short-term solutions and long-term consolidation. The events of the first five years of the reign of Elizabeth I may fairly be described as having provided the first and established the basis of the second. The turning-points, if they owed much to chance, were none the less real. The immediate questions as to the governmental capacity of the new Queen and her ability to fend off pressing dynastic and diplomatic dangers and, above all, command the loyalty of her people, had been satisfactorily answered.

Professor MacCaffrey has suggested that after

> about 1540 ... the balance between Crown and aristocracy began to shift in favour of the latter. Henry, desperately anxious for the future of his dynasty and for the continuance of the Crown's Supreme Headship, gave the lead to a group of his servants, by bestowing what were in effect lavish bribes. His death opened even wider opportunities for the ambitions of a newly formed aristocracy. The weakness of the Crown during the decade 1547–1558 allowed them to increase their wealth while gaining valuable experience.

One might add that the weakness and the mistakes of the Crown on the one hand and the ambition and rapacity of the nobility on the other exacerbated the religious, socio-economic and diplomatic problems of the period which were already in themselves serious enough. But the early years of the reign of Elizabeth I demonstrated that such royal weakness was now ended, that any experience gained during the relative atrophy of the decision-making competence of the Crown itself must now be geared quite strictly to the service of a monarch who was endowed with a judgement and a will that were fully equal to the tasks confronting her.[1]

Yet there remains the question of how and why the Tudor dynasty had survived the alarms and challenges – and its own failures – of the mid-century. Perhaps the key to this may be sought in the common factor which, despite the disparity in their nature, decided the outcome of all rebellions during the decade following 1547. This was quite simply loyalty to the Tudor dynasty, rooted in what can only be described as an instinctive identification of that loyalty with the interests of the political nation and the maintenance of the order and stability of society as a whole. In this context it cannot be too strongly emphasised that the only successful uprising against established *de facto* authority was that which swept Mary Tudor to her throne in 1553. In 1549, despite the differences in relative weight of religious and of social and economic causes in the major rebellions of that year, the nobility closed ranks against any threat to the established order; the same principle underlay Somerset's refusal to attempt to wage civil war in order to preserve his power, and the failure of Northumberland to command significant support in his effort to do so. Finally, it is indicative that the rebellion against a Tudor monarch which came nearest to success, that of Wyatt, did so despite the relative paucity of its support (in numerical terms) because of a momentary doubt within the ranks of the political nation as to whether, in face of the implications of a Spanish marriage, their interests were in fact coincident with those of Mary Tudor.

Fundamental identification of interest might secure loyalty to the dynasty, but there is still the question of the day-to-day provision of effective administration during the dangerous and turbulent mid-century years. In this connection we may recall the comment of Professor Elton, modifying his earlier condemnation of the quality of mid-Tudor government, that 'to speak of collapse, or anything remotely like it, is a mistake.... [For] government never lost control despite all the problems facing it.' The essential institutions of government – administrative, legislative and representative – remained unscathed or were even strengthened. The conciliar and parliamentary aspects of central government, and the voluntarily co-operative administrative and judicial functions of the justices of the peace in local government endured throughout. The processes of government need men to operate them, and there is ample evidence of a substantial element of politico-administrative continuity throughout the turbulent changes of the late Henrician, Edwardian, Marian and early Elizabethan regimes. It has been observed that such continuity was nurtured by self-interest in that 'such prudent politicians as Paget [with whom we may surely couple the name of Cecil] had to keep an eye on their retreat'. Indeed a contemporary, Ponet, selected the same example in sneering at 'Paget the master of practices . . ., that will have one part in every pageant; if he may by praying or paying put in his foot'. It is significant that other skilled administrators such as Mildmay and Gresham served the Crown almost throughout, contributing an element of bureaucratic competence, and that politiques such as Herbert unerringly distinguished the right 'bandwaggon' to join.[2]

Nor was the dexterity of these men completely self-seeking and disingenuous. Their actions, and indeed the general ground-swell of support for the established Tudor regime, must be related to the whole political philosophy of the age; and with 'political' we must couple 'social' and 'religious' in what was still essentially a unitary society. The rationale of their behaviour typifies the nation's acceptance, by and large, of the manner in which, like the 'grand old duke of York', successive regimes reversed the direction of official religious policy. For the suggestion that the Tudor nation-state was as much the instrument as the creation of the English Reformation has much to commend it in this respect: that by the 1530s Tudor England's vision of the majesty of kingship was such that Henry VIII's assumption of caesaro-papal power could readily be accepted.

It is instructive to recall that one of the most forthright statements of the position of the Crown as custodian of the political and religious welfare of its subjects, *De Vera Obedientia*, was written by Stephen Gardiner. Gardiner went a long way along the road to erastianism; his imprisonment for so much of the reign of Edward VI was for personal and political as well as doctrinal reasons. As for his rival, Cranmer, his intense loyalty to his monarch seems to have delayed (or at least concealed) his own doctrinal evolution. Indeed until the very hour of his martyrdom it had seemed likely that he would subordinate his own inner religious convictions to his ingrained sense of the propriety of bowing the neck to the will of the Lord's anointed. Moreover of those whose course to martyrdom was more unswerving the vast majority were resigned to the fact that this was the price of refusing to abandon beliefs which ran counter to the official religious creed. Tyndale's dying prayer before his martyrdom in exile – 'Lord, open the King of England's eyes' – was still more typical than Ponet's splenetic pamphleteering against Mary Tudor. In 1553 Ridley stood almost alone among the leading Protestants in citing the Catholic faith of Mary Tudor (whom he publicly stigmatised as a bastard) as justification for the attempt to exclude her from the throne. Even his fellow-martyr, Bradford, was to allude to 'the unjust Enterprise of the late Duke of Northumberland and what miserable success it had ... God will take Vengeance upon wrongful Doers. Otherwise the Queen's Majesty, that now is had not been Queen of England at this present.' Both Hooper and Knox, perhaps the most extreme representatives of 'orthodox' (as distinct from 'anabaptist') Protestantism, supported Mary throughout the succession crisis.[3]

For whether one sees it as the instrument or as the product of the English Reformation (or, to be more explicit, of the break with Rome), there is no doubt that the Tudor nation-state acquired an added dimension from that event. The divinity that 'doth hedge a king' could not but be enhanced by the formal attribution of spiritual as well as temporal leadership of the realm. Thus ironically an identification which, when challenged, was to help to ruin the Stuarts, did much to preserve the Tudors. For at least some of the inherited medieval belief that the teachings of and the loyalty owing to Holy Church were inextricably interwoven with the whole fabric of the social order was now transmuted into loyalty towards the person of the prince. It is in this context that we may grasp the full significance of the convention – in which there is such a curious parallel between Tudor England and Stalin's Russia – as to the expected and fitting behaviour of condemned 'traitors': that they should 'make a good end', admit their guilt, and profess their loyalty to the regime, their betrayal of which so richly merited death. Despite individual exceptions these generalisations held good for the vast majority of Tudor Englishmen. To the historically minded the Tudor dynasty stood for the nation's preservation from any recurrence of the civil strife of the late fifteenth century; to the upper orders of society it represented their guarantee of protection against the menace of attack upon the social order from within the realm, and against any threats to its integrity and to their own participation in the fruits of power from without; to the average citizen it was clearly the divinely ordained custodian of the whole political and religious complex of society. By the time that the Stuart dynasty in turn came to its test in the middle decades of the seventeenth century these assumptions had lost much of their force. But for the mid-Tudor crisis, despite the modifications of interpretation and the increase in our knowledge brought by the findings of recent research, the old verdict that 'Henry Tudor and son' had built well for their dynasty and their nation still has validity.

Short Titles and Abbreviations

This list includes short titles and abbreviations for primary and secondary works, including periodicals, which are cited throughout; in addition abbreviated versions of titles will be adopted in note references to other works where this may be done without ambiguity.

AgHR   *Agricultural History Review.*
AHEW   *The Agrarian History of England and Wales, IV, 1500–1640*, ed. J. Thirsk (Cambridge, 1967).
AHR   *American Historical Review.*
BIHR   *Bulletin of the Institute of Historical Research.*
Chronicle   *The Chronicle and Political Papers of King Edward VI*, ed. W. K. Jordan (Ithaca, N.Y., and London, 1966).
EconHR   *Economic History Review.*
English Reformation   *The English Reformation*, A. G. Dickens (London, 1964).
Jordan, I   W. K. Jordan, *Edward VI: the Young King* (London, 1968).
Jordan, II   W. K. Jordan, *Edward VI: the Threshold of Power* (London, 1970).
L. & P., Henry VIII   *Letters and Papers, Foreign and Domestic, of the Reign of Henry VIII*, eds. J. S. Brewer, J. Gairdner and R. H. Brodie (London, 1862–1932).
NCMH   *New Cambridge Modern History*, ed. G. N. Clark *et al* (Cambridge, 1957–).
PP   *Past and Present.*
Proclamations, I   *Tudor Royal Proclamations, I, The Early Tudors (1485–1553)*, ed. P. L. Hughes and J. F. Larkin (New Haven, 1964).
Proclamations, II   *Tudor Royal Proclamations, II, The Later Tudors (1553–87)*, ed. P. L. Hughes and J. F. Larkin (New Haven and London, 1969).
Scarisbrick   J. J. Scarisbrick, *Henry VIII* (London and Berkeley, Calif., 1968).
TRHS   *Transactions of the Royal Historical Society.*

Notes

CHAPTER 1: PAGES 1–6

1 G. R. Elton, *England under the Tudors*, pp. 193–4.
2 *Proclamations*, II, pp. 99, 103; W. T. MacCaffrey, *The Shaping of the Elizabethan Régime*, p. 16.
3 MacCaffrey, pp. 55–6; S. T. Bindoff, *Tudor England*, pp. 203–4.
4 Bindoff, p. 146.

CHAPTER 2: PAGES 7–34

1 H. W. Chapman, *The Last Tudor King*, p. 67.
2 L. B. Smith, *Henry VIII. The Mask of Royalty*, pp. 249–59.
3 L. B. Smith, 'Henry VIII and the Protestant Triumph', *AHR*, LXXI (July 1966), pp. 1240–3, 1249, 1253.
4 Chapman, pp. 60–1.
5 *Chronicle of the Grey Friars of London*, ed. J. G. Nichols (Camden Society, 1852) p. 53; S. Anglo, *Spectacle, Pageantry, and Early Tudor Policy*, pp. 292–3; Chapman, p. 117.
6 *Chronicle*, p. 107; Chapman, p. 268.
7 Chapman, p. 280.
8 S. T. Bindoff, 'A Kingdom at Stake', *History Today*, III (1953), pp. 642–8; Jordan, II, pp. 494–504, 510–20.
9 J. G. Ridley, *Thomas Cranmer*, p. 345; J. G. Nichols (ed.) *Narratives of the Reformation* (Camden Society, 1860), pp. 225–6.
10 C. Wriothesley, *A Chronicle of England during the Reigns of the Tudors*, ed. W. D. Hamilton (Camden Society) vol. II (1877), pp. 87–8.
11 *The Chronicle of Queen Jane and of Two Years of Queen Mary*, ed. J. G. Nichols (Camden Society, 1850), p. 7.
12 Ibid., p. 7; Ridley, *Cranmer*, p. 347.
13 H. F. M. Prescott, *Mary Tudor*, pp. 55, 179.
14 Prescott, pp. 64, 80, 83, 86, 93, 95; *L. & P., Henry VII*, VIII, no. 174, p. 58; X, no. 1137, p. 478; XVII, no. 371, pp. 220–1.
15 Prescott, pp. 124–6; *Chronicle*, p. 44.
16 S. T. Bindoff, *Tudor England*, p. 178; Prescott, p. 99.

17 G. R. Elton, *England under the Tudors*, p. 213; Prescott, p. 316.
18 Prescott, pp. 211–12, 217, 221–2, 227.
19 Wriothesley, II, pp. 108–9.
20 Prescott, p. 248.
21 Prescott, pp. 270–2, 277.
22 John Ponet, *A Shorte Treatise of politike power* (1556), D. iiii–D. iiiib.
23 Prescott, p. 378; J. Hurstfield, *Elizabeth I and the Unity of England*, p. 14.
24 W. Camden, *The History of the most renowned and victorious Princess Elizabeth late queen of England*, ed. W. T. MacCaffrey (Chicago and London, 1970), p. 9; M. Levine, *The Early Elizabethan Succession Question, 1558–1568*, pp. 5–7; J. E. Neale, *Queen Elizabeth*, p. 14.
25 Neale, p. 31.
26 Neale, pp. 38, 43.
27 Camden, pp. 28–9; MacCaffrey, pp. 63, 75, 77, 82.
28 Levine, pp. 11, 50.
29 Levine, pp. 31–4.
30 Levine, p. 48.
31 Levine, p. 32.

CHAPTER 3: PAGES 35–70

1 J. Hurstfield, 'Was there a Tudor Despotism after all?', *TRHS*, 5th Ser., 17 (1967), p. 105.
2 G. R. Elton, *Henry VIII: an Essay in Revision*, p. 7; Scarisbrick, pp. 643, 653n.
3 G. R. Elton, *The Tudor Revolution in Government*, pp. 8, 417, and *England under the Tudors*, p. 175.
4 G. L. Harriss, 'Medieval Government and Statecraft', *PP*, 25 (July 1963), p. 24; J. Hurstfield, 'Tudor Despotism', pp. 99, 102; G. R. Elton, *Policy and Police. The Enforcement of the Reformation in the Age of Thomas Cromwell*, p. 261.
5 Scarisbrook, p. 426; Elton, *Henry VIII*, p. 15.
6 Scarisbrook, pp. 655–6, 677; J. Hurstfield, 'Corruption and Reform under Edward VI and Mary: the Example of Wardship', *EHR*, LXVIII (1953), pp. 22, 25–7, 36.
7 G. R. Elton, 'The Tudor Revolution: A Reply', *PP*, 29 (Dec. 1964), pp. 47n. 52; P. Williams, 'A Revolution in Tudor History?', *PP*, 25 (July 1963), p. 53.
8 A. F. Pollard, *The Political History of England*, VI, *1547–1603*, pp. 1, 4; *Chronicle*, p. 4; J. Ponet, *Politike power*, I iii. b.
9 Jordan, I, pp. 75, 77; C. Wriothesley, *Chronicle*, II, p. 57.
10 W. T. MacCaffrey, 'The Crown and the New Aristocracy, 1540–1640', *PP*, 30 (April 1965), pp. 55–6; Jordan, I, p. 103;

Hurstfield, 'Political Corruption in Modern England', *History*, LII, no. 174 (Feb. 1967), p. 33.
11 Jordan, I, p. 349; F. W. Russell, *Kett's Rebellion in Norfolk*, pp. 55–6.
12 N. Pocock (ed.), *Troubles connected with the Prayer Book of 1549* (Camden Society, 1884), p. 29.
13 Ibid., pp. 44, 53.
14 John Heywood, *The Spider and the Flie* (1556), ed. J. S. Farmer (Early English Drama Society, London, 1908), p. 262; S. T. Bindoff, *Kett's Rebellion*, p. 15.
15 F. W. Russell, *Kett's Rebellion*, p. 107.
16 Jordan, I, p. 479; F. W. Russell, p. 151.
17 Jordan, I, p. 427.
18 *Proclamations*, I, p. 483; *Chronicle*, p. 17.
19 N. Pocock, *Troubles connected with the Prayer Book of 1549*, pp. 90–2, 95–101.
20 W. Turner, *The Huntyng of the Romyshe Wolfe* (c. 1554/5), A. iiii–A. iiii. b; Jordan, II, pp. 45–7, 56; *Chronicle*, pp. 59, 63, 78.
21 A. F. Pollard, *Political History*, V, p. 57.
22 C. Wriothesley, *Chronicle*, II, p. 63; *Chronicle*, pp. 87, 92, 119.
23 Jordan, II, p. 69; F. G. Emmison, 'A Plan of Edward VI and Secretary Petre for Re-organising the Privy Council's Work, 1552–3', *BIHR*, 31 (Nov. 1958), p. 205.
24 S. E. Lehmberg, *Sir Walter Mildmay and Tudor Government* pp. 32–9.
25 Jordan, II, pp. 450–5; F. G. Emmison, p. 205; G. R. Elton, *The Tudor Constitution*, p. 91; *Chronicle*, pp. 181–4.
26 Jordan, II, pp. 514–20.
27 S. E. Lehmberg, p. 40.
28 Elton, *Tudor Constitution*, pp. 99–100; H. F. M. Prescott, *Mary Tudor*, p. 261; C. Russell, *The Crisis of Parliaments. English History 1509–1660*, p. 135; J. D. Mackie, *The Earlier Tudors, 1485–1558*, p. 532.
29 D. M. Loades, *Two Tudor Conspiracies*, pp. 127, 244.
30 S. T. Bindoff, *Tudor England*, p. 173; *Chronicle of Queen Jane and ... Queen Mary*, p. 69; Loades, p. 56.
31 Loades, p. 70; *Proclamation*, II, p. 28; *Queen Jane and ... Queen Mary*, pp. 48–50; Loades, pp. 63, 74–6.
32 Loades, pp. 114–15.
33 J. E. Neale, *The Elizabethan House of Commons*, p. 274; G. R. Elton, *Tudor Constitution*, p. 295.
34 A. F. Pollard, *Political History*, VI, p. 148; Elton, *Tudor Constitution*, p. 295; E. H. Harbison, *Rival Ambassadors at the Court of Queen Mary*, pp. 273–4.
35 Elton, *Tudor Constitution*, p. 307; J. E. Neale, *Elizabeth I and her Parliaments, Vol. I, 1559–1581*, pp. 23–6; Pollard, pp. 143–6; Loades, p. 184.

36 C. Russell, *Crisis of Parliaments*, p. 133; J. Hurstfield, 'Corruption and Reform', *EHR*, LXVIII, pp. 23, 29–30; Elton, *Tudor Revolution in Government*, pp. 238–41.
37 Loades, pp. 245–6.
38 Ponet, *Politike power*, I. iii b; Elton, *England under the Tudors*, p. 405, and *Tudor Revolution in Government*, p. 417; MacCaffrey, *Shaping of the Elizabethan Régime*, p. 99; A. G. R. Smith, *The Government of Elizabethan England*, p. 14.
39 G. P. Gooch, *English Democratic Ideas in the Seventeenth Century*, 2nd edn., ed. H. J. Laski (Cambridge, 1927), p. 32; MacCaffrey, 'Elizabethan Politics: the First Decade, 1558–1568', *PP*, 24 (April 1963), p. 41; Neale, *Elizabethan House of Commons*, p. 278.
40 Neale, *Elizabeth I and her Parliaments*, Vol. I, p. 128; Elton, *England under the Tudors*, p. 395.

CHAPTER 4: PAGES 71–112

1 A. G. Dickens, *Reformation and Society in Sixteenth-Century Europe*, p. 11.
2 *English Reformation*, pp. 22–37; E. G. Rupp, *Studies in the Making of the English Protestant Tradition*, pp. 1–14.
3 Rupp, pp. 15–46; *English Reformation*, pp. 59–82.
4 *English Reformation*, p. 81; C. H. and K. George, *The Protestant Mind of the English Reformation*, p. 12; R. H. Bainton, *The Reformation of the Sixteenth Century*, p. 197.
5 Scarisbrook, pp. 517–47.
6 T. Cranmer, *Miscellaneous Writings and Letters*, II, ed. J. E. Cox (Parker Soc., Cambridge, 1846), pp. 83–114, espec. 97; A. G. Dickens and Dorothy Carr, *The Reformation in England to the Accession of Elizabeth I*, p. 74.
7 Scarisbrook, pp. 544–7; Dickens and Carr, p. 115; *English Reformation*, pp. 184–6.
8 Jordan, II, p. 532; B. Gilpin, *Sermon . . . before King Edward VI* (1552), printed in *Life of Bernard Gilpin*, by W. Gilpin (London, 1752), p. 20; Chapman, p. 94; N. Pocock, *Troubles connected with the Prayer Book of 1549*, p. viii; *Chronicle*, p. 159.
9 *English Reformation*, p. 202.
10 Ibid., p. 219; *The First and Second Prayer Books of Edward VI*, introd. E. C. S. Gibson (Everyman, 1957 edn), pp. 29, 67, 72, 225; R. H. Bainton, *The Age of the Reformation*, p. 57; *Chronicle*, pp. 35–6.
11 Pocock, p. 169.
12 L. B. Smith, *Tudor Prelates and Politics, 1536–58*, pp. 252–3; O. Chadwick, *The Reformation*, p. 120; J. Strype, *Ecclesiastical*

Memorials (Oxford, 1822), II, Pt. ii, pp. 69–71; *The Acts and Monuments of John Foxe*, ed. G. Townsend, VII (London, 1847), p. 435.
13 H. C. Porter (ed.), *Puritanism in Tudor England*, p. 20.
14 C. Wriothesley, *Chronicle*, II, p. 47; N. Ridley, *The Works of Nicholas Ridley*, ed. H. Christmas (Parker Society, Cambridge, 1843), pp. 319–24.
15 C. W. Dugmore, *The Mass and the English Reformers*, pp. 58, 130, 156–8; P. N. Brooks, *Thomas Cranmer's Doctrine of the Eucharist*, pp. xvi, 38–9, 60, 64, 68–9, 98.
16 W. P. Haugaard, *Elizabeth and the English Reformation*, p. 17; *English Reformation*, p. 234; J. Ridley, *John Knox*, pp. 75, 85.
17 Bainton, *Age of the Reformation*, p. 57; O. Chadwick, *The Reformation*, p. 121; *English Reformation*, p. 248; *Prayer Books of Edward VI*, ed. Gibson, p. 389.
18 *Prayer Books*, pp. 392–3; Haugaard, pp. 15–16.
19 *English Reformation*, pp. 251–3.
20 Ibid., p. 252; I. B. Horst, *The Radical Brethren. Anabaptism and the English Reformation to 1558*, passim; *Proclamations*, I, pp. 227–8; H. Robinson, ed., *Original Letters Relative to the English Reformation*, (Cambridge, 1846), I, p. 87; J. Veron, Introduction to H. Bullinger, *A most necessary & frutefull Dialogue* (Worcester, 1551), c. iii; *Chronicle*, pp. 28, 58; Veron, B. iiii; P. Hughes, *The Reformation in England*, II, pp. 261–3; *English Reformation*, p. 267; I. B. Horst, 'Anabaptism in England', *Mennonite Encyclopedia*, II, pp. 216–17, and *Radical Brethren*, pp. 142n. 3, 151–2, 156–8.
21 F. W. Russell, *Kett's Rebellion*, p. 17.
22 *Queen Jane and ... Queen Mary*, pp. 115–21.
23 D. M. Loades, *The Oxford Martyrs*, p. 110.
24 Ibid., pp. 106–9.
25 *Proclamations*, II, pp. 5–6.
26 C. H. Garrett, *The Marian Exiles*, pp. 1, 4, 7.
27 *English Reformation*, p. 260; *Proclamations*, II, pp. 36–7.
28 C. Wriothesley, *Chronicle*, II, p. 114; Loades, *Oxford Martyrs*, pp. 125–6; *English Reformation*, p. 263; J. A. Muller, (ed.), *The Letters of Stephen Gardiner* (Cambridge, 1933), pp. 464–7.
29 *Proclamations*, II, pp. 48–9; Loades. *Oxford Martyrs*, p. 149.
30 W. Turner, *The Huntying of the Romyshe Wolfe* (c. 1554/5), A. iii. b.
31 Loades, *Oxford Martyrs*, p. 148; Dickens and Carr, *Reformation in England*, p. 13; J. Strype, *Ecclesiastical Memorials*, III, Pt. ii, pp. 482–4, 506–7.
32 Loades, pp. 151–5, 174, 214–20; N. Ridley, *Works*, pp. 395n., 415; P. N. Brooks, *Thomas Cranmer's Doctrine of the Eucharist*, p. 110, n. 1; J. G. Ridley, *Thomas Cranmer*, pp. 394–411.

33 T. Cranmer, *Miscellaneous Writings and Letters*, II, pp. 563–570; Ridley, *Cranmer*, pp. 394–411; Loades, pp. 226–32; *English Reformation*, p. 271.
34 Ibid., pp. 266–7; C. H. Garrett, *Marian Exiles*, p. 41; Loades, p. 12 (map).
35 *English Reformation*, pp. 264–6; Prescott, *Mary Tudor*, pp. 300–5; Loades, pp. 157–8.
36 O. Chadwick, *The Reformation*, p. 123; A. G. Dickens, *The Counter Reformation* (London, 1968), p. 86, and *English Reformation*, pp. 280, 331; C. Russell, *The Crisis of Parliaments*, pp. 142–3.
37 J. E. Neale, *Elizabeth I and her Parliaments*, I, pp. 23–6; Garrett, *Marian Exiles*, p. 59; G. P. Gooch, *English Democratic Ideas in the Seventeenth Century*, p. 30.
38 P. Collinson, *The Elizabethan Puritan Movement*, p. 29; W. P. Haugaard, *Elizabeth and the English Reformation*, p. 129; C. Russell, p. 149.
39 Strype, *Ecclesiastical Memorials*, III, Pt. ii, p. 542; Collinson, p. 61; E. I. Watkin, *Roman Catholicism in England from the Reformation to 1950* (Oxford, 1957), p. 17.
40 *Proclamations*, II, pp. 3, 99–100, 103; J. Hurstfield, *Elizabeth I and the Unity of England*, p. 32; Neale, *Elizabeth I and her Parliaments*, I, pp. 57–8; *English Reformation*, p. 299.
41 Ibid., p. 298; Neale, pp. 59–84; Haugaard, pp. 98–9.
42 Neale, pp. 59–84; *English Reformation*, pp. 302–3; V. J. K. Brook, *Whitgift and the English Church*, pp. 18–19.
43 P. McGrath, *Papists and Puritans under Elizabeth I*, p. 13; V. J. K. Brook, p. 21; *Proclamations*, II, pp. 117–32, 146–9.
44 Neale, p. 89; Brook, p. 22; Haugaard, pp. 208, 233, 333.
45 Collinson, *Elizabethan Puritan Movement*, p. 47; *English Reformation*, p. 313; McGrath, p. 57.
46 Claire Cross, *The Royal Supremacy in the Elizabethan Church*, p. 25.

CHAPTER 5: PAGES 113–148

1 S. T. Bindoff, *Tudor England*, p. 146.
2 G. A. J. Hodgett, *Agrarian England in the Later Middle Ages*, pp. 7, 10, 13, 16.
3 J. Thirsk, 'Enclosing and Engrossing', *AHEW*, IV, pp. 247–9; P. J. Bowden, *The Wool Trade in Tudor and Stuart England*, p. 5.
4 E. Kerridge, *Agrarian Problems in the Sixteenth Century and after*, p. 66; C. M. Gray, *Copyhold, Equity, and the Common Law*.
5 J. Strype, *Ecclesiastical Memorials*, II, Pt. ii, pp. 361–2; Kerridge, p. 121.

Notes

6 T. Lever, *Sermons 1550*, ed. E. Arber (London, 1870), p. 37.
7 I. Blanchard, 'Population Change, Enclosure and the Early Tudor Economy', *EconHR*, 2nd Ser., XXIII (1970), p. 439.
8 P. H. Ramsey, *Tudor Economic Problems*, p. 37.
9 S. T. Bindoff, *Ket's Rebellion*, p. 9; F. W. Russell, *Kett's Rebellion in Norfolk*, pp. 55–6.
10 S. T. Bindoff, p. 20; R. L. Palmer, *English Social History in the Making. The Tudor Revolution*, pp. 79–80; *Proclamations*, I, pp. 514–18.
11 J. U. Nef, 'The Progress of Technology and the Growth of Large-scale Industry in Great Britain, 1540–1640', in E. M. Carus-Wilson, *Essays in Economic History*, I, pp. 88–9.
12 Anon., *A Discourse of the Common Weal of this Realm of England* (1549, J. Hales or Sir T. Smith), ed. Elizabeth Lamond (Cambridge, 1893), p. 88; N. Pocock, *Troubles connected with the Prayer Book of 1549*, p. 10.
13 Ramsey, *Tudor Economic Problems*, pp. 53, 86; F. J. Fisher, 'Commercial Trends and Policy in Sixteenth-Century England', *EconHR*, X (1940), pp. 95–99; L. Stone, 'State Control in Sixteenth-Century England', *EconHR*, XVII (1947), pp. 104–8; P. J. Bowden, *The Wool Trade in Tudor and Stuart England*, pp. xvii, 6, 112; J. D. Gould, *The Great Debasement*, pp. 114–160; G. D. Ramsay, *English Overseas Trade during the Centuries of Emergence*, pp. 21–2.
14 S. T. Bindoff, 'The Making of the Statute of Artificers', in S. T. Bindoff et al (eds.), *Elizabethan Government and Society*, p. 56.
15 R. B. Outhwaite, *Inflation in Tudor and Early Stuart England*, pp. 9–14; Gould, *The Great Debasement*; C. E. Challis, 'The Circulating Medium and the Movement of Prices in Mid-Tudor England', in *The Price Revolution in Sixteenth-Century England*, ed. P. H. Ramsey, p. 133; W. C. Richardson, 'Some Financial Expedients of Henry VIII', *EconHR*, 2nd Ser., VI (1954), pp. 47–8.
16 *Proclamations*, I, pp. 518–19, 525, 529–30; C. E. Challis, 'The Debasement of the Coinage, 1542–1551', *EconHR*, 2nd Ser., XX (1967), p. 454.
17 Outhwaite, p. 42.
18 W. G. Hoskins, 'Harvest Fluctuations and English Economic History, 1480–1619', *AgHR* XII, Pt. i (1964), pp. 28–9, 32–3, 35–7; C. J. Harrison, 'Grain Price Analysis and Harvest Qualities, 1465–1634', *AgHR*, XIX, Pt. ii (1971), pp. 138, 153; J. Ponet, *Politike power*, K. viii; Gould, p. 83.
19 F. J. Fisher, 'Influenza and Inflation in Tudor England', *EconHR*, 2nd Ser., XVIII (1965), pp. 120–9.
20 Anon., *Discourse of the Common Weal*, pp. 33, 80–1; J. Heywood, *The Spider and the Flie* (1556), ed. J. S. Farmer (1908), pp. 196–8; W. Cholmeley, *The Request and Suite of*

204   *The Mid-Tudor Crisis, 1539–1563*

    a True-Hearted Englishman (1553), ed. W. J. Thoms, *Camden Miscellany* II (1853), pp. 11–12, 17–18.
21 P. F. Tytler, (ed.), *England under the Reigns of Edward VI and Mary* (London, 1839), pp. 365–6.
22 *Proclamations*, I, pp. 499–503, 504–9, 520–2, 529–30; W. R. D. Jones, *The Tudor Commonwealth 1529–1559*, pp. 148–9, lists the large number of Proclamations devoted to this problem; N. S. B. Gras, *The Evolution of the English Corn Market*, pp. 448–9.
23 Gould, pp. 11–12, 58, 83, 88.
24 Ibid., p. 64; *Proclamations*, II, pp. 169–70; 179–81.
25 E. H. Phelps Brown and S. V. Hopkins, 'Wage-rates and Prices...', *Economica*, New Ser., XXIV (1957), pp. 289–306; J. Cornwall, 'English Population in the Early Sixteenth Century', *EconHR*, 2nd Ser., XXIII (1970), pp. 32–44; N. S. B. Gras; A. Everitt, 'The Marketing of Agricultural Produce', *AHEW*, IV, pp. 466–592.
26 P. H. Ramsey, *Tudor Economic Problems*, p. 16; J. E. T. Rogers, *Six Centuries of Work and Wages* (London, 1891), p. 326; J. H. Clapham, *Concise Economic History of Britain. From the Earliest Times to 1750*, pp. 211–13; Phelps Brown and Hopkins, pp. 289, 291–4, 299; J. D. Gould, 'The Price Revolution Reconsidered', *EconHR*, 2nd Ser., XVII (1964), pp. 251, 265; Phelps Brown and Hopkins, 'Seven Centuries of the Price of Consumables, compared with Builders' Wage-rates', *Economica*, New Ser., XXIII (1956), p. 363.
27 W. K. Jordan, *Philanthropy in England, 1480–1660*, pp. 243, 367.
28 T. Becon, *Early Works*, (c. 1542–43), ed. J. Ayre (Parker Society, Cambridge, 1843), p. 40.
29 *Proclamations*, I, p. 352; G. R. Elton, *England under the Tudors*, p. 207; C. S. L. Davies, 'Slavery and Protector Somerset; the Vagrancy Act of 1547', *EconHR*, 2nd Ser., XIX (1966), pp. 537–8, 541–5.
30 R. B. Smith, *Land and Politics in the England of Henry VIII*, pp. 87–91, 109; A. Everitt, 'Farm Labourers', *AHEW*, IV, pp. 398–9; P. J. Bowden, 'Statistical Appendix, Table XVI', *AHEW*, IV, p. 865.
31 W. G. Hoskins, 'English Provincial Towns in the Early Sixteenth Century', *TRHS*, 5th Ser., 6 (1956), pp. 14, 18, 19; J. F. Pound, 'The Social and Trade Structure of Norwich, 1525–1575', *PP*, 34 (July 1966), pp. 50–1, 56; R. B. Smith, p. 119.
32 L. Stone, 'Social Mobility in England, 1500–1700', *PP*, 33 (April 1966), pp. 20, 23, 40, 48.
33 J. H. Hexter, 'Storm over the Gentry', in his *Reappraisals in History* (Aberdeen, 1961), pp. 117–62 – some works of relevance by Everitt, MacCaffrey, Stone, Tawney and Trevor-Roper are listed in the Bibliography, but even an outline

book-list on this topic is impossible in the space available;
J. A. Youings, *The Dissolution of the Monasteries*, pp. 15, 19,
116, 125–8, 130, and 'Landlords in England. C. The Church',
AHEW, IV, pp. 338, 343–4, 349; H. J. Habbakuk, 'The Market
for Monastic Property, 1539–1603', *EconHR*, 2nd Ser., x
(1958), pp. 336, 366, 376–8, 380; G. W. O. Woodward, *The Dissolution of the Monasteries*, pp. 124, 130–4; R. B. Smith, p. 213.
34 *The Two Books of Homilies Appointed to be Read in Churches*, ed. J. Griffiths (Oxford, 1859), p. 105; W. Turner, *A new book of spirituall Physik* (1555), pp. 85, 85.b; P. F. Tytler, *England under ... Edward VI and Mary*, I, p. 209.
35 Turner, pp. 50.b, 52; J. Hales, 'Bill on Decay of Tillage' (1548), printed in *Discourse*, ed. E. Lamond, xlvi; T. Becon, *The Fortress of the Faithful* (1550), in *The Catechism of Thomas Becon*, ed. J. Ayre (Parker Society, Cambridge, 1844), pp. 598–600.
36 Anon., *The Institucion of a gentleman* (1555), pp. 39–42, 51–4; T. Cranmer, *Miscellaneous Writings and Letters*, II, pp. 398–9; Sir R. Morison, *A Remedy For Sedition* (1536), A.ii.b, B.i.b; Sir J. Cheke, *The hurt of sedition* (1549), printed in Raphael Holinshed's *Chronicles*, III (London, 1808 edn.), p. 990.
37 J. Heywood, *The Spider and the Flie* (1556), pp. 195–9; Cranmer, II, pp. 194–6; Cheke, p. 989; R. Crowley, *The Way to Wealth* (1551), in *Works*, ed. J. M. Cowper (London, 1872), pp. 132–3.
38 D. Wilkins, *Concilia Magnae Britanniae et Hiberniae*, III (London, 1837), pp. 727–32; Sir T. More, *The supplicacion of soules*, in *The Workes of Sir Thomas More Knyght* (London, 1557), p. 313.
39 I. B. Horst, *The Radical Brethren*, p. 107; T. Starkey, *Exhortation to the people* (1536), pp. 34, 72–72.ii; F. W. Russell, *Kett's Rebellion in Norfolk*, pp. 16–17; Tytler, I, p. 219; N. Pocock, *Troubles connected with the Prayer Book of 1549*, p. 90–2.

CHAPTER 6: PAGES 149–189

1 R. B. Wernham, *Before the Armada: the Growth of English Foreign Policy, 1485–1588*, pp. 13–16.
2 Ibid., p. 138.
3 Scaribrick, p. 470.
4 Wernham, p. 148.
5 C. J. Black and C. E. Challis, (eds.) *Henry VIII to his Ambassadors at the Diet of Ratisbon, 17 June 1541* (York, 1968); G. R. Elton, *England under the Tudors*, p. 196; Wernham, pp. 149–50; Scarisbrick, pp. 548–50.
6 G. Donaldson, in S. T. Bindoff *et. al.* (eds.), *Elizabethan*

Government and Society, p. 312; J. D. Mackie, *The Earlier Tudors, 1485–1558*, p. 406.
7 Mackie, p. 407; Donaldson, p. 284; Scarisbrick, p. 563; Wernham, p. 154; *Chronicle of the Grey Friars of London*, p. 45; Wernham, p. 155.
8 A. F. Pollard, *Political History*, VI, p. 10; J. Ridley, *John Knox*, p. 34.
9 J. R. Hale, 'Armies, Navies, and the Art of War', *NCMH*, II, p. 494; C. S. L. Davies, 'Provision for Armies, 1509–50', *EconHR*, 2nd Ser., XVII (1964), pp. 234, 244; Scarisbrick, p. 581.
10 Scarisbrick, p. 586.
11 C. Russell, *The Crisis of Parliaments*, p. 31; Wernham, pp. 161–1.
12 *The Letters of Stephen Gardiner*, ed. J. A. Muller (Cambridge, 1933), pp. 183–90, 198–9; Scarisbrick, p. 588.
13 A. Fraser, *Mary Queen of Scots*, p. 26; Scarisbrick, p. 602; Elton, *England under the Tudors*, p. 199.
14 Jordan, I, p. 238; Wernham, p. 164.
15 *Letters of Gardiner*, p. 267; Pollard, p. 11.
16 Jordan, I, pp. 263–4; Donaldson, pp. 285–7; Somerset's 'Epistle' printed in *Holinshed's Chronicles*, III (London, 1808), pp. 910–16.
17 Jordan, I, p. 295; E. H. Harbison, *Rival Ambassadors at the Court of Queen Mary*, p. 16.
18 Jordan, I, pp. 244, 247, 253, 300.
19 R. Crowley, *The Fable of Philargyrie The Great Gigant* (1551), ed. W. A. Marsden (London, 1931), D.vi.(a); Pollard, p. 48; Conyers Read, *Mr. Secretary Cecil and Queen Elizabeth*, p. 69; Wernham, p. 178.
20 Wernham, p. 189.
21 Jordan, II, pp. 137–41; *Chronicle*, pp. 56, 78; C. Read, p. 68.
22 Wernham, p. 200; Harbison, p. 15.
23 Harbison, pp. viii, 49.
24 Harbison, p. 29.
25 Harbison, 'French Intrigue at the Court of Queen Mary', *AHR*, XLV (April 1940), p. 548.
26 *Proclamations*, II, pp. 21–6.
27 Wernham, p. 218; *Proclamations*, II, pp. 33–4; *Chronicle of Queen Jane and ... Queen Mary*, pp. 34–5, 67.
28 Harbison, pp. 90–1; *Proclamations*, II, pp. 77–9.
29 Wernham, p. 232.
30 Harbison, p. viii; Pollard, p. 172.
31 Wernham, p. 239; C. Read, p. 124.
32 C. Read, p. 126.
33 W. Camden, *History of the ... Princess Elizabeth*, ed. W. T. MacCaffrey, p. 15; G. W. O. Woodward, *Reformation and Resurgence* (London, 1963), p. 139; J. E. Neale, *Queen Elizabeth*, p. 76.

34 Elton, *England under the Tudors*, pp. 264–5.
35 R. B. Wernham, *NCMH*, III, Chap. VIII, 'The British Question 1559–69', p. 210; G. Donaldson, in S. T. Bindoff *et al.* (eds.) *Elizabethan Government and Society*, p. 310.
36 J. G. Ridley, *John Knox*, pp. 299–301, 315, 318–30.
37 Ridley, p. 337; Neale, pp. 99–100.
38 *Proclamations*, II, pp. 141–4.
39 N. M. Sutherland, 'Queen Elizabeth and the Conspiracy of Amboise, March 1560', *EHR*, LXXXI (1966), p. 488; A. Fraser, *Mary Queen of Scots*, p. 97; Ridley, pp. 376, 386–7.
40 Fraser, p. 107; Ridley, p. 385.
41 C. Read, p. 316.
42 W. Camden, *History* . . ., p. 38; R. B. Wernham, private correspondence; C. Read, p. 260.
43 W. T. MacCaffrey, *The Shaping of the Elizabethan Régime*, pp. 55–6.

CHAPTER 7: PAGES 190–195

1 W. T. MacCaffrey, 'The Crown and the New Aristocracy, 1540–1600', *PP*, 30 (April 1965), p. 63.
2 Above, p. 40; C. Russell, *The Crisis of Parliaments*, p. 123; J. Ponet, *Politike power*, I.iii.b.
3 D. M. Loades, *The Oxford Martyrs*, p. 139; J. G. Ridley, *Cranmer*, p. 345.

Select Bibliography

This reading list is restricted to secondary works of particular relevance for the student of the mid-Tudor crisis. Primary sources are not included – a representative list of the type consulted may be found in *The Tudor Commonwealth, 1529–1559*, pp. 228–34.

Allen, J. W., *A History of Political Thought in the Sixteenth Century* (London, 1951).
Anglo, S., *Spectacle, Pageantry, and Early Tudor Policy* (Oxford, 1969).
Aston, M. E., 'Lollardy and the Reformation: Survival or Revival?' *History*, XLIX (1964), 149–70.
Bainton, R. H., *The Reformation of the Sixteenth Century* (London, 1953).
— *The Age of the Reformation* (Princeton, 1956).
Baumer, F. le V., *The Tudor Theory of Kingship* (New Haven, 1940).
Beresford, M. W., *The Lost Villages of England* (London, 1954).
— 'The Poll Tax and the Census of Sheep, 1549', *AgHR*, I (1953), 9–15, and II (1954), 15–29.
Bindoff, S. T., *Tudor England* (London, 1966).
— *Ket's Rebellion* (Historical Association Pamphlet No. 12, 1949).
— 'The Making of the Statute of Artificers', in *Elizabethan Government and Society*, ed. S. T. Bindoff et al. (London, (1961).
— 'A Kingdom at Stake', *History Today*, 3 (Sept. 1953), 642–8.
Blanchard, I., 'Population Change, Enclosure, and the Early Tudor Economy', *EconHR*, 2nd Ser., XXIII (1970), 427–45.
Bowden, P. J., *The Wool Trade in Tudor and Stuart England* (London, 1962).
— 'Wool Supply and the Woollen Industry', *EconHR*, 2nd Ser., IX (1956), 44–58.
— 'Agricultural Prices, Farm Profits, and Rents', in *AHEW*, IV, 593–695.
Brenner, Y. S., 'The Inflation of Prices in Early Sixteenth-Century England', *EconHR*, 2nd Ser., XIV (1961), 225–39.

— 'The Inflation of Prices in England, 1551–1650', *EconHR*, 2nd Ser., xv (1962), 266–84.
Brook, V. J. K., *A Life of Archbiship Parker* (Oxford, 1962).
— *Whitgift and the English Church* (London, 1964).
Brooks, P., *Thomas Cranmer's Doctrine of the Eucharist* (London, 1965).
Brown, E. H. Phelps and Hopkins, S. V., 'Seven Centuries of the Price of Consumables, compared with Builders' Wage-rates', *Economica*, New Ser., xxiii (1956), 296–314.
— 'Wage-rates and Prices: Evidence for Population Pressure in the Sixteenth Century', *Economica*, New Ser., xxiv (1957), 289–306.
Carr, Dorothy *see* Dickens, A. G.
Caspari, F., *Humanism and the Social Order in Tudor England* (Chicago, 1954).
Chadwick, O., *The Reformation* (London, 1964).
Challis, C. E., 'The Debasement of the Coinage, 1542–1551', *EconHR*, 2nd Ser., xx (1967), 441–66.
— 'The Circulating Medium and the Movement of Prices in Mid-Tudor England', in P. H. Ramsey (ed.), *The Price Revolution in Sixteenth-Century England* (London, 1972), 117–46.
— 'Currency and the Economy in Mid-Tudor England', *EconHR*, 2nd Ser., xxv (1972), 313–22.
Chapman, H. W., *The Last Tudor King* (London, 1958).
Clapham, J. H., *A Concise Economic History of Britain: From the Earliest Times to 1750* (Cambridge, 1949).
— and Power, E., (eds), *The Cambridge Economic History of Europe, I, Agriculture* (Cambridge, 1941).
Collinson, P., *The Eizabethan Puritan Movement* (London, 1967).
Cornwall, J., 'English Population in the Early Sixteenth Century', *EconHR*, 2nd Ser., xxiii (1970), 32–44.
Cross, M. Claire, *The Royal Supremacy in the Elizabethan Church* (London and New York, 1969).
Darby, H. S. *Hugh Latimer* (London, 1953).
Davies, C. S. L., 'Provision for Armies, 1509–50', *EconHR*, 2nd Ser., xvii (1964), 234–48.
— 'Slavery and Protector Somerset; the Vagrancy Act of 1547', *EconHR*, 2nd Ser., xix (1966), 533–49.
Dickens, A. G., *Lollards and Protestants in the Diocese of York, 1509–1558* (Oxford, 1959).
— *Thomas Cromwell and the English Reformation* (London, 1959).
— *The English Reformation* (London and New York, 1964).
— *Reformation and Society in Sixteenth Century Europe* (London, 1966).
— *The Age of Humanism and Reformation* (New Jersey, 1972).
— 'The Radical Reformation', *PP*, 27 (April 1964), 123–5.

Dickens, A. G. and Carr Dorothy, *The Reformation in England to the Accession of Elizabeth I* (London, 1967).
Dietz, F. C., *English Government Finance, 1485–1558* (Urbana, 1921).
Donaldson, G., 'Foundations of Anglo-Scottish Union', in S. T. Bindoff et al. (eds), *Elizabethan Government and Society* (London, 1961), 282–314.
Dugmore, C. W., *The Mass and the English Reformers* (London, 1958).
Elliott, J. H., 'Revolution and Continuity in Early Modern Europe', *PP*, 42 (Feb. 1969), 34–56.
Elton, G. R., *The Tudor Revolution in Government* (Cambridge, 1953).
— *England Under the Tudors* (London, 1957).
— *The Tudor Constitution* (Cambridge, 1960).
— *Henry VIII: an Essay in Revision* (Historical Association Pamphlet No. 51, 1962).
— *Policy and Police. The Enforcement of the Reformation in the Age of Thomas Cromwell* (Cambridge, 1972).
— (ed.), *The New Cambridge Modern History, II, The Reformation* (Cambridge, 1958).
— 'Thomas Cromwell's Decline and Fall', *Cambridge Historical Journal*, 10 (no. 2, 1951), 150–85.
— 'The Political Creed of Thomas Cromwell', *TRHS*, 5th Ser., 6 (1956), 69–92.
Emmison, F. G., 'A Plan of Edward VI and Secretary Petre for Re-organising the Privy Council's Work, 1552–3', *BIHR*, 31 (Nov. 1958), 203–10.
Everitt, A., 'The Marketing of Agricultural Produce', in *AHEW*, IV, 466–592.
— 'Social Mobility in Early Modern England', *PP*, 33 (April 1966), 56–73.
Feaveayear, A. E., *The Pound Sterling*, ed. E. V. Morgan (Oxford, 1963).
Ferguson, A. B., *The Articulate Citizen and the English Renaissance* (Durham, N.C., 1965).
Fisher, F. J., 'Commercial Trends and Policy in Sixteenth-Century England', *EconHR*, x (1940), 95–117.
— 'The Development of the London Food Market. 1540–1640', in E. M. Carus-Wilson (ed.), *Essays in Economic History*, I (London, 1955).
— 'The Sixteenth and Seventeenth Centuries: the Dark Ages in English Economic History?', *Economica*, New Ser., XXIV (1957), 1–18.
— 'Influence and Inflation in Tudor England', *EconHR*, 2nd Ser., XVIII (1965), 120–9
— (ed.), *Essays in the Economic and Social History of Tudor and Stuart England* (Cambridge, 1961).

Fisher, H. A. L., *The Political History of England*, V, *1485–1547* (London, 1913).
Fraser, A., *Mary Queen of Scots* (London, 1969).
Garrett, C. H., *The Marian Exiles* (Cambridge, 1938).
George, C. H. and K., *The Protestant Mind of the English Reformation, 1570–1640* (Princeton, New Jersey, 1961).
Gould, J. D., *The Great Debasement* (Oxford, 1970).
— 'The Price Revolution Reconsidered', *EconHR*, 2nd Ser., XVII (1964), 249–66.
— 'Y. S. Brenner on Prices: a Comment', *EconHR*, 2nd Ser., XVI (1963), 351–60.
Gras, N. S. B., *The Evolution of the English Corn Market* (Cambridge, Mass., 1915).
Gray, C. M., *Copyhold, Equity, and the Common Law* (Cambridge, Mass., 1963).
Habbakuk, H. J. 'The Market for Monastic Property, 1539–1603', *EconHR*, 2nd Ser., X (1958), 362–80.
Hale, J. R., 'Armies, Navies, and the Art of War', in *NCMH*, II, *The Reformation*, ed. G. R. Elton (Cambridge, 1958), 481–509.
Harbison, E. H., *Rival Ambassadors at the Court of Queen Mary* (Princeton, 1940).
— 'French Intrigue at the Court of Queen Mary', *AHR*, 45 (April 1940), 533–51.
Harrison, C. J., 'Grain Price Analysis and Harvest Qualities, 1465–1634', *AgHR*, 19, pt.ii (1971), 135–55.
Harriss, G. L., 'Medieval Government and Statecraft', *PP*, 25 (July 1963), 8–39.
Haugaard, W. P., *Elizabeth and the English Reformation* (Cambridge, 1968).
Heaton, H., *The Yorkshire Woollen and Worsted Industries* (Oxford, 1920).
Heckscher, E. F., *Mercantilism*, trans. M. Shapiro, revised edn, ed. E. F. Söderbund, 2 vols (London, 1955).
Hexter, J. H., *Reappraisals in History* (Aberdeen, 1961, New York and Evanston, Ill., 1963).
Hodgett, G. A. J., *Agrarian England in the Later Middle Ages* (Historical Association, Aids for Teachers No. 13, 1966).
Hopf, C. L. R. A., *Martin Bucer and the English Reformation* (Oxford, 1946).
Hopkins, S. V., *see* Brown, E. H. Phelps.
Horst, I. B., *The Radical Brethren. Anabaptism and the English Reformation to 1558* (Nieuwkoop, 1972).
— 'Anabaptism in England', in *The Mennonite Encyclopedia*, ed. H. S. Bender and C. H. Smith, II (Scottdale, Penn., 1956), 215–21.
Hoskins, W. G., *Essays in Leicestershire History* (Liverpool, 1950).

Hoskins, W. G., 'English Provincial Towns in the Early Sixteenth Century', *TRHS*, 5th Ser., 6 (1956), 1–20.
— 'Harvest Fluctuations and English Economic History, 1480–1619', *AgHR*, XII, pt.i (1964), 28–46.
Hughes, P., *The Reformation in England, II, The King's Proceedings* (London, 1950).
— *The Reformation in England, II, Religio Depopulata* (London, 1953).
Hughes, P. L., and Larkin, J. F., (eds), *Tudor Royal Proclamations, I, The Early Tudors (1485–1553)* (New Haven, 1964).
— *Tudor Royal Proclamations, II, The Later Tudors (1553–87)* (New Haven and London, 1969).
Hurstfield, J., *Elizabeth I and the Unity of England* (London, 1960).
— (ed.), *The Reformation Crisis* (London, 1965).
— 'Corruption and Reform under Edward VI and Mary: the Example of Wardship', *EHR*, LXVIII 1953), 22–36.
— 'Political Corruption in Modern England', *History*, LII, no. 174 (Feb. 1967) 16–34.
— 'Was there a Tudor Despotism after all?', *TRHS*, 5th Ser., 17 (1967), 83–108.
Jones, W. R. D., *The Tudor Commonwealth, 1529–1559* (London, 1970).
Jordan, W. K., *The Development of Religious Toleration in England*, I (London, 1932).
— *Philanthropy in England 1480–1660* (London and New York, 1959).
— (ed.), *The Chronicle and Political Papers of King Edward VI* (Ithaca, N. York, and London, 1966).
— *Edward VI: the Young King* (London, 1968).
— *Edward VI: the Threshold of Power* (London 1970).
Kerridge, E., The Agricultural Revolution (London, 1967).
— *Agrarian Problems in the Sixteenth Century and after* (London and New York, 1969).
— 'The Movement of Rent, 1540–1640', *EconHR*, 2nd Ser., VI (1953), 16–34.
  'The Returns of the Inquisitions of Depopulation', *EHR*, LXX (1955), 212–28.
Kramer, Stella, *The English Craft Gilds* (New York, 1927).
Larkin, J. F., see Hughes, P. L.
Lehmberg, S. E., *Sir Walter Mildmay and Tudor Government* (Austin, Texas, 1964).
Leonard, E. M., *The Early History of English Poor Relief* (Cambridge, 1900).
Levine, M., *The Early Elizabethan Succession Question, 1558–1568* (Stanford, 1966).
— *Tudor England, 1485–1603* (Bibliography) (Cambridge and New York, 1968).

Loades, D. M., *Two Tudor Conspiracies* (Cambridge, 1965).
— *The Oxford Martyrs* (London, 1970).
MacCaffrey, W. T., *The Shaping of the Elizabethan Régime* (Princeton, 1968, and London, 1969).
— 'Elizabethan Politics: the First Decade, 1558–1568'. *PP*, 24 (April 1963), 25–41.
— 'The Crown and the New Aristocracy, 1540–1600', *PP*, 30 (April 1965), 52–64.
Mackie, J. D., *The Earlier Tudors, 1485–1558* (Oxford, 1957).
— 'Henry VIII and Scotland', *TRHS*, 4th Ser., 29 (1947), 93–114.
McConica, J. K., *English Humanists and Reformation Politics* (Oxford, 1965).
McGrath, P., *Papists and Puritans under Elizabeth I* (London, 1967).
Mattingly, G., *Renaissance Diplomacy* (London, 1955).
Morris C., *Political Thought in England. Tyndale to Hooker* (Oxford, 1953).
Neale, J. E., *Queen Elizabeth* (London, 1960).
— *The Elizabethan House of Commons* (London, 1963).
— *Elizabeth I and her Parliaments, Vol. I, 1559–1581* (London, 1969).
Nef, J. U., *Industry and Government in France and England, 1540–1640* (Philadelphia, 1940).
— 'The Progress of Technology and the Growth of Large-scale Industry in Great Britain, 1540–1640', in E. M. Carus-Wilson (ed.), *Essays in Economic History*, I (London, 1955).
— 'Prices and Industrial Capitalism in France and England, 1540–1640', *EconHR*, VIII (1937), 155–85.
Outhwaite, R. B., *Inflation in Tudor and Early Stuart England* (London, 1969).
Palmer, R. L., *English Social History in the Making. The Tudor Revolution* (London, 1934).
Parker, T. M., *The English Reformation to 1558* (Oxford, 1952).
Pollard, A. F., *England under Protector Somerset* (London, 1900).
— *The Political History of England, VI, 1547–1603* (London, 1910).
Porter, H. C., (ed.), *Puritanism in Tudor England* (London, 1970).
Pound, J. F., 'An Elizabethan Census of the Poor: the Treatment of Vagrancy in Norwich, 1570–1580', *University of Birmingham Historical Journal*, 8 (No. 2, 1962), 135–61.
— 'The Social and Trade Structure of Norwich, 1525–1575', *PP*, 34 (July 1966), 49–69.
Power, E., *see* Clapham, J. H.
Prescott, H. F. M., *Mary Tudor* (London, 1952; published as *Spanish Tudor*, New York, 1940).
Ramsay, G. D., *The Wiltshire Woollen Industry in the Sixteenth and Seventeenth Centuries* (Oxford, 1943).

Ramsay, G. D., *English Overseas Trade during the Centuries of Emergence* (London, 1957).
Ramsey, P. H., Tudor Economic Problems (London, 1963).
— (ed.), *The Price Revolution in Sixteenth-Century England* (London, 1971).
Read, C., *Mr. Secretary Cecil and Queen Elizabeth* (London, 1955).
— (ed.), *Bibliography of British History: Tudor Period, 1485–1603* (Oxford, 2nd edn, 1959).
Richardson, W. C., 'Some Financial Expedients of Henry VIII', *EconHR*, 2nd Ser., VII (1954), 33–48.
Ridley, J. G., *Nicholas Ridley* (London, 1957).
— *Thomas Cranmer* (Oxford, 1962).
— *John Knox* (Oxford, 1968).
Rose-Troup, F., *The Western Rebellion of 1549* (London, 1913).
Rupp, E. G., *Studies in the Making of the English Protestant Tradition* (Cambridge, 1947).
Russell, C., *The Crisis of Parliaments. English History 1509–1660* (Oxford, 1971).
Russell, F. W., *Kett's Rebellion in Norfolk* (London, 1859).
Scarisbrick, J. J., *Henry VIII* (London and Berkeley, Calif., 1968).
Slavin, A. J., *Politics and Profit. A Study of Sir Ralph Sadler 1507–1547* (Cambridge, 1966).
Smith, A. G. R., *The Government of Elizabethan England* (London, 1967).
Smith, L. B., *Tudor Prelates and Politics, 1536–58* (Princeton, N. J., 1953).
— *Henry VIII. The Mask of Royalty* (London, 1971).
— 'Henry VIII and the Protestant Triumph', *AHR*, 71 (July 1966), 1237–64.
Smith, R. B., *Land and Politics in the England of Henry VIII* (Oxford, 1970).
Stone, L., *The Crisis of the Aristocracy, 1558–1641* (Oxford, 1965).
— *Social Change and Revolution in England, 1540–1640* (London, 1965).
— 'State Control in Sixteenth-Century England', *EconHR*, XVII (1947), 103–20.
— 'Social Mobility in England, 1500–1700', *PP*, 33 (April 1966), 16–55.
Sutherland, N. M. 'Queen Elizabeth and the Conspiracy of Amboise, March 1560', *EHR*, LXXXI (1966), 474–89.
Tawney, R. H., *The Agrarian Problem in the Sixteenth Century* (London, 1912).
— *Religion and the Rise of Capitalism* (London, 1942).
— 'The Rise of the Gentry, 1558–1640', *EconHR*, XI (1941), 1–38.
Thirsk, J., *Tudor Enclosures* (Historical Association Pamphlet No. 41, 1959).

— (ed.), *The Agrarian History of England and Wales, IV, 1500–1640* (Cambridge, 1967).
Trevor-Roper, H. R., *The Gentry, 1540–1640* (EconHR Supplements, No. 1, Cambridge, 1953).
— *Historical Essays* (London, 1957).
Unwin, G., *Industrial Organisation in the Sixteenth and Seventeenth Centuries* (Oxford, 1904).
— *The Gilds and Companies of London* (London, 1908).
Webb, S. and B., *English Local Government: English Poor Law History: Part I. The Old Poor Law* (London, 1927).
Wernham, R. B., *Before the Armada: the Growth of English Foreign Policy, 1485–1588* (London, 1966).
— (ed.), *New Cambridge Modern History, III, The Counter-Reformation and Price Revolution, 1559–1610* (Cambridge, 1968).
Williams, G. H., *The Radical Reformation* (Philadelphia and London, 1962).
Williams, P., and Harriss, G. L., 'A Revolution in Tudor History?', *PP*, 25 (July 1963), 3–58.
Woodward, G. W. O., *The Dissolution of the Monasteries* (London, 1966).
Youings, J. A., *The Dissolution of the Monasteries* (London and New York, 1971).
— 'Landlords in England: The Church', in *AHEW*, IV, 306–56.
Zeeveld, W. G., *Foundations of Tudor Policy* (Harvard, 1948).

Index

Africa, 172
Agriculture, 113, 114–21, 128, 134, 139; *see also* Enclosure, Open Fields, Pasture, Rents, Tillage
Alderney, 175
Alva, Ferdinand Alvarez de Toledo, Duke of, 26
Amboise, Conspiracy of, 184, 186
America, New World, 133, 172, 173
Anabaptism, Anabaptists, 80, 89–91, 100, 109, 146, 194
Ancrum Moor, Battle of, 157
Angers, Treaty of, 167
Anglicanism, Church of England, 2, 89, 106, 109–10, 111–12
Anne of Cleves, Queen of England, 8–9, 15, 152
Antwerp, 125, 131, 172, 188
Arable: *see* Tillage
Aragon, 13
Ardres, Treaty of, 159, 162, 164
Aristocracy: *see* Nobility
Armada, the Spanish, 22, 188
Armed forces: *see* Crown, military resources of
Arran, James Hamilton, 2nd Earl of, and Duke of Châtelherault, 156, 183, 186
— James Hamilton, 3rd Earl of, 186
Arthur, Prince of Wales, 7, 8, 15
Articles of Religion, the Ten, 77; the Six, 2, 77, 78, 81, 82–3, 95, 152; the Forty-two, 89, 110; the Thirty-nine, 89, 109, 110, 111; the Eleven, 109
Artificers, Statute of: *see* Statutes
Arundel, Henry Fitzalan, Earl of, 19, 61
Ascham, Roger, 28
Augmentations, Court of, 57
Augsburg, Interim of, 160

Bacon, Sir Francis, 104, 107
Barnes, Robert, 73, 77
Beaton, David, Cardinal, 151, 155, 156, 159
Becon, Thomas, 136
Bedford, Earl of: *see* Russell, Lord John
Beggars, begging, 136, 137, 138–9; *see also* Charity, Poverty, Vagabonds
Berwick, Treaty of, 184
Bible, Scriptures, 73–4, 79, 81, 83, 85, 86, 156, 162
— the 'Great', 78
Bindoff, S. T., 4, 16, 22, 62, 113, 125
Bishops, 76, 78, 94, 97, 102, 105, 109, 110, 111
Bishops' Book, The, 76–7
Bocher, Joan ('Joan of Kent'), 90
Bodmin, 47
Body, Archdeacon William, 47
Boleyn, Anne, Queen of England, 7, 8, 15, 20, 31
Bonner, Edmund, Bishop of London, 84, 100, 101, 102
Bothwell, James Hepburn, Earl of, 31
Boulogne, 46, 138, 157–68 passim, 174–5, 176
Bowden, P. J., 116
Bradford, John, 194
Brandon, Charles, Duke of Suffolk, 15, 16
— Frances, 15, 16
Brighton, 158
Brittany, 163
Brook, V. J. K., 108
Brooks, P. N., 86, 87
Brussels, 172
Bucer, Martin, 87

Index

Bullinger, Johann Heinrich, 87, 90, 146
Burgundy, Burgundian, 25, 149, 171, 172, 179

Calais, 152, 161, 168, 174–5, 177, 178, 183, 187
Calvin, John, 80, 85, 87, 103, 185
Calvinism, Calvinists, 79, 82, 86, 87, 89, 106, 107, 109, 110, 111
Cambridge, 19, 27, 73
— University, 87
Camden, William, 179
Caraffa, Gian Pietro: *see* Paul IV, Pope
Carlos, Don, 33, 171
Castilian, 172
Cateau-Cambrésis, Treaty of, 107, 175, 178–9, 180
Catherine de Medici, 185–6, 187
Catherine of Aragon, Queen of England, 7, 8, 15, 20, 31, 169
Catholicism, Catholics, 2, 3, 4, 10, 11, 16, 21, 54, 65, 71–111 passim, 147, 160, 176, 185, 186
— Roman: *see* Papacy, Papistry, Rome, Church of
Cecil, William, later Lord Burghley, 4, 30, 57, 68, 107, 120, 131, 148, 167, 182, 187, 192
Challis, C. E., 127
Channel, the English, 160; *see also* Narrow Seas
Chantries, Dissolution of, 81
Chapuys, Eustace, Imperial Ambassador, 20
Charing Cross, 56
Charity, 135–7, 138, 145; *see also* Beggars, Poverty
Charles V, Emperor, 20, 21, 23, 60, 151–72 passim
Charles IX, King of France, 185
Châtelherault, Duke of: *see* Arran, Earl of
Cheape(side), 95
Cheke, Sir John, 11, 17, 27, 100, 144
Cholmeley, William, 130, 131
Church, the, 71–111 passim, 194
 income, property, wealth, 3, 39, 73, 74, 81, 83, 84, 91, 96, 154
 lands, 43, 96, 97, 141–2, 159

 Royal Supremacy over, 20, 36, 37, 74–6, 92–6 passim, 105–111 passim, 154, 191, 194; *see also* Statutes
 see also entries under Religion
Church of England: *see* Anglicanism
Churchill, Sir Winston, 180–1
Clapham, Sir J. H., 134
Clergy, regular: *see* Religious houses
 secular, 74, 91, 95, 104, 105, 106, 108, 111
 see also Bishops, Convocation
Cleves, 3, 152
— House of, 152
Cloth, 115
 -manufacture, 122, 123–4, 125, 140
 export of, 114, 123, 124, 130, 148
 -subsidy, 120
 -workers, 123, 124
 see also Prices
Coinage, debasement of, 3, 39, 114, 124–33 passim, 159
— 'calling-down' of, 114, 125, 132
— Elizabethan reform of, 4–5, 114, 125, 132–3, 148
 see also Prices, Exchanges
Collinson, P., 103
Common Fields, Commons, 118, 119, 120, 143; *see also* Open Fields, Enclosure
Commons, House of, 24, 30, 66, 83, 94, 96, 106–7, 108, 138
Commonwealth Ideals, Men, 13, 42, 54, 119, 131, 137, 138, 147–8
Communion: *see* Eucharist
Condé, Henry, Prince de, 187
Convocation of Clergy, 83, 88, 97, 109, 110, 111, 152
Copyhold, 116
Corn, Grain, 115, 128, 129
Cornwall, 47
Council, King's, Privy, 2, 10, 14, 17, 19, 22, 25, 26, 38–70 passim, 87, 88, 89, 90, 96, 107, 124, 142, 167, 169, 170, 172, 173, 175, 190
— Regency, 10–11, 41, 80
Counter-Reformation, Catholic Reformation, 97, 102, 111
Courtenay, Edward, Earl of Devon, 24, 25

— House of, 47
Court, Royal, 21, 101, 169
Courts, Royal, of Revenue: see Augmentations, Exchequer, Wards
Coverdale, Miles, Bishop of Exeter, 110
Coventry, 140
Cox, Richard, Bishop of Ely, 11, 12, 106
Cranmer, Thomas, Archbishop of Canterbury, 8, 10, 17, 53, 73, 76–90 passim, 98–9, 143, 144, 193
Crediton, 47
Crépy, Treaty of, 157
Cromwell, Thomas, Earl of Essex, 2, 3, 8, 21, 36–8, 39, 40, 68, 72, 75, 77, 150, 152
Cross, M. Claire, 111
Crowley, Robert, 145; *Philargyrie*, 165
Crown, power and prestige of, 1–2, 37, 40, 44, 56, 64, 72, 149, 150, 191, 194–5
  succession to, 1–9 passim, 14–35 passim, 59, 69, 92, 149, 150, 154, 155, 160, 161, 170–1, 180, 186, 190; see also Statutes
  finance, revenue, and expenditure of, 39, 46, 57–8, 66–7, 114, 127–8, 130, 131, 132–3, 149, 159, 175; see also Taxation
  lands of, 43, 97, 127, 141–2, 159, 166
  military resources and expenditure of, 3, 39, 46, 114, 127, 130, 157–9, 166, 175, 177
  revenue, Courts of: see Courts, Statutes
  see also Government, State, Church, Royal Supremacy over

Darnley, Henry Stuart, Lord, 15, 31
Davies, C. S. L., 138
Depopulation, 115, 117, 119
Devon, Earl of: see Courtenay, Edward
Devonshire, 47, 62
Dickens, A. G., 75, 88, 89, 100, 108
Dieppe, 187
Disraeli, Benjamin, 169

Divorce, the Royal, 72
Donaldson, G., 154, 180
Dormer, Jane, Duchess of Feria, 9, 11
Dudley, John, Lord Lisle, Earl of Warwick, Duke of Northumberland, 11–22 passim, 25, 28, 30, 42, 43, 50–9 passim, 83, 84, 92, 120, 125, 160, 161, 164–8, 169, 173, 176, 177, 192, 194
— Lord Guildford, 15, 16, 19, 25
— Robert, Earl of Leicester, 4, 30–31, 33, 68, 187, 190
Dudley Conspiracy, the, 64, 66, 173
Dugmore, C. W., 86
Dunbar, 156
Dussindale, Battle of, 50, 52

East Anglia, 18, 47, 92
Edinburgh, 156, 162
Edinburgh, Treaty of, 185
Edward VI, King of England, 1, 2, 8–17 passim, 21, 22, 27, 28, 34, 40, 41, 43, 54, 57–60 passim, 67, 68, 72, 79, 83, 84, 88–91 passim, 100, 106, 107, 108, 124, 129, 132, 141, 151, 154, 155, 160, 161, 167, 169, 176, 189, 190, 193
  his *Chronicle*, 22, 52, 55, 56, 82, 167
  his 'Discourse', 57, 79
Edward the Confessor, Arms of, 10
Elizabeth I, Queen of England, 1–5 passim, 8, 9, 13–34 passim, 67–70, 72, 78, 103–11 passim, 129, 132, 133, 154, 169, 176, 177–180, 182–9, 190–1, 192
Elton, G. R., 3, 36–7, 38, 40, 138, 153, 192
Emden, 188
Empire, Holy Roman, 168
Enclosure, 49, 114, 115, 116, 117, 118–20, 138, 143
  governmental policy towards, 114, 119, 120–1
  Commissions on, 117, 118, 120
  see also Engrossing, Statutes (Tillage)
Engrossing, of land, 117, 118
Erastianism, 81, 193
Essex, 55, 90

Index

Essex, Earl of: *see* Cromwell, Thomas
Eucharist, Communion, Mass, 22, 74, 77, 80–1, 82, 85, 86–7, 87–8, 89, 95, 99, 107, 108, 109, 110
  see also Prayer Books, Sacramentarianism, Transubstantiation
Everitt, A., 140
Exchanges, foreign, 124–5, 130, 131
Exchequer, Court of, 67
Exeter, 47, 48
Exiles, for religion, 66, 94, 102, 103, 105, 106, 109
Exports, export trade, 124–5, 130

Feria, Gomez, Count of, 61, 179
Firth of Forth, 184
First-fruits and Tenths, Clerical, 66
Fisher, F. J., 129
Fitzroy, Henry, Duke of Richmond, 7, 8, 10
Flanders, 21
Fleet Street, 63
Flowerdew, John, 49
Food and drink, Englishmen's diet of, 129, 135
  marketing/supply of, 115, 116, 123, 129, 131, 134
  government's concern with supply of, 119, 132
  see also Prices
Foxe, John, 73, 100, 101; *Acts and Monuments* (*Book of Martyrs*), 111
France, French, 3–6 passim, 16, 26, 31, 32, 46, 149–89 passim
Franche-Comté, 171
Francis, I, King of France, 151, 158, 161
Francis II, King (formerly Dauphin) of France, 4, 15, 32, 163, 180, 181, 183
Frankfurt-am-Main, 103, 106
Freehold, 116
Frith, John, 73, 74
Frederick the Great, King of Prussia, 146
Fuel, 66

Gardiner, Stephen, Bishop of Winchester, 11, 24, 25, 38, 39, 41, 43, 61, 63, 65, 80, 82, 84, 94–101 passim, 158, 161, 172, 193
  De Vera Obedientia, 193
Garret, Thomas, 77
Garrett, C. H., 94
Garter, Order of the, 57
Gates, Sir John, 55
Geneva, 87, 103, 105, 182
Gentry, Gentility, 19, 49, 61, 64, 67, 141–2, 143, 144
Germany, Germans, 8, 77, 84, 105, 145, 151, 152, 157, 159, 160, 168
Gilds, 122–3, 125
Gilpin, Bernard, 79
Gladstone, William E., 169
Gloucester, 97
Gooch, G. P., 69
Goodman, Christopher, *How Superior Powers Oght to be Obeyd*, 103
Gould, J. D., 129, 132
Government, organs of: *see* Crown, Council, Parliament
  allegation of corruption in, 39, 40, 43–4
  social and economic responsibilities and policies of, 44, 119, 125, 131–2, 136–9, 147–8
  see also Coinage, Enclosure, Industry, Prices, Poverty
Grain: *see* Corn
Gravelines, Battle of, 175
Gray, C. M., 117
Greenwich, Treaty of, 155, 161
Gresham, Sir Thomas, 193
Grey, Henry, Duke of Suffolk, 15, 19, 25
— Lady Catherine, 15, 31
— Lady Jane, 15, 16, 17, 18, 19, 25, 31
Grindal, Edmund, Bishop of London (later Archbishop of Canterbury), 106, 110
Guise, House of, 179, 180, 184, 185, 186, 187
— Francis, Duke of, 175, 183, 186, 187
— Mary of (and of Lorraine), Queen-Mother Regent of Scotland, 15, 151, 155, 163, 170, 180, 181, 182, 183, 184, 185
Guisnes, 175

Index

Habbakuk, H. J. 141
Haddington, 163, 164
Hales, John, 117
Hampshire, 100
Hampton Court, 52
Hanse, 172
Habsburg, House of, 24, 149, 150, 151, 153, 154, 168, 169, 170, 171, 173, 176, 177
Harbison, E. H., 65, 169
Harvests, 66, 126, 129, 132
Harwich, 21
Haugaard, W. P., 104, 109
Heath, Nicholas, Bishop of Worcester, Archbishop of York, 84
Henry VII, King of England, 7, 15, 17, 32, 45, 67–8, 149, 151, 195
Henry VIII, King of England, 1–16 passim, 20–3 passim, 27, 31, 36–45 passim, 59, 68, 72–80 passim, 84, 94, 95, 96, 111, 121, 124, 129, 143, 149–60 passim, 164, 169, 177, 181, 190, 193, 195
  Defence of the Seven Sacraments, 75
  will of, 9, 16, 17, 31, 33, 41
Henry II, King of France, 5, 25, 32, 160, 161, 163, 169, 173, 174, 180
Herbert, Sir William, Earl of Pembroke, 48, 52, 53, 61, 146, 174, 193
Herefordshire, 62
Heresy, Heretics, 3, 71, 73, 77, 90, 95, 96, 97, 98, 145, 152, 167; *see also* Anabaptism, Lollardy
Hertford, Earl of: *see* Seymour, Edward
Heywood, John, 144
Hierarchy, Concept of: *see* Society
Holbein, Hans, 8
Hooper, John, Bishop of Gloucester, 78, 80, 83, 84–5, 86, 89, 90, 97, 98, 131, 194
Horst, I. B., 91
Hoskins, W. G., 129, 140
Howard, House of, 10, 11, 39, 80
— Catherine, Queen of England, 9, 15, 152
— Henry, Earl of Surrey, 10
— Thomas, Duke of Norfolk, 10, 39, 49, 152, 154, 158

— Mary, wife of Henry Fitzroy, 10
Huguenots, 5, 184, 186, 187
Hurstfield, J., 37, 106
Hus, John, 73

Imports, 130
Impropriators, Lay, 66
Industry, 113, 121–5, 128; workers in, 121, 122, 123
Inflation: *see* Prices
Influenza, 126, 130, 134
Injunctions, Religious, 109
Inquisition, 167
Ireland, Irish, 153, 163, 166
Italy, Italians, 97, 150, 173, 176

James IV, King of Scotland, 15, 154
James V, King of Scotland, 15, 31, 151, 154, 155, 159–60
James VI, King of Scotland, and I, King of England, 15, 32
Jerome, William, 77
Jewel, John, Bishop of Salisbury, 106
'Joan of Kent': *see* Bocher, Joan
John O'Groats, 32, 179
Jordan, W. K., 16, 41, 51, 59, 79, 136, 164, 167
Julius III, Pope, 96
Justices of the Peace, 35, 44, 120, 132, 138–9, 192
Justification by Faith, 76–7, 110

Kent, 24, 90
Kerridge, E., 117
Ket, Robert, 49–51; *see also* Rebellions
King's Book, The, 76, 77
Kingston-on-Thames, 63
Kingston, Sir Anthony, 66
Knightsbridge, 63
Knollys, Sir Francis, 107
Knox, John, 83, 84, 86, 87, 88, 89, 103, 109, 161, 182, 185–6, 194
  First Blast of the Trumpet, 182–3

Labour, position of, 115, 116, 117, 122, 128, 129, 134–5, 140
Lancaster, House of, 150
Land, use of: *see* Agriculture
  enclosure of: *see* Enclosure
  sale of: 131, 141–2; *see also* Church, lands of; Crown, lands of

Index

Land—*contd.*
  tenure of: *see* Commons, Copyhold, Freehold, Leasehold, Open Fields
  demand for, 115, 118, 128
  -lords, 115, 116, 117, 118, 119, 120
  see also Rents
Langland, William, *Piers Plowman*, 144
Latimer, Hugh, Bishop of Worcester, 13, 54, 73, 77, 80, 98, 100, 120
Leasehold, 116, 118
Leather, 123, 125
Le Havre, 187, 190
Lehmberg, S. E., 60
Leicester, Earl of: *see* Dudley, Robert
Leicestershire, 62
Leith, 183, 184
Lever, Thomas, 118
Levine, M., 32
Litany, the English (1544), 78
Living standards, 115, 129, 134–5
Loades, D. M., 61, 92, 100
Lollardy, Lollards, 73, 86, 145
London, 18, 19, 20, 24, 25, 47, 50, 51, 52, 53, 55, 62, 63, 64, 91, 97, 106, 116, 121, 124, 134, 139, 162, 170, 171
London Bridge, 63
Long Acre, 56
Lords, House of, 83, 96, 107, 108
Lords of the Congregation, Scottish, 181, 182, 183, 185, 186
Low Countries: *see* Netherlands
Loyola, St Ignatius, 102
Ludlow, 20
Luther, Martin, 73, 76, 85, 86
Lutheranism, Lutherans, 8, 73, 74, 77, 79, 82, 86, 151, 152, 159

MacCaffrey, W. T., 4, 31, 43, 188, 191
Mackie, J. D., 61
Maldon, 21
Margaret, Duchess of Burgundy, 149, 151
Margaret Tudor, Queen of Scotland, 15, 31, 154
Marketing, 113, 115, 122, 123, 124; regulation of, 132

Martyrs, religious, 90–1, 92, 97–102, 104–5, 111
Mary I, Queen of England, 1, 2, 7–30 passim, 34, 43, 44, 58–72 passim, 83, 91–107 passim, 120, 129, 132, 141, 160, 165–80 passim, 189, 190, 192, 194
Mary Stuart, Queen of Scots, 4, 15, 31–4, 155, 156, 162, 163, 167, 169, 178, 180–90 passim
Mary Tudor, Duchess of Suffolk, 15, 16
Mary Rose, 158
Mass: *see* Eucharist
McGrath, P., 109, 110
Melanchthon, Philip, 87
Mercenary troops, foreign, 46, 48, 50, 162, 163, 166, 174
Merchant Adventurers, 172
Merchants, middlemen, 131, 132
Merton, Statute of, 120
Metallurgy, 121, 122, 123
Middle Ages, 71
Middlemen: *see* Merchants
Mildmay, Sir Walter, 45, 57, 67, 193
Military expenditure: *see* Crown
Monasteries: *see* Religious houses
Montreuil, 157
More, Sir Thomas, 74, 145
Morison, Sir Richard, 143–4
Mousehold Heath, 49, 50
Mühlberg, Battle of, 160, 162
Münster, 146

Napoleon Bonaparte, 146
Narrow Seas, 158, 174
Neale, Sir J. E., 28, 65, 69, 107, 183
Netherlands, the, 25, 26, 149, 150, 167, 171, 172, 173, 175, 179, 188
— Revolt of the, 188
Nice, Truce of, 151
Noailles, Antoine de, French Ambassador, 24, 169, 170
Nobility, the, 43, 141–2, 143, 191
Norfolk, 18, 48, 49, 119; *see also* Rebellions
Norfolk, Duke of: *see* Howard, Thomas
Norman Conquest, 141
Northampton, Marquis of: *see* Parr, William

Index

North-east Passage, 172
North-west Passage, 172
Northumberland, Duke of: *see* Dudley, John
Norwich, 19, 49, 50, 121, 140

Open Fields, 118
Ordinal, the English (1550), 84, 87
Osiander, Andreas, 79
Outhwaite, R. B., 128
Oxford, 97
  University, 102

Paget, Sir William, Lord, 38, 41, 45, 46, 47, 53, 55, 56–7, 60–1, 68, 91, 95, 96, 146, 158, 159, 161, 172, 192–3
Palmer, Sir Thomas, 55
Papacy, papal, 66, 74, 75, 76, 93, 95, 96, 97, 99, 105, 150–1, 152, 160, 167
Papal states, 173
Papistry, Papists, papal/Roman Catholicism, 4, 11, 14, 21, 25, 28, 31, 32, 72, 93, 151, 182; *see also* Rome, Church of
Paris, 30
Parker, Matthew, Archbishop of Canterbury, 50, 87, 100, 105, 109
Parliament, 25, 32, 33, 36, 37, 44, 54–9 passim, 65–70 passim, 74, 75, 81, 93–7 passim, 103–11 passim, 121, 170, 171, 175
  see also Commons, Lords, Statutes
Parr, Catherine, Queen of England, 9, 13, 15, 28
— William, Marquis of Northampton, 50, 56
Pasture, 115, 116
Passau, Treaty of, 168
Paul III, Pope, 151
Paul IV, Pope (Caraffa), 32, 172–3
Paulet, Sir William, Marquis of Winchester, 45, 67
Peasantry, peasant-farmers, 115, 116, 117, 118, 120, 129
Peasants' Revolt (1381), 144
Peasants' Revolt (1524–25) (Germany), 145–6
Pembroke, Earl of: *see* Herbert, Sir William
Perth, 182

Petre, Sir William, 38, 45, 53, 58, 61
Philip II, King of Spain (and of England, 1554–58), 15, 23–6 passim, 30, 33, 60–1, 65, 97, 101, 157, 170–4, 175, 176, 179, 183, 184, 186, 188
Pilgrimage of Grace, 3, 46, 62, 119, 143
Pinkie Clough, Battle of, 162, 163
Plague, 115
Plantagenet, House of, 150
— Edward, Earl of Warwick, 8
Pole, Reginald, Archbishop of Canterbury, Lord Cardinal, Legate, 21, 23, 24, 63, 93, 95–102 passim, 105, 151, 152, 160, 173
Pollard, A. F., 41, 42, 56, 156, 164
Ponet, John, Bishop of Winchester, 26, 84, 100, 129, 192, 194
  Short Treatise of politike power, 103
'Poor Pratte, Epistle of', 92
Population, 113, 115, 116, 128–9, 130, 133–5; *see also* Depopulation
Portsmouth, 100
Portugal, 172
Potter, Gilbert, 92
Pound, J. F., 140
Poverty, 113, 119, 131, 133, 134–41
  Relief of, 135–9, 148
  see also Beggars, Charity, Statutes (Poor Law)
Prayer Book, English, First, 21, 47, 81–2, 85, 87, 88, 108
  Second, 87–9, 106, 107, 108
  'Black Rubric', 88, 108
  Elizabethan, 108
Precisians: *see* Puritans
Predestination, 89, 110
Prescott, H. F. M., 21, 22, 101
Prices, food, 66, 131, 132, 134, 140; fuel, 66; wool, 116
  inflation of, 66, 113–14, 118, 126–129, 130, 131–2, 133–5, 140, 141
Primer, the English (1545), 78
Privy Council: *see* Council
Protestantism, Protestants, 2, 10, 11, 12, 14, 28, 29, 49, 61–2, 69, 71–110 passim, 145, 152, 156,

Protestantism, Protestants—*contd.*
  157, 159, 161, 162, 165, 176, 181, 182, 185, 186, 194
  see also Anglicanism, Calvinism, Lollardy, Lutheranism, Puritanism, Zwinglianism
Purgatory, 81, 89, 110
Puritanism, Puritans, Precisians, 109, 110
Pyrenees, 32, 179

Ramsey, P. H., 124
Ratramn (Ratramnus of Corbie), 86, 88
Read, Conyers, 178, 187
Rebellion, in the West, 2, 18, 21, 46–8, 53, 82–3, 118, 192
  in Norfolk (Ket's), 2, 18, 44, 48, 49–51, 53, 64, 83, 118, 119–120, 121, 144, 192
  Wyatt's, 2, 18, 24–5, 26, 28, 61–4, 94, 170, 171, 173, 192
  of the Northern Earls, 46, 119
  see also Pilgrimage of Grace
Reformation, the Protestant, 37, 71, 73, 74, 84, 85, 86, 162, 181, 193, 194
Regensburg (Ratisbon), Diet of, 152, 153
Religion: *see* Anabaptism, Anglicanism, Articles of Religion, Bible, Calvinism, Catholicism, Church, Chantries, Clergy, Convocation, Eucharist, Exiles, Heresy, Injunctions, Lutheranism, Papacy, Papistry, Prayer Books, Protestantism, Puritanism, Reformation, Religious Houses, Vestments, Zwinglianism
  contention and uncertainty in, 2, 4, 71, 77–8, 91, 146
  innovation in, and social subversion, 145–6
Religious Houses, charity of, 135–6
  dissolution of, 74, 114, 141, 142, 162
  proposed restoration of, 97
  use of confiscated estates and wealth, 141, 152, 159
Renard, Simon, Imperial Ambassador, 24, 60, 61, 65, 97, 101, 102, 169

Rents, 118, 120, 131
  Rack-renting, 118, 119, 131, 143
Requests, Court of, 45, 117
Richmond, Duke of: *see* Fitzroy, Henry
Ridley, J. R., 185
Ridley, Nicholas, Bishop of Rochester and London, 18, 73, 79–80, 84, 85, 86, 88, 98, 100, 194
Robespierre, Maximilien, 101
Robsart, Amy, 30
Rogers, J. E. T., 134
Rogers, John, 97
Rome, 102, 173, 179
  Church of, 65, 72, 74, 75, 96, 97, 98, 103, 150, 158, 172, 173–174, 194; *see also* Papacy, Papistry
Rupp, E. G., 73
Russell, C., 66, 102
Russell, Lord John, Earl of Bedford, 47–8, 50, 51, 52, 53, 124, 146
Russia, 172, 194

Sacramentarianism, 95
Sadler, Sir Ralph, 38
St Andrews Castle, 159, 161
St Paul's, 13, 85
St Quentin, Battle of, 174, 175
Sampford Courtenay, 47, 48
Scarborough Castle, 64, 173
Scarisbrick, J. J., 39, 76, 151, 153
Schmalkalden, League of, 152
Schoolmen, medieval, 86
Scory, John, Bishop of Chichester and Hereford, 84
Scotland, Scots, 3, 4, 16, 31, 32, 34, 46, 109, 149, 151, 153–69 passim, 173–7 passim, 180–8 passim
  Parliament of, 156, 181, 185
Scriptures: *see* Bible
Secretary, Principal, 36, 38
Seymour, Edward, Earl of Hertford, Duke of Somerset, Lord Protector, 10–14 passim, 21, 31, 38–57 passim, 79–83 passim, 117, 119, 120, 138, 142, 144, 146, 147, 156–7, 161–9 passim, 176, 177, 181, 182, 192
  'Epistle to the Nobility of Scotland', 162–3
— Edward, Earl of Hertford, 15, 31

Index

— Jane, Queen of England, 8, 10, 15, 151
— Sir Thomas, of Sudeley, Lord Admiral, 12, 13, 28, 52, 164
Shaxton, Nicholas, Bishop of Salisbury, 77
Shakespeare, William, 142, 178
Sheep
 -farming, 116, 120
 -tax, 120; *see* Statutes
Smith, L. B., 11, 83
Smith, R. B., 142
Smith, Sir Thomas, 53
Smithfield, 97
Society, hierarchical concept of, 139, 141, 142, 143–4
 concern for stability of, 139, 141, 143, 144–6, 191, 194
 occupational groupings of, 139–140
 social mobility, upstarts', 139, 141, 142–4
 social orders: *see* Gentry, Nobility, Peasantry
Solent, the, 158
Solway Moss, Battle of, 154–5, 162
Somerset, Duke of: *see* Seymour, Edward
— Duchess of: *see* Stanhope, Anne
Somerset House, 52
Southampton, Earl of: *see* Wriothesley, Thomas
Southwark, 62, 63
Spain, Spanish, 3, 16, 24, 25, 26, 29, 65, 101, 149, 151, 152, 169–79 passim, 184, 188
 Spanish colonial trade, 172, 173
 Spanish marriage (1554), 24–6, 65, 94, 95, 101–2, 170–1, 172, 177, 192
 Spanish treasure, 128, 133
Stafford, Thomas, Conspiracy of, 64, 173
Stalin, Joseph, 194
Stanhope, Anne, Duchess of Somerset, 42
Starkey, Thomas, 146
State, concept of, 37
 Church and, 37, 71, 74, 81, 105
 see also Crown, Government
Statutes: 'Against Revilers and for Receiving in Both Kinds', 80; Apparel, 143; Artificers, 114, 121, 126, 139; Attainder, 13, 52, 78; Chantries, 81; Courts of Revenue, 45, 58; *de Haeretico Comburendo*, 81; Merton, re-enactment of, 120; Poor Law, 137, 138; Proclamations, 37–8; re-enactment of Medieval Heresy Laws and repeal of Henrician anti-papal legislation, 96; repeal of Edwardian Religious legislation, 94; repeal of Treason Statutes, 42; Sheeptax, 120; Six Articles, 77, 81; Succession, 7, 9, 20; Supremacy, 108; Tillage, preservation/restoration of, 120, 121; Uniformity, 82, 89, 108; Unlawful Assemblies, 120
Stone, L., 141
Strassburg, 84, 87
Stuart, House of, 31, 32, 70, 151, 177, 179, 180, 188, 194, 195
Suffolk, Duke of: *see* Brandon, Charles
Surrey, Earl of: *see* Howard, Henry
Sutherland, N. M., 184
Switzerland, Swiss, 84, 108, 109

Tawney, R. H., 114, 117
Taxation, 120, 127, 140, 159, 171, 175
Textiles: *see* Cloth
Thames, River, 63
Tillage and husbandry, Arable, 115, 117, 118, 120–1, 143; *see* Statutes
Timber, 128
Titian, 24
Tower Hill, 14
Tower of London, 10, 20, 25, 31, 56, 63, 82
Towns, 122, 125, 128, 129, 134, 140–1
Trade, Commerce, 122
 overseas, 124–5
 boom and slump in, 123–5, 129, 140
 terms of, 124–5, 131
 see also Cloth, Exchanges, Exports, Imports, Merchants, Wool
Transubstantiation, 73
Trent, Council of, 161

Troubles begun at Frankfurt, The, 103
Troyes, Treaty of, 187
Tudor Despotism, Concept of, 37
Tunstall, Cuthbert, Bishop of Durham, 84, 110
Turner, William, 54, 96–7
　Huntyng of the Romyshe Wolfe, 97
Tyndale, William, 73–4, 85, 193

Unemployment, 113, 116, 119, 121, 123, 134, 135
Uniformity, Statutes of: *see* Statutes
Upstarts, 142, 143, 144

Vagabonds, Vagabondage, 136, 137, 138, 139
Valois, House of, 32, 150, 153, 163, 173, 179, 180, 188
Vassy, Massacre of, 186
Vestments, controversy regarding, 80, 85, 108

Wages, 128, 130, 134–5, 140
Wales, Union of England with, 36
Wards, Court of, 39, 57, 67
Wars of Religion, French, 5–6, 186, 188
Warwick, Earl of (d. 1499): *see* Plantagenet, Edward
Warwick, Earl of: *see* Dudley, John
Wash, the, 100
Welfare State, 147
Wernham, R. B., 150, 153, 158, 171, 180, 187

West Country, 46–8, 124; *see also* Rebellions
West Riding of Yorkshire, 139
White Horse Inn, 73
Wight, Isle of, 158
Williams, P., 40
Winchester, 26
Winchester, Marquis, of: *see* Paulet, William
Windsor, 53, 63
Wittenberg, 87
Wokingham, 55
Wolsey, Thomas, Archbishop of York, Lord Cardinal, Legate, 36, 73, 74, 150, 151
Woodward, G. W. O., 142
Wool, 115, 132
　industry, 124
　export of, 124
　see also Cloth, Prices
Wriothesley, Charles, *Chronicle* of, 85, 95
Wriothesley, Thomas, Earl of Southampton, 38, 43, 45, 83, 151, 159
Wyatt, Sir Thomas, 25, 62, 63; *see also* Rebellions
Wycliffe, John, 73

Yarmouth, 19, 121
York, 154, 186
Youings, J., 141

Zeeland, 183
Zurich, 84, 87, 90
Zwingli, Ulrich, 85, 87–8, 90, 103
Zwinglian, 73, 74, 79, 85, 86, 87–8, 95